Relational Databases: Theory and Practice

Val Occardi

British Library Cataloguing In Publication Data

Occardi, Val

    Relational Databases.

    I. Title

    000.00

    ISBN 1-85554-065-7

© Val Occardi, 1992

All rights reserved. No part of this publication may be reproduced, stored in a retrieval system, or transmitted, in any form or by any means, without the prior permission of NCC Blackwell Limited.

First published in 1992 by:

NCC Blackwell Limited, 108 Cowley Road, Oxford OX4 1JF, England.

Editorial Office: The National Computing Centre Limited, Oxford House, Oxford Road, Manchester M1 7ED, England.

Typeset in 10pt Times by ScribeTech Ltd, Bradford, West Yorkshire; and printed by Hobbs the Printers of Southampton

ISBN 1-85554-065-7

To My Mother

Contents

Page

Preface

Acknowledgements

Part 1   Preliminaries

1   The Database Concept   1

   1.1   Introduction   1
   1.2   The User's Requirement   1
   1.3   Technical Implications   4
   1.4   Summary   13

2   Information and Storage Basics   15

   2.1   A Multi-Level View of Data   15
   2.2   The User's View of Information   16
   2.3   The Analyst's View of Information   16
   2.4   The Machine View of Information – Computer Data Storage   20
   2.5   Mapping Information Structures to Storage Structures   33

3   Data Models   35

   3.1   Background to Data Models   35
   3.2   Database Models   37
   3.3   Semantic Data Models   47

4   Introduction to Modern methods of Analysis and Design   51

   4.1   Introduction   51
   4.2   Background   51
   4.3   Structured Analysis   54
   4.4   Structured Design   65
   4.5   Object Oriented Design   73

Part 2   Relational Database Theory   81

5   Tables, Relations and First Normal Form   83

   5.1   Background   83
   5.2   Relational Tables   83
   5.3   Table Headers and Bodies   85
   5.4   Mathematical Relations, the Table Body   86
   5.5   The Table Header   89
   5.6   First Normal Form   90
   5.7   Relationships   92

6   The Relational Model Operators   95

   6.1   Introduction   95
   6.2   Cartesian Product   96
   6.3   Restriction   97
   6.4   Projection   98
   6.5   Division   99
   6.6   Join   100
   6.7   Union   102
   6.8   Intersection   104
   6.9   Difference   104
   6.10   Relational Completeness   105
   6.11   User Views   106

7   Relational Model Integrity Rules   109

   7.1   Nulls   109
   7.2   Entity Integrity   110
   7.3   Referential Integrity   111

8   Further Normal Forms   113

   8.1   Introduction   113
   8.2   Functional Dependency   113
   8.3   Second Normal Form (2NF)   115
   8.4   Third Normal Form (3NF)   117
   8.5   Boyce-Codd Normal Form (BCNF)   118
   8.6   Multi-Valued Dependency   120
   8.7   Fourth Normal Form (4NF)   122
   8.8   Fifth Normal Form (5NF)   124

Part 3   Information Models   129

9 Information Modelling and the Relational Model   131

9.1   Introduction   131
9.2   E-O Model Concepts   133
9.3   Normalisation and the Information Model   155
9.4   Applicability of the E-O Model   162

10 The Entity-Object (E-O) Semantic Data Model   163

10.1   The Objects of the E-O Model   163
10.2   The Integrity Rules of the E-O Model   165
10.3   The Operators of the E-O Model   165

11 Constructing Information Models   171

11.1   Introduction   171
11.2   Identifying the use of Information in serving the Goals of an Enterprise   172
11.3   Identifying the Information Sources   173
11.4   Partitioning the Problem   174
11.5   Producing the Information Model   174
11.6   Balancing the Information Model with the Functional Model   181
11.7   Adding Supplementary Information to the Model   184

Part 4   Relational Database Management Systems   189

12 Introduction to the SQL Language   191

12.1   Introduction   191
12.2   Example Database   192
12.3   Creating and Deleting Databases   193
12.4   Creating, Indexing and Deleting Tables and Views   195
12.5   The SQL SELECT Statement   197
12.6   The SQL INSERT Statement   207
12.7   The SQL DELETE Statement   208
12.8   The SQL UPDATE Statement   209
12.9   The SQL CREATE and DROP VIEW statements   209
12.10   Access Control in SQL   211
12.11   Transaction Control in SQL   211
12.12   Embedded SQL   213

13 Relational Database Management Systems   221

13.1   Introduction   221
13.2   General Overview of RDBMSs   222
13.3   Overview of INGRES™   226
13.4   Overview of ORACLE™   247

14 Developing Relational Database Systems

265

14.1	Data Driven versus Function Driven Developments	265
14.2	The Relational Database System Project Life Cycle	266
14.3	The Analysis Phase	269
14.4	The Design Phase	272
14.5	The Coding/Application Generation Phase	273

Appendix A: Object Oriented Databases

279

Bibliography and References

295

Index

297

Acknowledgements

Writing a technical book in isolation would be a worrying activity. The book cannot tell you whether you are making sense and, if you are, whether you are getting that sense across to the reader. The availability of technically aware colleagues and friends who are willing to take time both to discuss complex technical matters and to read and comment on sections of the book, is, therefore, of great benefit to the writer.

I am very grateful to my colleagues Steve Hayes, Dave Metcalfe and Terry Glennon for many technical discussions and for reading and commenting on particular sections of the text. Peter Pearson made many useful comments on the presentation of the material in Parts 1 and 2. I am particularly grateful to Dr Geoff Haig who read large sections of the text and made many valuable comments both on technical matters and on the layout and presentation of the material.

Nevertheless, any errors, omissions or obscurities in the book lie entirely at my door.

Val Occardi
Lymington, Hants
January 1992

Preface

Purpose of the book

The purpose of this book is to equip its readers with the theoretical knowledge and practical know-how they require to enable them to develop relational databases and their applications, making use of commercially available relational database management systems (RDBMSs).

The internal design of RDBMSs is not covered, however the interfaces they present to their users, in particular the analyst/designer user, are discussed in some detail.

The book is aimed primarily at computer system managers, analysts and programmers who are already, or will be, involved in the analysis, design and implementation of relational databases and their applications. It will also be of interest to those computer science students who wish to obtain a practical as well as a theoretical orientation on the topic.

The text is tutorial in style and assumes no previous knowledge on the reader's part of relational databases, or, indeed, of database technology in general. However, the reader is assumed already to have a good understanding of computer systems together with some systems analysis and/or programming background whether obtained by training, by experience, or both.

Benefits to be obtained from the book

On completion of this book, the reader should have acquired . . .

- A good general understanding of the different types of database management systems available.
- Knowledge of the particular benefits of relational database management systems.
- A sound knowledge of basic relational database theory.
- A sound knowledge of information modelling techniques which are appropriate to the design of relational databases.
- A practical feel for the kind of development facilities provided by typical relational database management systems.
- The practical know how needed for the tasks of systems analysis and design of relational databases and their applications.

Preface

- A broad understanding of modern methods of analysis and design and how to fit relational database system developments into their context.

Emphasis of the book

To the reader who is unfamiliar with database system development practice it may appear surprising that the development of application programs using a relational database is not stressed in the earlier parts of the book. There are two reasons for this. Firstly, the initial stages of a relational database system development must be concentrated on getting the design of the database itself correct. The overriding consideration is that the information needs of the user community be fully researched and understood and properly integrated into a database design and that this design should be produced to a specified level of quality. This initial emphasis in the development process will ensure a sound basis for the development of the database application software. Secondly, relational database management systems provide a variety of easy to use 'application generation' facilities which enable quite sophisticated on line database applications to be developed without recourse to traditional programming methods. An understanding of these facilities must predicate any decisions as to how particular applications will be developed.

The development of systems which are based on the use of an RDBMS is a special software engineering discipline in its own right requiring its own set of analysis, design and programming methods. The techniques described in this book provide the developer with a structured, but at the same time a natural and common sense, way of going about relational database design. This method, which is based on simple and well proven techniques of information modelling, guides the developer towards the production of relational database designs which are fully correct according to relational database theory. Relational database theory itself need not necessarily be known in depth to apply this information modelling technique, but knowledge of it will provide the analyst with a powerful method of checking that errors have not been inadvertently introduced into his or her design. To this end, the theoretical aspects of the relational model have not been neglected.

Relevance of modern methods of analysis and design

Increasingly, analysts and programmers may have to work within the environment provided by some overall system analysis and design method supported by some CASE (Computer Aided Software Engineering) tools. Such, so called, modern methods of systems analysis and design require the use of information modelling techniques as part of the overall analysis activity. In general, however, the literature and training associated with these methods give sparse instruction on information modelling techniques, and none on what techniques are appropriate when the resulting information model is to be implemented in whole or in part as a relational database. This book attempts to remedy this deficiency.

Preface

Structure and content of the book

The book is divided into four parts. Part 1 provides general background information and terminology as a setting for the parts specific to relational databases and information modelling which follow. It introduces the overall database concept, the special properties of databases and the need for a specialist technology (database management systems) to support their development and use. Fundamental information modelling concepts are introduced and explained. Against this background of information modelling concepts, conventional computer physical and logical storage mechanisms are reviewed in terms of how information can be represented using them. The topic of data models is introduced and their different practical uses, whether as the basis for the development of database management systems or for the development of information models, is discussed. The various database models which have been introduced over time, including the hierarchic, network, relational and entity-relationship models are outlined, discussed, and compared. An overview of modern methods of analysis and design is given.

Part 2 covers the essentials of relational database theory. The treatment has been kept as non mathematical as possible, but does fully cover and explain all the relational database concepts and terminology that the reader is likely to encounter in the course of his or her work. The bibliography and reference section, included at the end of the book can be consulted by readers who wish to pursue their studies of relational database theory into greater depth.

In Part 3, the topic of information modelling is returned to in more detail and a semantic data model, whose object, integrity rules and operators can be used in the construction of information models, which in turn can serve as the basis for complete and correct relational database designs, is described.

Part 4 opens with an introduction to SQL, the standard relational database programming language. It continues with a description of the facilities commonly provided by commercially available relational database management systems (RDBMSs). Two of the major RDBMS products from independent suppliers, ORACLE™ and ASK INGRES™ are then overviewed in terms of how they provide these facilities. Finally, the overall steps to be followed when developing relational database systems are described.

The book closes with an appendix on the topic of Object Oriented Databases.

Part 1
Preliminaries

The first part of this book provides general background reading to the later parts which are dedicated to the topics of information modelling and relational databases.

Chapter 1 introduces the general concept of a database from the point of view of the requirements of the end user and derives from these requirements the technical features required of database management systems (DBMSs).

Chapter 2 covers the fundamentals of information analysis and storage. Information is discussed in terms of how it is viewed in the real world of the end user. The notions of entities, attributes and relationships are introduced and explained to show how real world information can be systematically analysed and organised in the mind of the data analyst. Conventional computer storage is described at the physical and logical levels.

In Chapter 3, the ability of such conventional storage mechanisms to support the database concept is discussed and its deficiencies in this respect, leading to the need for a specialist DBMS technology, are explained. The various database models which have been introduced over time to remedy this deficiency, including the relational model, are outlined, discussed, and compared.

System development staff, including those involved with relational database work, are increasingly likely to have to work within the framework of some overall analysis and design methodology usually supported by the use of a CASE tool. Chapter 4 introduces such modern methods of analysis and design, and, in doing so, also introduces some useful graphical and textual notations which are extensively used in later parts of the book.

1
The Database Concept

1.1 Introduction

The word "database", which originated in computing terminology, has come into common use in the language to the point where its definition can be found in recent editions of the standard, non-technical dictionaries. A typical dictionary entry would be, *"A store of a large amount of information, especially in a form that can be handled by a computer"*. This expresses very well the general public's conception of a database.

However, the word has been in use amongst the computing community, since the 1960s and has acquired a much more specialised and complex meaning within that community. It expresses a concept which has evolved and changed gradually over the years since the term was coined. Implementation of the concept has been made possible by the improving hardware and software technology as made available to the providers of computing services. It has also developed over time to support the changing control and communications philosophies within organisations as seen by the users of these services.

Implementation of this database concept requires a major shift in attitude by a computer user community to the distribution and sharing of information within their organisation and, just as importantly, it necessitates a watershed change to the traditional techniques employed by computer staff responsible for the analysis, design and implementation of systems for those users. It also requires the selection, purchase and use of specialist and expensive tools.

Thus, in discussing the concept during the rest of this chapter, two views will be taken of it . . .

- The requirements of and on the user for the sharing and distribution of information.
- The technical implications of these requirements.

1.2 The User's Requirement

This topic is best introduced by asking the question, "What purpose does a database serve for the computer user community within an organisation?"

Going back to the dictionary, a "datum" is defined as, "a fact or proposition from which inferences can be drawn" and " base" as "the bottom or supporting part of anything". Thus, the earlier definition of a database can be expanded to become: *"A store of a large amount of information in a form which can be handled by computer which*

2 The database concept

provides the basis upon which an organisation can draw inferences in conducting its business". An item of information can be a fact, like sales figures for last month, or a proposition, like target sales for next month.

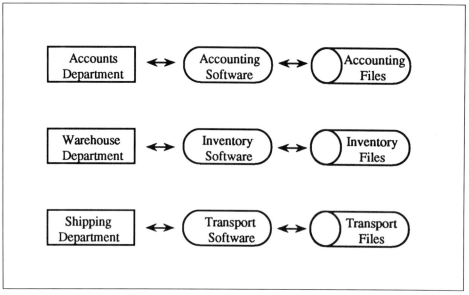

Figure 1.1 Dedicated department files

This definition is much better, but still lacks precision in the context of this book. As it stands it could apply collectively to the files illustrated in Figure 1.1. In this system arrangement, each department may share a common computer system using the same data processing (DP) department's services, but each has its own dedicated software which in turn has its own dedicated filing system. This gives rise to problems should, for instance, the shipping department need to develop a software application which requires access to account department files. Discussion of the technical problems involved in this will be left until later in this chapter. For the present it needs no great stretch of the imagination to see that political problems are likely to occur. The behaviour of people within organisations being what it is, there is likely to be a strong, adverse reaction from the accounting department to the release of its data to the shipping department. This will stem partly from a simple, protectionist attitude to its own "property", but also, and perfectly reasonably, from concern that their data may, in some way, be interfered with. Should the accounting department's views prevail, an opportunity to improve overall organisational performance might be lost. Suppose, for example, that the shipping department wanted access to customer accounting information in order to give priority to high value deliveries and thus improve cash flow?

Any organisation wishing to establish a database in the modern, computer systems sense of the word is likely to run into severe internal problems of a political nature. To overcome these, an organisation wide policy has to be established that all data created or collected by whichever department must, in the first instance, be considered for inclusion in a common "pool" which is accessible to all parts of the organisation with a need to know that information. Figure 1.2 illustrates this concept of a database. Note that the data in this database need to be "integrated" in the sense that they must not just represent isolated facts and propositions about the real world but should also represent naturally occuring relationships between them. For example, if the database contains data about orders and customers, it must show which orders were placed by which customers.

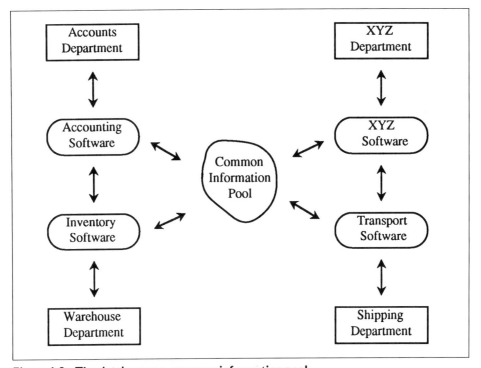

Figure 1.2 The database as a common information pool

To succeed, the policy must also take into account the genuine concern of departments that information they are responsible for may be interfered with by others. Thus, the policy must be extended to include the concept of "private ownership of data". Whilst a department might make its data available to other departments, it retains ownership of those data and it has the sole right to amend them or create new data of the type at any time.

The earlier definition given of a database can now be expanded to become: *A large, integrated, shared pool of information in a form suitable for handling by a computer which is a basis upon which the computer user community within an organisation can draw inferences in conducting its business.*

This database is an *integrated, shareable* repository for all the information needed to run the business of the organisation owning it. In its effect it becomes a computerised model of the operations of the business of the organisation.

4 *The database concept*

1.3 Technical Implications

1.3.1 Technical Requirements

In addition to being *integrated* and *shareable*, the database must have certain additional technical properties if it is to be acceptable to its users.

The larger and more comprehensive a database becomes, the more valuable and vital an asset it will be to the organisation which uses it. It must be protected against accidental or malicious damage. A database must be *reliable, secure* and *recoverable.*

The database will contain information about the tactical and strategic operations of an enterprise which could be of great value to its competitors. Its contents must not be accessible except to those within the organisation who have a need to know. A database must have *privacy.* Note that in many countries this is now a legal requirement where the database contains data about people.

The database will be accessed in parallel by diverse people and functions within the organisation. It is of vital importance that different users of the database obtain exactly the same understanding of the operational status of the organisation from it at any point in time. For example, warehousing and sales departments must see exactly the same information about the quantity of some item in stock at any instant in time, otherwise commitments might be made to customers about delivery times which will not be met. A database must present a *consistent* picture of the real world of the organisation's operations to all its users.

The database must be immediately accessible to its users where and when they require to use it. A database must be *available.*

The database must be capable of being extended with regard to its information content over time, in line with the changing requirements of the organisation it serves. A database must be *flexible* to change.

1.3.2 Database Management Systems

The technology required to satisfy the above user's needs of a database, is, in practice, provided by a special kind of software tool called a Database Management System – DBMS for short. A number of different types of DBMS have been evolved over time, including Relational Database Management Systems (RDBMSs) which are, of course, the kind of main interest to this book. The various types of DBMS available will be described in Chapter 3. However, the fundamental user's requirements as discussed above must be satisfied regardless of which type of DBMS is used and the technical implications of each of these requirements are now discussed.

1.3.3 Shareability – Multiple Access

Data in computers, of course, are not directly accessed by people, but, rather, by software acting on their behalf. Putting that aside for the moment, the data will be accessed for one of four main purposes with four corresponding access types.

- Simple retrieval – query

For example, the user may wish to know the numbers of a specific line item in stock, the credit status of a customer, the availability of seats on a specific aeroplane flight and so forth.

- Update of existing data

The user may, as the result of a real world transaction, wish to record the reduction of the numbers of a specific line item held in stock, or the number of seats available on a flight, etc.

- Insertion of new data

The user may wish to introduce data about a new type of line item into the database, or a new customer, or a new flight and so forth.

- Deletion of old data

The user may wish to delete all information about some specific line item, no longer sold by his organisation, from the database, or about a past flight about which information is no longer required, or about a customer no longer on its books and so forth.

The terms *retrieve* or *query, update, insert* and *delete* will be used in the above meanings throughout this book.

Since the data must be shareable amongst different users, the above operations must be carried out in a multi-access environment, an environment where many users can be using the system to carry out the above database operations concurrently. This can be put another way by stating that multiple users require to carry out multiple *transactions* concurrently with respect to the database. A transaction can be defined, informally, as any complete interaction between the computing system and a user which results in a useful input to and/or output from the system. A transaction will usually involve a sequence of database accesses. The term is most commonly used in the context of on line systems, that is, where the user interacts with the system via a computer terminal and receives a more or less immediate response to his input, as illustrated in Figure 1.3. Different users can be carrying out the same or different transactions types with the system concurrently. In the figure, user 1 is retrieving inventory information, user 2 is entering a sales order, user 3 is also entering a sales order and user 4 is adjusting an employee's salary. Users 2 and 3 are performing the same type of transaction which is different from the types performed by users 1 and 4 which are themselves different from each other.

Transactions are carried out by software (acting on behalf of the user) on data within the system. Many types of transaction will be supported by a system, each transaction type being associated with particular programs or program modules. In earlier transaction-oriented systems, it was usual for separate copies of the relevant software to be provided in the computer's main memory by the system for each concurrent activation of a specific transaction type. However, this method is constrained by the size of main memory available and can result in unacceptable restriction being placed on the number of concurrent transactions which can be serviced concurrently by the system. It is possible, however, for the software to be *re-entrant* such that a single copy of it can support multiple activations of the transaction type it services. Re-entrant programs contain instructions which do not vary when the program runs and consist of logically separate code and data segments. Each activation of a transaction which uses re-entrant software will be allocated its own working data space. After the transaction activation has run to completion, its working space will be returned to the system for use by other transaction activations.

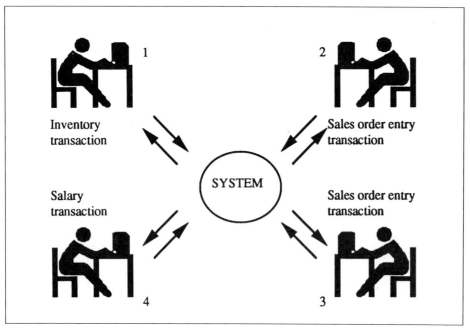

Figure 1.3 Multiple concurrent transactions

Whether or not the software supporting it is re-entrant, a transaction can be associated with two distinct types of data. The data held in the transaction activation's working space are *private* to that transaction activation. They are of no interest to any other activation of the same or different transactions. Data which need to be accessed by multiple activations of the same or different transaction types, on the other hand, cannot be held within the transaction's private working space and must be held in some publicly accessible data area. Examples of private data could include a store holding a variable used as a loop count, or a store used to hold the intermediate results of some calculation being carried out by transaction code during its activation. *Public* data include any data which might be required for access by different types of transaction, or by multiple activations of one transaction type. These public data in a transaction-oriented system correspond to the data which must be held in a database. Modern DBMSs are designed to support thousands of users entering into transactions with the system concurrently.

1.3.4 Consistency

Given multi-access to the database in the manner which has just been described, it is vital that the database present a consistent picture of the operations of the enterprise it models to all of its users at any given point in time.

Consider the following case. At some point in time there are 30 tourist class seats available on an aeroplane flight and this is the figure recorded in the database. Sales clerk A receives a call from a customer wishing to book 20 tourist class seats on the flight. He/she performs a retrieval transaction with the database and, finding 30 seats free, accepts the booking. Simultaneously, sales clerk B is asked for 15 seats on the flight and, also seeing thirty seats free, accepts this booking. Both sales persons now go on to update the database, reducing the number of seats available on the flight to minus 5. The system may not allow overbooking (or if it does, as is usually the case, some limit will have been set) and may flash an error to one or other of the sales persons, but the business transactions have been completed and, in the real world, the flight has been overbooked (accidentally rather than deliberately).

The retrieval and update transactions could be combined into a single transaction. When a sales clerk receives a booking request, a single transaction could be initiated which first retrieves the number of available seats, then checks whether these are enough to satisfy the booking. At this point a decision is made by the program either to inform the sales person that insufficient seats are available, or to go ahead and confirm the booking after performing the necessary update operation on the database. At first sight this may appear to solve the problem, but this is not the case. It is perfectly possible to have a situation where one transaction activation has just successfully completed its database query sequence and found sufficient seats available, but has not yet completed its update sequence and, at about the same time, for another transaction to enter into its query sequence. If the first transaction activation does not complete its update sequence before the second enters its query sequence, the latter will also find the number of seats available satisfactory and proceed into its update sequence. The net effect is exactly the same as in the earlier example. The probability of the users seeing inconsistent information in the database has been reduced because the period of time between querying and subsequent update of the database has been reduced, but the problem has not been eliminated.

The solution universally adopted to solving this problem of database inconsistency is the introduction of a *locking mechanism* for use with public data (as previously defined) within the system. Assume that one transaction is the first to obtain access to some required public data and further suppose that in the course of the transaction these data may be updated. It immediately locks them against any access by any other transaction activation of whatever type. If a second transaction now comes along and attempts to read the same data, the attempted access will be rejected and queued because the data is locked. This second transaction activation, in a frequently implemented algorithm, will be restarted from the beginning to try again, may find the data still locked and may be restarted yet again and so forth until the first transaction runs to completion and the data are unlocked by it. At this point the second transaction can obtain access to the data, lock them, read them, update them, then unlock them again. The next transaction requiring the data, which might or might not have been in a queued state, can now obtain access to them, and so forth.

This all works well up to a point. However, the locking mechanism itself introduces a further, very serious problem. Consider the following situation. Three transaction activations, one, two, and three, which could be of the same or different transaction types need access to three database items A, B, and C. Suppose that:

8   *The database concept*

- One needs to read A, then read B, and as a result of its findings, update C in some manner.
- Two needs to read B and as a result update C in some manner.
- Three needs to read C and as a result update B in some manner.

Suppose now that transaction one manages to access and lock A first, transation two manages to access and lock B and transaction three manages to access and lock C first. One cannot proceed further because it runs into a lock on B. Two cannot proceed further because it runs into a lock on C. Three cannot proceed further because it runs into a lock on B. Since none of the transaction activations can proceed, it is impossible for any of the locks to be removed and the transactions are all hung up. This situation is commonly referred to as a *deadlock* (or, more vividly, as a *deadly embrace*).

Operator interaction is needed to fix this problem if it is allowed to occur, with consequent long delays for users (who might be directly interacting with customers) and the need for requisitely skilled operations staff. The only satisfactory solution is, quite simply, not to allow deadlocks to happen, that is, to stop transaction activations which could be about to enter into a deadlock situation and only restart them when it is possible for them to proceed. At one extreme, implementing this solution might simply mean leaving it all to the application programmer who keeps trying to obtain and lock all the data resources he/she requires before proceeding into the main body of his/her transaction routine. At the other extreme, sophisticated system software which detects and avoids potential deadlocks with minimal support from the application software may be provided. Note that a data resource can be locked against both read and write operations or against write operations only. A lock which locks against write operations only permits concurrent transactions to retrieve locked data but not to update or delete them.

Up until now the problems of maintaining consistent views of the database should data be replicated within it have not been considered. The locking and deadlock avoidance mechanisms we have been discussing would have to be applied to all copies of such replicated data items, making the problem even more difficult to solve. This is one reason why replication of data within a database is highly undesirable. There are others and this important topic will be the subject of much further discussion in the course of this book.

1.3.5   Reliability

Computer hardware has become increasingly more reliable over the years. Nevertheless, it does break down on occasion and the database must be protected against such incidents. At the very least this means taking regular dumps of the database from its normal storage on magnetic disk to a back up magnetic media – usually to magnetic tape because of its relative cheapness. In modern practice two, complementary types of back up dump are taken. The entire database will be backed up at regular intervals. Since this is usually a very lengthy and computer resource expensive operation, it is done relatively infrequently and usually as an overnight operation. This full back up of the database will be supplemented by the maintenance of some form of transaction log which keeps a record of changes to the database since the last dump was taken. In the event of a major failure affecting the database, it can be restored by reloading the full back up and applying the transaction log to it. This will bring the database back up to the state it was in at the final point of failure.

1.3.6 Security and Privacy

These topics are grouped together, since essentially the same technical mechanisms are required to implement both requirements. Security means security of the database contents from accidental of malicious damage. This means that there must be control over access to the database. Privacy means that the database contents should be available only to those with a need to know them to do their jobs and who therefore are given the corresponding authority. Again, control over access to the database contents is the prerequisite.

Access to the database will be controlled at a number of levels. The first level of access control will be to the system as a whole, which in practice means to the facilities provided by the operating system in use. All modern operating systems provide log on/off facilities by which a user gains access to the system. This access is controlled by the issuing of user names and passwords by the installation's system manager. Having logged on to the system successfully, the user must then have the appropriate permission to be able to use the database management system at all. In this case the permission issuing authority is likely to be the DBA (Database Administrator). Access to the contents of a database by account holders will be controlled at various levels of granularity, from access to a database as a whole, down to access to specific parts of it. The exact manner in which this granular access control is exerted is dependent on the DBMS in use. The type of access method available to a database user for specified parts of the database is also controlled, that is whether for insertion, update, deletion or retrieval of the specified part or some combination of these. Access control mechanisms are the means of enforcing the private ownership of data concept which was discussed earlier in this chapter.

1.3.7 Availability – Networking and Distribution of Databases

The information resource of an organisation, its database, must be available to the user community when and where they require access to it. Since these users could be scattered over one large geographical site or over many such sites at many different locations, it is inevitable that some form of telecommunications network must be invoked in support of database access. The simplest arrangement – for users who are all located at one private geographical site, is illustrated in Figure 1.4. One computer system (there can be many others) serves as a *database server* within the network. It might be dedicated to this task, or it might share it with other tasks. Users may be directly connected to the network, or connected to other computers which are in turn connected to the network. Regardless of how they are connected, each user has transparency of access to the database within the limitations only of the access control permissions allocated to them.

In modern practice, the network illustrated will almost certainly be a *local area network* (LAN) having a bus or ring topology and will conform to some standard, such as the Ethernet LAN standard, in its implementation.

If users are scattered over many geographically separate sites, or if a single site spans a large area, then some users will have to be connected to the database server via the public telecommunications network, generally known as a *wide area network* (WAN). This is illustrated in Figure 1.5. Connection from the LANs to the WAN is effected by the use hardware/software devices known as *communications gateways*. Once again the location of the database server is completely transparent to the end user. Full support for LAN/WAN networking is provided by typical DBMS products.

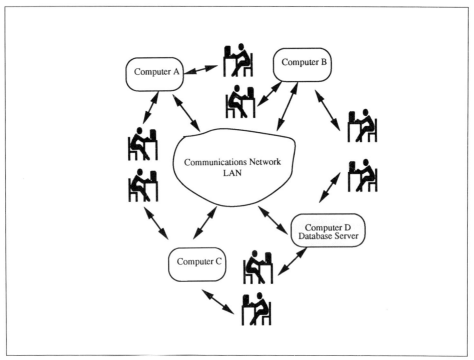

Figure 1.4 Local area network with central database server

The computers within a network may be homogeneous, all from one manufacturer, or heterogeneous, from diverse manufacturers. Typical RDBMSs as described in Part 4 support both homogeneous and heterogeneous working across networks.

The kind of centralised database server described so far fits in well with an organisation control philosphy where control of the enterprise is centralised, that is, invested to a large degree in some corporate headquarters function. As public and commercial organisations have grown larger and larger, the inefficiencies inherent in this kind of monolithic control have led to its falling out of favour. Corporate philosophy has moved more to the distribution of control and decision taking to management at branches and/or departments of the enterprise. This in turn has led to the bulk of the database accesses required being to locally held data. Thus, whilst centralised databases still have a role to play in many organisations, they are increasingly being, superseded by *distributed databases*. In this arrangement, as illustrated in Figure 1.6, the database is distributed over the network. The networking facilities are similar to the previous examples, however, branch A has its own local database which covers local operations, branch B has its local database covering its operations and so forth. A slimmed down central database can still exist, but local databases can now be tailored to branch needs using local analyst/ designer/programmer skills. Access to non-local databases, for less frequently used data, is possible from any node in the network to any other node. Full support for distributed databases is provided by the typical RDBMS products described in Part 4.

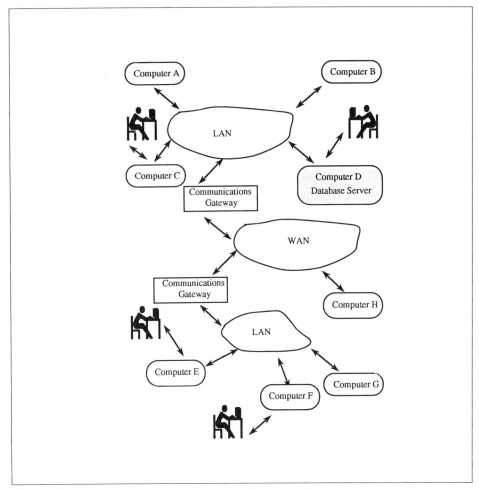

Figure 1.5 Local and wide area networks with central database server

1.3.8 Flexibility

No organisation can anticipate at any given point in time what all its information needs will be for the future. They will change as the needs of the organisation change. Thus it must be possible not only for a database to grow in terms of the volume of the specific types information it contains at any time, but it must also be capable of accommodating new types of information as time goes on. Equally, organisations will not be able to anticipate at any point in time the uses they will put their database to, that is, the software applications which will be developed to make use of it. Thus it must also be possible for the variety of programmed applications written against a database to grow over time.

12 The database concept

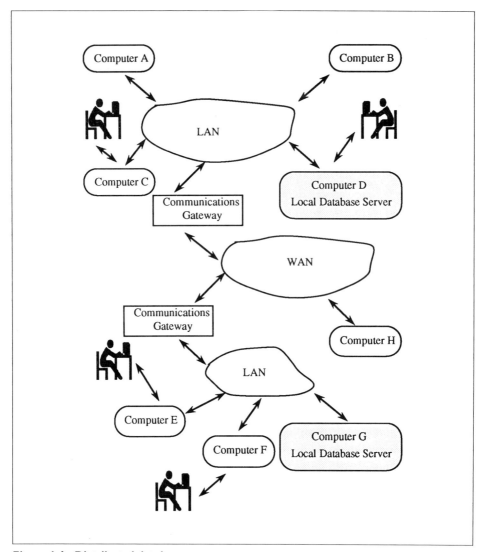

Figure 1.6 Distributed database

If the addition of new types of data to a database to support new applications or enable change to some existing applications has a 'ripple effect' upon existing programs not requiring change, causing them to require amendment, then the database itself is intrinsically inflexible to change. This is because of the expense involved in amending already working programs, the high risk involved of introducing errors into them whilst doing so and the consequent disruption of the users' day to day work. It is, therefore, a basic requirement of DBMSs, that their use results in flexibility of the databases constructed. What they try to achieve in this respect is to de-couple the logic of programs accessing databases from the structure of the database, so that change to the database structure does not necessitate change to the accessing programs. Private data as defined earlier in this chapter, are accessible only by particular programs which support particular transaction types. They are part of the logic of individual programs. If the nature of private data belonging to code sequences is subject to change, then only the specific program which uses them is affected. Change to the nature of public data, data in the database, on the other hand, can result in change to any or all of the programs accessing it unless this de-coupling is achieved.

1.3.9   Integration

Earlier, during discussion of the user's requirements is was seen that a common pool of information was required rather than a series of departmental files, that is, the database has to be integrated. This is clear enough in plain English, but the technical implications are less easily defined. In fact, a good deal more about the nature of information and about the structure of data must be discussed before the technical implications of database integration can be fully understood. This topic will be dealt with in the next chapter. Meanwhile, it can be stated that for a database to be integrated, its structure must reflect the naturally occurring relationships between items of information which exist in the real world so that the user is provided with all necessary access paths to each item of information and all other items of information related to it.

1.3.10   Database Administration

Mention was made earlier of the need for the user community to accept a radical change to their traditional attitudes to the sharing of information as a preliminary to the introduction of the database concept into an organisation. A basic change of attitude is also required on the part of staff developing and providing computer services to the user community. Apart from learning a new approach to system development, such staff soon realise that overall control of the database and its ongoing development has to be centralised within the data processing organisation itself. This realisation has led to the creation of a new role within such departments in the years since database management systems were introduced, the role of the *database administrator* (DBA). This role may be filled by one person or may constitute a whole sub-department depending on the size of the database and the organisation it serves.

1.4   Summary

In this chapter we have learned the meaning of the term database from the point of view of the computer user community within an organisation and have defined this as: *"A large, integrated, shared pool of information in a form suitable for handling by a computer which is a basis upon which the computer user community within an organisation can draw inferences in conducting its business."*

For the successful introduction of a database corresponding to this definition into an organisation, we have seen that the organisation must adopt an across the board policy for the sharing of information whilst ensuring that control of change to specific items

14   *The database concept*

of information is invested in the right hands. To satisfy the user community, the database must be integrated and capable of concurrent access by multiple transactions of the same of differing types. Additionally, it must be:

- Reliable.
- Secure against unauthorised access.
- Consistent in the information it presents to its multiple users.
- Available at all points where the user requires access to it.
- Flexible to change.

To meet these requirements database management systems (DBMS) of various kinds have been introduced. All DBMS of whatever type have to satisfy certain basic technical requirements, namely:

- Multi-access transaction management.
- Lock/unlock and deadlock avoidance facilities.
- Database back up and restore.
- Control of access to data.
- Networked and distributed database facilities.
- De-coupling of database structure from the accessing programs' logic.

2
Information and Storage Basics

2.1 A Multi-level View of Data

In dealing with data, analysts deal with three "worlds" as illustrated in Figure 2.1. Firstly, they must deal with the world of reality, the world in which they breathe and which is perceived through their five senses. This is the world of the computer user community. Secondly, they deal with the world of information, the information about this real world which has been selectively abstracted into their minds. Thirdly, they deal with the world of the machine, the computing equipment into which a representation of that selectively abstracted information will be stored.

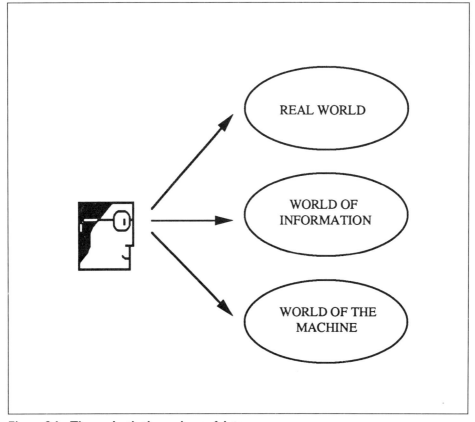

Figure 2.1 The analyst's three views of data

16 *Information and storage basics*

Corresponding to these three worlds, information can be looked at from three points of view; that of the end user, that of the analyst/designer and that of the machine.

2.2 The User's View of Information

The user is interested in certain things in the real world which appertain to his business, in certain characteristics of these things and in the relationships of these things to each other. For example, he will be interested in his customers and certain characteristics about them such as where they are, what their credit status is and so forth. He will be interested in the state of his order book, what orders have been placed, their value, etc. But he will also be interested in relationships between these things which are of interest to him. Obviously, for example, he will wish to know which customers placed which orders.

2.3 The Analyst's View of Information

The analyst, of course, is interested in exactly the same real world information as the users, but needs to analyse the users' information requirements in a methodical and structured way and, as a result of this analysis, produce some structured representation of the requirement in the form of a document. The term *information model* or *data model* is currently used to describe such a document. Some fundamental notions which have become widely accepted in the industry and which underpin all modern methods of information modelling (or data analysis) are introduced in this chapter. These notions, which will be more fully discussed in Part 3, centre around the terms *entity, attribute* and *relationship*.

Entities

The word entity conveys the meaning of a thing's existence as opposed to the properties it possesses or its relationships with other things. Thus, 'John Smith is an entity' simply means that John Smith has existence. An entity can exist in the past, the present or the future. John Smith could be an ancestor, a living parent or a future child. So long as he can be conceived of, he is an entity. In observing the real world, we group like entities together and give them a general name, such as 'ship', 'harbour', 'person', 'animal'. Such groupings are referred to as *entity types*. An entity type does not have to be a generalisation of something concrete as in the examples just given. It can also be a generalisation of some kind of abstract thing. For example, 'Mathematical theorem' is a perfectly valid entity type. During systems analysis we will be selective in our choice of entity type abstractions from the real world, taking interest only in those entity types of interest to the organisation for which a system is being developed.

Attributes

The fact that we have conceived of an entity type means that we have observed a group of things which have certain classes of properties in common. For example, all ships have a length, a hull colour, a means of propulsion and so forth. Such property classes are referred to as *attributes* of an entity type. Again, the analyst will be selective in his or her choice of attributes during systems analysis. He/she will only be interested in those attributes of entity types which are also of interest to his/her end users.

When dealing with an entity type, a clear distinction must be made between the class of thing it represents as a whole and individual occurrences of that class of thing. The entity 'Warrior', for example, is an occurrence of the entity type 'ship'. Specific *attribute values* will be associated with an occurrence of an entity type. Warrior, for instance, has a black hull, is 420 feet long and is propelled by both steam and sail. These attribute values can, of course, vary between one occurrence of an entity type and another. Other ships may have different values for hull colour, length etc. Figure 2.2 illustrates an entity type, its attributes and specific attribute values for some of its occurrences. The figure deals with the entity type 'ship' (using as examples nineteenth century warships) which has the attributes 'length', 'breadth' and so forth. Specific occurrences of the entity type are listed in the figure together with their attribute values.

Entity Type: Ship				
Ship__Name	Length (ft)	Breadth (ft)	Displacement (tons)	Speed (knots)
Duncan	252	58	7000	13
Orlando	336	52	5643	13
Warrior	420	58	9137	14
Gloire	255	55	2500	12.5

Figure 2.2   Entity type, attributes and attribute values

Identifying Attributes

Note that one attribute in Figure 2.2, 'Ship__Name', is intended to identify uniquely each ship. Whilst other attributes may take on the same value for different ships, for example a ship's speed, the value of the attribute 'Ship__Name' must be unique in each case, otherwise it would not be possible to know which ship was being considered. An attribute which must have a unique value for each occurrence of an entity type is referred to as an *identifier attribute,* or *identifier* for short. On occasion, a single attribute may be insufficient to provide the unique identification required. For example, when dealing with merchant ships, the ship's name is only unique in the context of the port in which she was registered. To identify a merchant ship uniquely, we must know both her name and her port of registration. Where two or more attributes are required to form an identifier, is is referred to as a *concatenated identifier.*

18   *Information and storage basics*

Relationships

One could, if one wished, have information available about the entity types 'ship' and 'harbour' and keep these as completely separate pieces of information. However, in the real world, a systematic *relationship* exists between these entity types. The relationship between ships and harbours is that ships can take shelter in harbours. In order to integrate our separate pieces of information about ships and harbours we need to know about occurrences of this relationship. A relationship can be expressed by a connecting verb between the nouns naming entity types, for example, 'Harbour *shelters* ship'. Note that all such relationships are bi-directional, 'Ship *takes shelter* in harbour' means exactly the same as 'Harbour *shelters* ship'.

Again, a distinction must be made between a generalised relationship type between two entity types, like 'harbour shelters ship' and actual occurrences of such relationships. For example, 'Portsmounth harbour shelters HMS Warrior' is an occurrence of the relationship 'harbour shelters ship'. An occurrence of a relationship is identified by concatenating together the identifier values of the entities participating in it. Thus, the identifier attributes of the entity types on each side of a relationship, taken together, constitute a concatenated identifier for the relationship.

An entity type can have a relationship with itself. Assuming an entity type 'employee' which represents all the staff of a company, some of these employees will manage others and the relationship 'employee manages employee' will exist. These are referred to as *loop relationships*.

Two entity types can partake in more than one relationship with each other. The relationship 'Ship takes shelter in harbour' has been discussed. A port is a special type of harbour and the relationship 'Ship takes shelter in port' is also valid. The further relationship 'Ship has home port' also occurs in the real world. 'Ship takes shelter in port' is not the same relationship as 'Ship has home port' although both relationships are between the same entity types. This also applies to loop relationships. For example, the end user may not only be interested in the relationship 'Employee manages employee' but also in the different relationship 'Employee trains employee'.

A very important property of a relationship is defined in this book as its *proportion*. Consider the relationship 'Customer places order'. A single customer can place many orders, so the proportion of this relationship is *one to many*, which is usually written as '1:m'. For one occurrence of a customer many occurrences of orders related to that customer can occur. On the other hand, the relationship 'child has father' has a *many to one* (m:1) proportion, since many children can belong to one male parent. Note that the direction of the relationship is important when dealing with its proportion. Had the previous relationship been expressed as 'father has child', the proportion expressed would be 1:m. The relationship between parents and children is *many to many* (m:n), because a parent can have more than one child and a child can have more than one parent. *One to one* (1:1) relationships are also possible, as for example in the relationship 'employee drives company car', the assumption being that each employee is allowed only one company car at a time.

(*Note:*   Proportion, in the literature, is sometimes referred to as *cardinality*. This can be very confusing because the term cardinality has a completely different meaning when used in relational database theory. The term *multiplicity* has also been used.)

Another important property which needs to be known about a relationship is the obligatory or otherwise nature of the participation of occurrences of the related entity types in the relationship. This will be referred to in this book as the relationship's *insistency*. Consider again the 1:m relationship between customers and the orders they place. It is possible for one or more customers to have no orders placed, therefore it is not obligatory that each customer entity take part in an occurrence of the relationship. But it is not possible to have an occurrence of an order entity without a corresponding occurrence of the customer entity who placed it, therefore all occurrences of orders must take part in an occurrence of the relationship. The obligatory or otherwise participation of entity types on either side of a relationship can be shown by the absence or presence of the letter 'c' qualifying the proportion of the relationship. The 'Customer places order' relationship, case would be qualified as 1:mc. To take a further example, an occurrence of the ship entity type, 'HMS Warrior', does not necessarily mean an occurrence of the m:n relationship 'Harbour shelters ship'. HMS Warrior could be at sea.

Associative Object Types

It is possible for a relationship to have non-identifier attributes of its own. Consider the relationship 'Plane *lands* on runway'. ''lands on'' expresses a relationship between the entity types 'plane' and 'runway'. But this relationship has attributes of its own, for example the time of the landing and the wind speed and direction at that time are attributes of the relationship itself, not of the plane or the runway. Relationships of this kind are referred to as *associative entity types*.

Supertype/Subtype

Entity types may be further generalised from subtypes into supertypes. For example, one could generalise from the entity types 'bridge', 'pontoon' and 'ford' to the super-type 'river crossing'. Bridge, pontoon and ford would then become subtypes of the super-type 'river crossing'. For this type of generalisation to be useful, the subtypes must have some, but not all classes of attributes in common before being generalised into a super-type. The supertype can then have these common attribute classes and the subtypes can each have attribute classes which are particular to them alone. For example, the super-type 'river crossing' might have attributes like 'length' and 'width' which are common to all the subtypes, but not 'height', since this is not an attribute of a ford. By the same coin, 'ford' could have the attribute 'depth' which is irrelevant to bridges and pontoons.

Accessing Information − The Use of Identifiers

In accessing information about specific entity types or relationships, whether in his mind, from a colleague or from some written form in which it is catalogued, the analyst uses identifier values. He identifies individual occurrences of ships by giving a value to the identifier 'name', such as 'HMS Warrior'. Just as importantly, he accesses naturally occurring relationships between entity types by associating identifier values together. For example, he associates the identifier value 'HMS Warrior' (for ship) with the identifier attribute value 'Portsmouth' (for harbour) to access the information that HMS Warrior is in Portsmouth harbour.

2.4 The Machine View of Information – Computer Data Storage

2.4.1 Data Structure

The analyst can organise information in a systematic way into entity types, their attributes and their relationships and this information can be accessed by the use of identifiers. In moving from the analyst's view of information into that of the manner in which it is stored in a computer, the information has to be mapped into the computer's data storage mechanisms. In the discussion about entities, attributes and relationships care was taken to distinguish between general types of things and specific occurrences of them. This

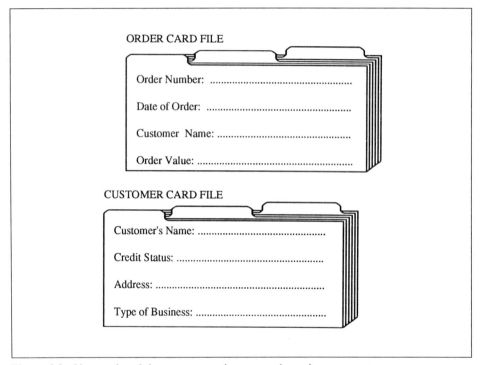

Figure 2.3 Unpopulated data structure (storage scheme)

distinction is reflected in the way information is stored as data in a computer. Types of entities, attributes and relationships are represented by the *data structure,* or *storage schema* created for holding data in the computer; occurrences of them are represented by the data which is embedded in that structure/schema.

Consider Figure 2.3 in which a simple, manual card filing system is depicted. There is one card file for 'customer' and another for 'order'. Each of these cards files represents an entity type. The cards are preprinted and this is a further aspect of the data structure, since individual attributes of the entity types are clearly designated on the cards. A pack of cards with only the preprinted information on them, as in Figure 2.3, corresponds to an 'empty' data structure or storage schema. This data structure becomes *populated* with occurrences of the customer and order entity types as the cards are filled in with information about individual entities as shown in Figure 2.4. Note that the identifier attributes 'Customer Name' for customer and 'Order Number' for order are placed first in the cards to highlight them, but this is not absolutely necessary, just useful. Note also that space has been provided in the order card for the name of the customer who placed the order. This is an example of the use of identifiers to indicate relationships which was spoken of earlier.

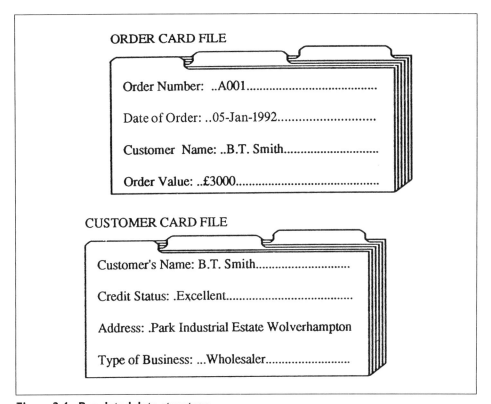

Figure 2.4 Populated data structure

2.4.2 Conventional Computer Storage Structures

2.4.2.1 Type and Occurrence

The card files with their preprinted cards were an example of a form of data structure which is used to represent *types* of entities, attributes and relationships. The blank space on the cards can be filled in with *occurrences* of entities, attributes and relationships. With this distinction between data structure and the data which are used to populate it in mind, conventional data storage structures available in computers and the manner in which entities, attributes and relationships types and their occurrences can be mapped onto them can be discussed.

22 *Information and storage basics*

2.4.2.2 Physical Storage

The physical characteristics of computer storage media are largely hidden from the analyst and programmer by the facilities provided by today's operating system software. However, a brief recapitulation of those characteristics will be useful as a setting for the discussion of the more advanced storage facilities provided by such software, and they must also be understood and taken into account when considering database performance.

Computer storage is commonly divided into 'main memory' and 'backing store', the former providing the fastest access to data and the latter being relatively much slower.

Main Memory

In modern systems this is almost invariably provided by RAM (Random Access Memory) chip technology which allows both reading and writing of data at sub-microsecond speeds. ROM (Read Only Memory) chips of various types are also used in main memory, but these are only suitable for program storage, or storage of constant data since their contents cannot be altered on line in the computer.

As seen by the programmer, main memory is divided into *words* of storage. Each word has a unique address which can be used by machine language or assembler level programs to access its contents directly. The length of a word varies from machine to machine and may be fixed or, in some limited fashion, variable. As a general rule, the longer the word length of a computer is, the more powerful is that computer. As seen by the programmer, the word length in commercial computers is invariably a multiple of a *byte*, a byte being eight times a binary *bit* in length.

The size of main memory available with computers has increased dramatically and its cost has reduced just as dramatically, since the introduction of RAM/ROM chip technology, in line with the increasing numbers of bytes which have been engineered onto a single chip. Whilst eight megabytes of main memory was considered exceptional on a late seventies mainframe computer, one hundred megabytes would not be considered exceptional on today's mini computer. Nevertheless, the kinds of database we are considering in this book may contain many gigabytes of data and for this reason, because of the still relatively high cost per byte of main memory compared to backing store and because of its vulnerability to power failures (the contents of main memory are not retained when power is removed from the equipment), databases are still, for the most part, held in backing store.

Backing Store

Backing store can be broadly categorised into *immediate access* storage which is used to hold data which must be accessed on line and slower *archive* storage which is used to hold back up copies of the on line data and programs or simply to file away data which will only be required very infrequently.

Magnetic tape storage is used for archiving purposes and for software distribution. It consists of a magnetic tape onto which bytes of data can be written and read sequentially. With tape storage there is no quick way of accessing data which are written far down the tape. They have, as it were, to be plodded to wherever they are. WORM (Write Once Read Many (times)) disk storage is also coming into favour as an archiving media.

Magnetic disk storage is the most frequently used immediate access storage media. It is essentially serial in nature, like magentic tape. However it is divided up into concentric tracks, each of which can be accessed separately by either a fixed or moving read/write head assembly. With disc storage it is possible to move quickly to the track containing the data required and then to perform the short search required through that track for them. WORM disk storage is also coming into use as an immediate access media but only where the data do not need to be inserted, deleted or updated on line. For example geographic (map/chart) data which is subject to very infrequent change can be held on WORM media for immediate access on line. On the infrequent occasions when change to the geographic data is required, the WORM disks can be replaced with new ones containing the more up to date data.

Figure 2.5 shows how data are arranged physically on magnetic tape. The tape contains a number of parallel tracks. Nine track tape is illustrated but it is still possible to find seven or eight track tape units. On nine track tapes a byte of data is written across the tracks, one bit per track in parallel. Nine track tape allows a full eight bit byte to be written plus a parity bit for checking purposes. Tape units also provide facilities for writing and reading inter record gaps which indicate the end of one record of information and, therefore, the start of the next. Some units provide facilities for writing *end of file markers* which indicate the end of a group of records which together constitute a file of data. We will be discussing files and records in more detail later. Most tapes have short, reflective tabs attached which the tape unit can detect and which indicate the beginning and the end of the tape. Tape units will usually be specified as operating at a density of so many bits per inch or centimetre, frequently with a choice of densities, and as operating at a speed of so many inches or centimetres per second. From this information the analyst or programmer can calculate the minimum time needed for, say, a back up dump of his disk based database to magnetic tape.

Figure 2.6 shows how data are arranged on a simple magnetic disk. The data is written in bit serial fashion, invariably as bytes, on the disk's tracks. A moving read/write head can be shifted from track to track in any order required. Extra bits may be added to each byte to enable parity checking and more elaborate checks against data corruption may be included for each track. A track is divided (by software) into *blocks*. The size of a block is set by the operating software and may be selectable by the user. The most common block sizes are 512, 1024 and 4096 bytes.

On simpler disk systems such as those provided with personal computers, blocks on a track may be *interleaved*. Blocks are arranged on the disk in a staggered manner such that an interval of one or more blocks may intervene between block accesses. Interleaving allows time for checksum calculations to be made for the block, and for data transfer delays between the computer and the disk to be catered for. The size of the interleave gap in bytes is usually selectable when the disk is formatted and can have a very distinct effect on database performance. In more sophisticated equipment, RAM buffering will be provided to hold one or more tracks full of information at a time, thus removing the need for interleaving.

More elaborate arragements than those shown in Figure 2.6 are possible, particularly for the disk head unit. It is possible to have a multiple head assembly, thus covering several tracks at one time and to have single of double sided disk platters thus enabling quicker search algorithms to be developed. It is also possible to have a disk spindle with several disk platters, which may be single or double sided, mounted on it and single or multiple

24 Information and storage basics

heads for each disk platter on the spindle. In this arrangement, the search is across twice as many tracks as there are disks and the combination of tracks which can be accessed at any one time is referred to collectively as a *cylinder*.

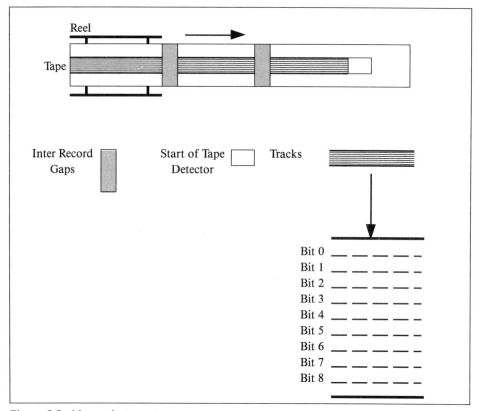

Figure 2.5 Magnetic tape storage

2.4.2.3 Logical Storage. Files and Records

The physical details of computer storage media are hidden from the programmer by operating systems which support the *logical* files and records described in this section.

Data Items

The term *data item* is used to mean the smallest discrete unit of data which can be identified in a computer system. Different programming languages use their own terminology to describe data items. For example, in Fortran a data item is known as a field, in Cobol as an elementary item and in Ada as a scalar data type. The meaning is the same in each case in that the terms are used to describe an item of data which cannot be subdivided within the system, one which can have no component parts. Data items are given names and each named data item will have a possible set of values.

Logical storage data items 25

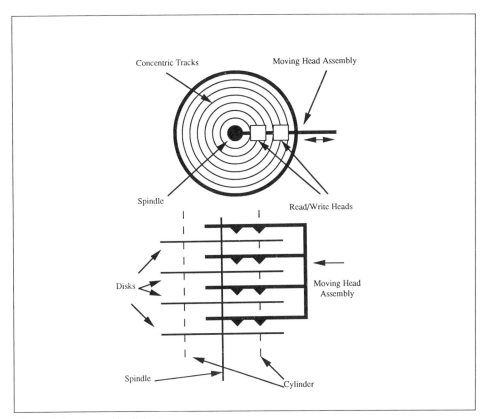

Figure 2.6 Magnetic disk storage

The type of value which a named data item can take on whether by input from some device or as a result of some calculation are usually predefined (declared) in some way in programming languages. In older languages such as Fortran and Cobol, a data item type may be declared as *numeric, alphabetic* or *alphanumeric*. Numeric types can be sub-classified as either *integers* (whole numbers; no fractional parts) or *real* (numbers with fractional parts; floating or fixed point numbers). The more modern languages such as Pascal and Ada allow for *enumeration types* in addition to the integer and real types. An enumeration data type can be defined against the set of values which the data item can take. Predefined enumeration types may be available within the language, Ada for example supports Boolean and Character as predefined enumeration types.

The physical characteristics of data item storage are hidden from the programmer if an HOL (Higher Order Language) such as Cobol, Fortran or Ada is in use. Only assembler language programmers need concern themselves with them. However, the analyst may be interested in them when sizing a database. In modern systems, text (all printable characters) is invariably stored at one byte per character. However, numbers are stored in some binary form to reduce their storage occupancy and make calculations easier.

26 Information and storage basics

In most cases integers and real numbers are stored in two or four bytes of memory and this is usually specifiable by the programmer.

Records

A record is a named collection of data items which can be of the same or different data types. Data items within records are usually referred to as *fields*. An example of a simple record could be:

Data Item Description	Data Item Name	Data Item Type
Customer order number	ord__num	Integer
Date of order	date	Character
Customer identification	cust__id	Character
Value of order	ord__val	Real
Delivery date required	deliv__date	Character

Records can have a more complex structure, for example:

Data Item Description	Data Item Name	Data Item Type
Customer order number	ord__num	Integer
Date of order	date	Character
Customer identifier	cust__id	Character
{Line item identifier	lintm__id	Integer
Numbers of line item	num__lintm	Integer}

In this example, the offset data items shown enclosed within the braces can repeat as many times as required to represent all the line items in the order, making the record variable in length. Other, more complex arrangements still are possible, particularly in modern languages like Ada. Each language must be examined for its possibilities with respect to record structures. This is mentioned here because there can be difficulties in mapping all the possible record structures available with programming languages onto the logical storage structures provided by relational database management systems. Logical records may or may not map directly onto the physical features of the storage media. How this mapping is achieved by the underlying system software is normally transparent to the programmer.

Files

A file is a named collection of records which may be of the same or different types. Files may contain records of fixed length of variable length, or both. Files fall into various categories depending on the method used to access records within them. The most common categories in this respect are serial, sequential, indexed, direct, and inverted.

Storage—files 27

The treatment of each of these categories which follows is intended only to give a general idea of the traditional filing techniques available. The topic is by no means trivial and the published literature on it runs to very many volumes. Some of the standard works on the subject are listed under [1], [2], [3], [4], [5] and [6], in the Reference and Bibliography section at the end of the book for readers who wish to pursue the topic into depth.

A *serial file* is simply a collection of records arranged sequentially in no particular order. Serial files may be a temporary form of storage for data prior to their being further processed, usually into one or other of the file categories which follow. They are also often used for permanent storage of archives and journals. Serial files are accessed record after record in the order in which the records were stored.

Sequential files: A *sequential file* is a collection of records sorted into some particular order, but which can still only be accessed sequentially. A file consisting of customer order records might be sorted in either ascending or descending order of the key, say, 'order_number' field values, or simply in the order that they were written to the file. But it might equally well be sorted chronologically by other record fields such as 'date_of_order' or 'delivery_date' if this were the most useful order for production of a report from it. Sequential files are used most frequently when a long series of repetitive calculations have to be carried out on each record sequentially within a file, for example in pay-roll applications.

Serial or sequential files can be used with both disk and tape storage. The file structures which are now described are more complex and can only be implemented practically by using disk storage.

Indexed files: The fundamental use of indexes is to speed up retrieval of data from files. Suppose each record of a particular file contains the (unique) name of a supplier and further data about him such as his address, telephone number, the goods he supplies and so forth. In the simplest form of indexed file arrangement, an index table, itself held as a file, would contain an ordered list of, for example, the supplier's names and the corresponding logical locations on disk of their records. Various techniques can be used to search quickly through the records of the index using an individual supplier's name in order to find and access the record for that particular supplier. Since the index file is physically smaller than the file it indexes, fewer disk input/outputs (I/Os) are required and the record will be found more quickly than if the search had been through the main file. Using the index, a search might also be made against a range of values, for example to retrieve all suppliers whose names start with 'P'. Several indexes might be created on one file. For example, an index based on the values of addresses in the supplier file would enable a rapid response to the query *Find me all suppliers who are located in London.*

A simple index file arrangement means that for each record in the file containing the data, a corresponding entry must exist in the index file. This can lead to impracticably large amounts of storage space for index files being required. A compromise technique which is very widely used is for the index entry to point to a sequential group of records. The principle is illustrated conceptually in Figure 2.7. Records are grouped into disk blocks, each block holding a group of records which correspond to a sequential range of keys. The block is represented in the index file by the highest key. Thus the index file contains entries only for individual blocks each of which contains a number of data file records. A search through the index is made to identify the block holding the desired record and the block is then itself scanned until the desired record is found by matching

28 Information and storage basics

keys. Indexed sequential files of this nature are usually referred to as ISAM (Indexed Sequential Access Method) files in the literature.

The example in Figure 2.7 has been idealised for simplicity in that the records are shown neatly falling into a pattern of four records per block. In practice, however, this ideal distribution is most unlikely to happen. Keys are unlikely to be of the very simple numeric form illustrated and there is likely to be an uneven distribution of key values within the ranges defined in the index, resulting in an uneven distribution of records requiring space in a particular block. If a block size which can accommodate the maximum number of records possible within the ranges of values defined in the index is defined, then space will be wasted on the disk, since many blocks will be sparsely populated. The procedure normally adopted to avoid this is to define an optimum, compromise block size and introduce a facility for providing *overflow blocks* as required.

The underlying physical arrangement of ISAM files, including the manner in which the disc locations of files are addressed is in general transparent to programmers. However, they must usually calculate and specify the number of disk blocks required by the file and they must take note of possible block overflows and define overflow areas accordingly.

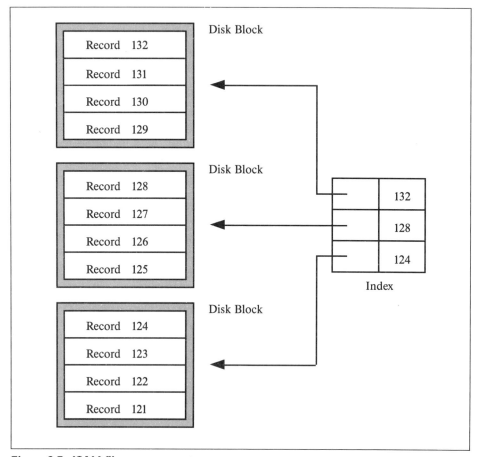

Figure 2.7 ISAM file arrangement

ISAM files can be used for repetitive record processing in the same manner as sequential files, but have the added advantage of providing quick access to individual records or records falling within a particular range of key values where this is required. Note, however, that entering or deleting a record within an ISAM file entails the overhead of creating or deleting the index entry for it, whereas updating (assuming that the update does not alter an indexed field value) or retrieving existing records does not. If the index records are simply held sequentially in storage, then each time a new entry or deletion takes place, the index file will have to be adjusted accordingly and this can be a slow operation. To overcome this to some extent it is common to hold the index file in a *chain* or *ring structure*.

In a chain structure, records are related together by pointers, that is, each record contains a pointer to the physical or logical location of the next record as in the two simple arrangements illustrated in Figure 2.8.

Three records with keys ABC, ABD and ABE are shown. These are linked together by pointers in alphabetical order of key. In the first two examples, each record points to the location of the next in daisy chain fashion. The figure shows two variations of this basic structure, one way, uni-directional and two way, bi-directional chains. In the latter each record points both to the next and previous record allowing bi-directional searching through them, but necessitating the use of multiple pointers. In the second two examples, the first and last records in a chain are connected together forming a *ring*. Searching can begin at any point in the ring and proceed to anywhere else in the ring. Pointers may be embedded in records or stored as a separate array to speed up access times.

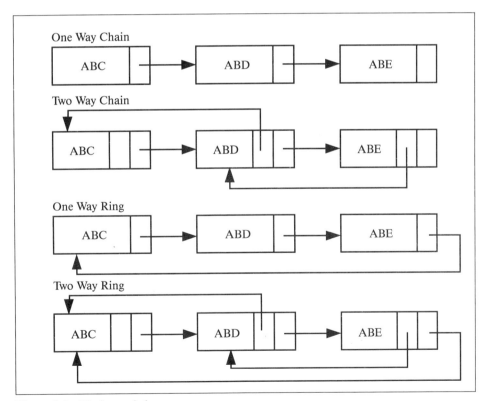

Figure 2.8 Chains and rings

30 *Information and storage basics*

When used in indexes, chain or ring structures speed up the process of inserting or deleting entries because the chain or ring can simply be broken and new links inserted or existing links removed as necessary. It is also very useful in dealing with overflow blocks since these can be 'stitched in' as required. This type of structure is also used for many other purposes and variations of it will be discussed in Chapter 3 where the various database models are introduced.

The prime purpose of indexes, as stated earlier, is to speed up retrieval, of data from files. Since indexes are themselves files, further indexes can be constructed to speed up searches through them and further indexes still to speed up searches through those and so forth. This is known as *multi-level* (or *tree structured*) indexing and the principle of this form of indexing is illustrated in Figure 2.9. The first level index contains records which contain pointers to groups of records in the second level index as illustrated. Suppose that it was desired to retrieve the record whose identifying key was 107. The first index would be searched for a value equal to or nearest to and greater than 107. This would result in the retrieval of the record containing 116 in the level 1 index. This points to the group of records shown in the level 2 index and once again a search would be made for a record containing a value equal to or nearest to and greater than 107 and would result in the record containing 108 being retrieved. This record would contain a pointer to the disk block containing the required record which would be found by a scan through this block until a matching key was found.

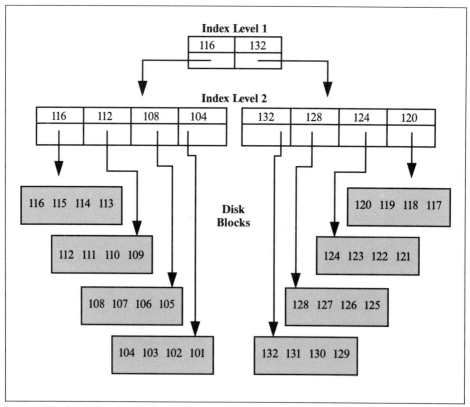

Figure 2.9 Multi level indexing

As for the ISAM example in Figure 2.7 earlier, the example in Figure 2.9 has been idealised for simplicity and takes no account, for example, of the need for overflow blocks. However it does serve to illustrate the principle of how faster access to records can be obtained by dramatically reducing the disk I/Os needed. Suppose, for example, that a 100000 record ISAM file used a single level index containing 10000 records and suppose that the index records could be retrieved from backing store into main memory in groups of 100 at a time. Suppose also that each disk access (to retrieve 100 index entries) took on an average 300 milliseconds. To find the index entry pointing to a given disk block (the block containing the required main file record) would take an average of 50 disk I/Os or 1.5 seconds. Now suppose that the index were arranged on two levels with the level 1 index containing 100 records and the level 2 index 10000 as before. To obtain the level 1 index would take one disk I/O and to obtain the 100 level 2 index records pointed to by this entry would take a further I/O giving 0.06 seconds in total. The computer processing time required has, of course, been ignored in this calculation but in most cases this is negligible in practice compared with the effect of disk I/O times.

Direct files: A *direct file,* often referred to as a hashed random file, differs from sequential and ISAM files in that the record required is fetched directly from the disc when the identifying key field is presented without any intermediate search. No index file is required, but an algorithm, generally known as a *hashing algorithm*, must be used to calculate the location of the record from the record's key field value. The basic elements in a direct access file are *buckets*, an addressable group of disk blocks each containing a sequentially ordered sub-group of the total records in the file, a *hashing technique*, a mathematical algorithm for converting key field values into the address of a bucket and a means of handling *overflows* from buckets.

Many hashing algorithms exist, indeed there is an extensive literature on them. One of the simplest techniques uses the *remainder algorithm*. Suppose that 500 records with keys 000 through 499 have to be distributed over 25 buckets, giving an average of 20 records per bucket. The hashing algorithms is simply to divide the key value with the number of buckets and take the remainder as the address of the bucket. For example, if the key value is 123, then the bucket address is obtained by,

$$123/25 = 4 \text{ remainder } 23$$

and the bucket address is 23. The principles of direct file access are illustrated in Figure 2.10 using the remainder algorithm.

A file length of 16 records has been assumed and four disk buckets capable of holding 4 records each. The record key consists of a three alphabetic character code. To obtain a bucket address, the key is first converted into an integer, in this case by assigning the values 10 through 35 to the letters A through Z respectively. For example, ABC becomes $10+11+12 = 33$. This integer is then divided by the number of buckets (4) and the remainder gives the bucket address which must be 0, 1, 2 or 3. Records are arranged in their respective buckets in ascending alphabetic order. Bucket 0 has overflowed and Bucket 3 is sparsely populated. Records in the disk buckets are usually linked together with pointers in a ring or chain structure, as discussed earlier. This facilitates rapid search through them and simplifies the problem of dealing with overflows, as the chain can be broken and relinked to include overflow buckets in their correct order.

Although much of the underlying complexity in setting up direct access files is made transparent to the analyst and programmer, they have to take many complex factors into

32   *Information and storage basics*

consideration. In addition to the choice of hashing algorithm, the size of disk buckets may be taken into account, as well as the size of overflow areas for them, against the likely number of records and the probable statistical distribution of their key field values across the full range possible. Despite its relative complexity, the direct access method is sometimes the only one suitable for on line systems where rapid response to queries and updates at terminals is important.

Key	Key/4	Remainder/Bucket Address
VAZ	19	0
TTT	21	3
LBS	15	0
KKK	15	0
HJY	17	2
ABC	4	1
XYC	19	3
NLQ	17	2
DBD	9	1
PQR	19	2
RST	21	0
VNQ	20	0
VAC	13	1
QLN	17	2
FST	18	0
GAB	9	1

Overflow	Bucket 0	Bucket 1	Bucket 2	Bucket 3
VNQ FST	VAZ RST LBS KKK	VAC GAB DBD ABC	QLN PQR NLQ HJY	XYC TTT – –

Figure 2.10   Direct access

Inverted Files: An *inverted file* is one which supports access to records via multiple key field values. Such files can be fully inverted supporting access by any field, or partially inverted supporting access by a restricted set of key fields. In a fully inverted file, the index itself in effect becomes the file (hence the use of the word inverted). Every field value of every record can be used as a key and has an entry in the index, together with the address of the record or records within which it is contained. (Note that the same field value could occur in different records.) Since all field values are held within the index and the record structure is therefore implicit within it, there is no need to store these values separately as such. However, facilities are needed to create the records and, as a basis for this, at each record location pointers are stored for each data item in the record which locate the item in the inverted file. In a partially inverted file, the index holds only a selection of key field values for every record, together, as before, with the identity of the record or records holding them and with pointers to the locations of the actual records since, in this case, the records, or at least part of them, must be explicity stored.

2.5 Mapping Information Structures to Storage Structures

2.5.1 Storage Schemata

The earlier part of this chapter discussed how information could be analysed using the notions of entities, attributes and relationships. In order to implement a database, the information obtained by this analysis must be mapped into a computer representation of it using the storage structures available in the computer. In doing this an overall data structure which represents the entity, attribute and relationship *types* identified in the information model will be created. (This structure will later be populated with actual *occurrences* of entities, attributes and relationships.) This overall data structure is referred to as a *storage schema*.

2.5.2 Mapping Entity Types and Attributes to Files and Records

The entity types abstracted from the real world can conveniently be equated with named files in the computer storage schema, one entity type per file. Customer files, order files and so forth can be defined. Occurrences of an entity type will then be accommodated in records of its file, one entity occurrence per record. With each record within a file containing an occurrence of the entity type the file is named for, each field in the record will correspond to an attribute of that entity. When the storage schema is populated, each field of each record will contain an attribute value for a given entity occurrence.

2.5.3 Mapping Relationships between Entities to Files and Records

Assuming that sequential or ISAM based customer and order files existed corresponding to the simple card file example of Figures 2.3 and 2.4, the relationship between customers and orders could be expressed in exactly the same way by cross referencing between one file and the other, using key attribute values to do so. In this case the relationships are established using the *content* of records. It is also possible to use a chain or link structure to represent relationships by linking the related records (entity occurrences) together. In this case the relationships are established using the *position* of records in storage. Alternatively, a combination of both methods could be used.

It has now been established that it is possible to map from an information model which represents the analyst's view of the information into a storage schema which represents the machine view of the same information. However, it is yet to be established whether such storage schemas, based on the conventional logical storage facilities as provided by most modern operating systems can be used to construct databases which meet all the user and technical requirements we established in Chapter 1. This question is addressed in the following chapter.

3
Data Models

3.1 Background to Data Models

The topic of database management systems (DBMSs) was introduced in Chapter 1. The need for such software tools arose out of the concept of a database to satisfy the user community which was described there. Recapitulating what was said, such a database has to be integrated, and capable of concurrent access by users entering into multiple transactions of the same or differing types with it. Additionally, it must be reliable, secure against unauthorised access, consistent in the information it presents to multiple users, available at all points where the user requires access to it and flexible to change in line with change and extension to the user's requirements. It was implicit to this database concept that a database be defined and maintained under the overall control of a separate database administration department.

A database in line with this concept could in principle be constructed using the logical storage facilities described in Chapter 2, but in practice the problems faced would be very severe. For a start, no comprehensive facility for describing the required data structure to the computing system would exist. The operating system would allow the naming of files, but that is about all. Data items and records could not be defined outside of the programming language(s) in use and different languages have their own conventions in this respect. The database design, of course, could be put down on paper and programmers could be instructed to follow that design in the relevant sections of their code, but this is extremely difficult to police, particularly where a mixture of languages is used to build a system. Moreover, it would mean that the larger part of the data structure was coded into programs, making it extremely difficult to change the database's structure without having to revise the code of already working programs. Leaving aside the cost of this revision, it is almost certain to introduce errors into the working programs with consequent disruption to the work of the system's users. In fact, any approach to database construction based directly on the use of traditional file management tools is bound to result in database systems which are intrinsically inflexible to change.

The basis of a solution to these problems is to have an independent *data definition language* (DDL). This language is used to define the required data structure for the database to the system. In order to access this structure and insert, update, retrieve and delete data within it, programs need to be able to use a *data manipulation language* (DML), which is companion to the DDL. The DDL and DML must be capable of being embedded in the common languages in use, Cobol, Fortran and so forth. That is, must be capable of being embedded in a number of *host languages*. Mention was made earlier of the transaction, user terminal orientation of database systems. Ideally, a variation

36 Data models

of the DDL/DML is required which can be entered interactively at a terminal by users to access the data base without the need to embed it within a host language. This is usually referred to as an *interactive query language*. Although this term is in general use, it is inaccurate since such 'query' languages usually also support data definition, insertion, update and deletion operations.

A DBMS is a software package whose essential purpose is to provide DDL, DML and, perhaps, interactive query language facilities. Additionally, it will provide facilities to meet all the other technical capabilities (multi-access, security and privacy and so forth) which were discussed earlier.

Before a DBMS can be developed there must be a concept in the mind of the developer of the type of data structure which can be described using the DDL and how data can be manipulated within this structure using the DML. Where such an underlying concept has been formally defined, it is commonly referred to as a *data model*. To be complete, a data model definition must include definitions of all the possible *objects* which can be represented by it, all the possible *operations* which can be performed on these objects and any rules necessary to preserve the *integrity* of a database constructed by its use. The meaning of 'objects' here corresponds closely to that of data structures as discussed in Chapter 2. The operators supported must, at minimum, permit access to enable insertion, update, deletion and retrieval of data. An example of an integrity rule might be that in a data model supporting ISAM files, each key occurrence in a file must be unique in value.

Over the years a number of data models have been introduced which have been used as the basis for DBMS implementations. These are referred to as the *hierarchic, network, inverted list, relational* and *entity-relationship* models and they are briefly overviewed in the next section in terms only of the objects (data structures) they support. Before going onto these overviews, however, a number of points need to be made.

Firstly, the hierarchic and network models were not defined prior to the development of DBMSs which follow the approaches they dictate. The hierarchic model was arrived at by a process of abstraction from existing implementations, principally from IBM's IMS™ database management system. The network model was abstracted from the CODASYL model and the terms 'network' and 'CODASYL' have, for practical purposes, become synonymous. Thus 'hierarchic' and 'network', although frequently referred to in the literature as models, are really just a convenient way of classifying a certain group of DBMS products into the two broad sub-categories. This group of DBMSs relies principally (but by no means entirely) on *position* in logical storage as a means of representing relationships and they are usually referred to as *formatted* models. The above remarks also apply to the inverted list model, except that in this case the *content* of database storage is of greater importance than position in representing relationships.

The first formal data model definition produced was that for the relational model. All genuine RDBMSs were produced subsequent to that definition and conform to it. The model is, of course, the prime topic of this book. Indeed the idea of having a formal data model at all can be said to have originated with E.F. Codd who defined the relational model. The relational and entity-relationship models depend entirely on the *content* of logical data storage to represent relationships, specifically by the use of key attribute values.

Secondly, the later (and continuing) work on data models has been directed to improving their semantic capability, that is, to improving their capability to represent the meaning of data as such rather than the manner in which it is to be stored. The objects of such models can be used to construct *information models* which represent the information requirements of an organisation. Consequently they have become an important component of modern methods of systems analysis. Thus, whatever original motivation there might have been for their definition, one can conveniently think of two types of data model: *database models*, which have served as the basis for DBMS implementations; *semantic data models,* which serve as the basis for production of an organisation's information model. These two types of data model are not mutually exclusive in principle, but tend to be so in practice.

3.2 Database Models

3.2.1 The Hierarchic Model

The hierarchical database model concept evolved from early practical DBMS implementations. The model can be equated with a *hierarchical tree structure*. This structure, as illustrated in Figure 3.1, can be used to construct a hierarchy of records in the form of nodes and branches. The top or *root* node 'owns' all the 'member' nodes connected to it by branches beneath it and each lower node similarly owns the branch nodes underneath it. The effect is to create sets of 'member' records which are related to the master 'owning' record. In the example given, the root record represents some product entity occurrence which is composed of parts A, B and C. Each of these parts can itself be composed of sub-parts, A1, A2, .., An, B1, B2, .., Bn and so forth. The bottom half of the figure shows how an hierarchical tree structure might be implemented using simple pointer chains. If bidirectional chains (not shown) were to be used, the structure could be searched in both directions enabling owner records to be found from member records.

A basic problem occurs with hierarchical tree structures in that they are not flexible enough to represent all the relationship proportions which occur in the real world. In the Figure 3.1 example there was an implicit assumption that each sub-assembly had a unique set of parts and, therefore that the 'product consists of parts' relationship was 1:m. However, it is very common for sub-assemblies to have parts which are also used by other sub-assemblies, thus forming an m:n relationship between products and parts. This cannot be represented in a hierarchical tree file organisation except by duplicating the information in one node about a part which is already held at another node. In terms of the relationship proportions discussed earlier, the hierarchical tree can support 1:1 and 1:m but not m:n relationships. IBM's IMS DBMS is now described briefly to illustrate the implementation of the concept.

IMS was made available in 1969, being one of the very earliest DBMS products. It has been subject to continual improvement ever since and is still in very widespread use. It is a very comprehensive and complex product and only few of its major features can be highlighted here.

IMS terminology is somewhat idiosyncratic. The product is based on the concepts of so called physical and logical 'data bases'. Physical and logical data bases are described by data base descriptions (DBDs). A collection of physical and logical data base DBDs

38 *Data models*

describes an entire database in the currently accepted use of the word. A program control block (PCB) defines those parts of a database of interest to particular groups of users, that is to particular groups of application programs. All the PCBs for a given user are collectively referred to as a program specification block (PSB). The DDL and DML are incorporated into one language called Data Language/One (DL/1). Each physical or logical 'data base' is a hierarchical tree structure supporting 1:m (or 1:1) relationships. Nodal points of the tree structure are occupied by a segment type. Many occurrences of a segment type are possible at the nodal position. An occurrence of a segment type corresponds to the occurrence of a record in the meaning of that term which has been used previously. A segment occurrence is the smallest unit in the structure for access purposes. An occurrence of a tree in total is referred to (somewhat confusingly) as a record. The segment type at any node is 'parent' to 'children' at the next lower level branches in the hierarchy. Figure 3.2 illustrates the physical data base structure. Logical data bases use the same hierarchical structure.

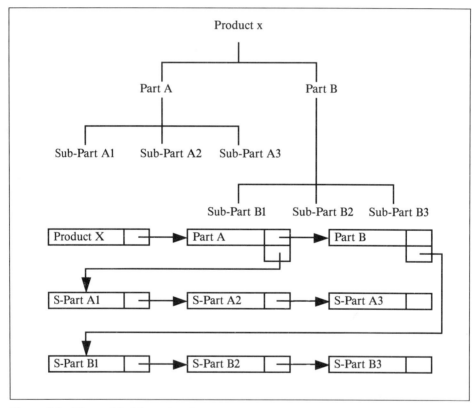

Figure 3.1 Hierarchical tree structure

In the top half of the figure, a physical database type is exemplified. It consists of a parent 'course' segment type and the three 'student', 'time' and 'location' child segment types of this parent. In the bottom half of the figure two occurrences of this physical database type, that is two 'record' occurrences in IMS terminology, are shown, the first for a French course and the second for a German course. The former has three students and is held in Room 1 on Mondays, Wednesdays and Fridays. The latter also has three students and is held in Room 6 on Tuesdays, Thursdays and Fridays.

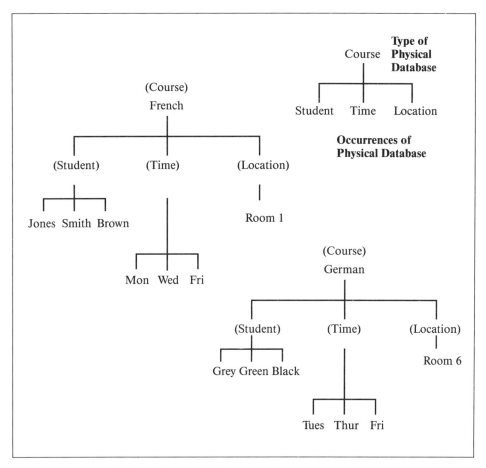

Figure 3.2 A physical 'database' in IMS

Earlier it was seen that it was not possible to represent an m:n relationship in a hierarchical tree structure without introducing redundancy. In the above example it would not be possible to show Smith attending both French and German courses without repeating data about him and introducing redundancy into the database. IMS gets around this by its use of logical data bases. Using these, it is possible to define 'logical children' in one physical data base of 'logical parents' in another. The underlying physical database is not affected by this although a penalty has to be paid in terms of the effect on performance.

A PSB, one user's view of the database, is a collection of logical trees, each of which represents a physical tree or some subset of it, including the logical children, if any, associated with it. Subsets can omit any segment type of the physical tree except the

40   *Data models*

segment at the root node. If a segment type is omitted from a logical tree, all of its subordinate types in the hierarchy are also omitted. If it is included, all its superior types in the hierarchy up to the root segment must also be included. Thus, although some flexibility is possible, the PSB, a logical sub-set representing a user's view of the overall database schema, may contain a high degree of redundant information so far as a particular user is concerned.

An entity type can be represented in IMS by a segment type and attributes of the entity type by the data items in a segment. One to many or one to one relationships between entity types are easily represented in the physical structure and many to many relationships can be introduced by the use of logical children. Occurrences of entity types correspond to occurrences of segments and occurrences of relationships correspond to occurrences of records (physical data bases) and the logical children associated with them.

3.2.2 The Network Model

The network database model concept can be equated with a *network file structure* as exemplified in Figure 3.3 which supports 1:1, 1:m and m:n relationships. In this structure it is possible for one node to share ownership of a node at a lower level in the structure with another node on a separate branch of the tree. It is now possible, for example, for the same part to be owned by different sub-assemblies without need for the information in that part record to be duplicated.

The bottom half of the figure indicates how pointers might be used to implement a network structure. The use of chains or rings is not feasible since linking in the shared member records between owners would cause the linking together of other records which were unrelated. This means that each owner record must have pointers to all its member records and, in order to enable owner records to be found from member records, that each member record needs to have pointers back to all of its owners. The resultant structure is very complex, requiring a large number of pointers and the difficulties presented are such that it is rarely used in practice.

The term 'network model' has, in practice, become synonymous with 'CODASYL model' and the latter is overviewed here.

CODASYL stands for 'Conference on Data System Languages' which is the name given to an informal organisation of computer manufacturers, users, government institutions and so forth whose objective is to oversee the development of standard techniques and languages to assist in analysis, design and implementation of computer systems. The original initiative for CODASYL came from the US Department of Defence who created it to investigate the feasibility of a Common Business Oriented Language (COBOL) during the fifties. In the late sixties CODASYL directed its attention to the problem of a common model for DBMS implementations and, as a result, a specification was produced in the early seventies which has been widely implemented in DBMS products such as IDBMS from the Cullinane Corporation and DBMS from DEC. The CODASYL model is quite complex and only its key structural features are highlighted here.

The basic objects in the model are data items, data aggregates, records and sets, all of which can be named. As always, distinction must be made between types and occurrences of these. One or more data items constitute a data aggregate and one or more data aggregates constitute a record type. The name of a record type must be unique within

The network model 41

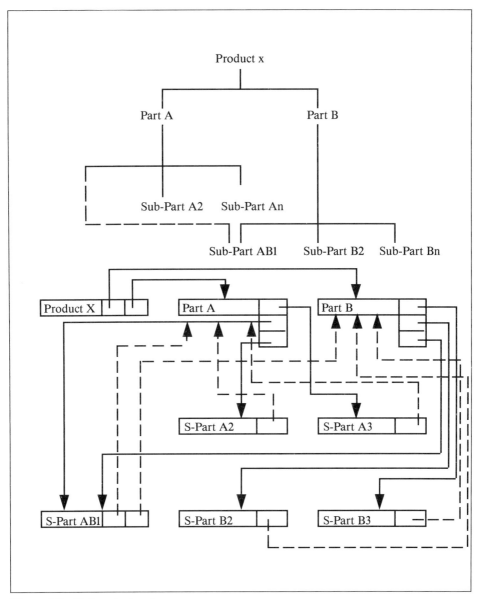

Figure 3.3 Network structure

a database. A set type is defined as a collection of one owner record type and one or more member record types. A record type can participate either as a member or owner in many diffferent set types, but cannot be both an owner and a member in the same set type. The name of a set type must be unique within a database.

Sets are, essentially, hierarchical tree structures and as such cannot represent many to many relationships. CODASYL does not support the network structure based on

42 *Data models*

pointers which was described earlier in this section, because of the complexity of pointer maintenance that this would introduce. It achieves the same effect, however, by the use of *link records* which contain pairs of key values for the record occurrences to be associated and can also hold attribute values which belong to the relationship itself rather than to the associated record occurrences.

The set constructs discussed up till now do not provide a convenient way of searching through all record occurrences of one record type. There is likely to be a requirement to process information on, for example, all customers, all line items and so forth; that is, to search through owner records independently of any consideration of the members of the sets they own. Since a record cannot be both an owner and a member of the same set type, a special category of set called a *system set* is supported by the model. Such a set consists of a dummy 'system' record type and one member record type, for example one could have the set system-orders. Only one instance of such a set can occur and for that reason it is also knowm as a *singular set*.

In the CODASYL model entity types are represented by record types, with each record corresponding to an occurrence of an entity. Attributes correspond to named data items within records and relationships are represented by non-singular set types. Each occurrence of a relationship corresponds to a set occurrence for 1:1 and 1:m relationships and to the occurrence of a pair of sets sharing a link record type for m:n relationships.

3.2.3 The Inverted List Model

Once again no formal inverted list database model has actually been defined. The term is used to group together a number of DBMSs whose underlying design is based on the inverted list file structure described in Chapter 2. The actual manner in which this structure is used varies considerably from DBMS product to product and it is difficult to find a typical example, although many excellent, well liked and widely used products are based on the principle. Since inverted list products use storage content as the main means of expressing relationships, they have a strong family likeness to products based on the relational model which will be described next. The difference is in the level of abstraction presented at the interface with the analysts and programmes using the system. The user of these products is more aware of the underlying file structures than is the user of RDBMSs. Most such products have acquired SQL (the standard relational database language) 'front ends' in recent years.

3.2.4 The Relational Model

This model will, of course, be discussed in great detail in the course of this book. At this point a very simple treatment of it is given with the sole purpose of showing how it handles entities, attributes and relationships.

Tables

An entity type in the relational model is represented as a named table of values. Named table columns represent attributes of the entity type and each row in the table corresponds to an entity occurrence. One or more columns must contain attribute values which enable each entity occurrence (row) to be uniquely identified. In Figure 3.4 the entity type 'customer' is represented by the table CUSTOMER. The first column of the table holds values for the primary key attribute 'name' whose value, in the example, is assumed to be unique for each occurrence of a CUSTOMER entity. The names of primary key attributes are shown in bold faced type in the figure. (This convention will be followed in further examples of tables given in this book.) The second column holds values for the attribute 'credit status', the third for 'business_type' and so forth. The first row contains attribute values for the customer entity 'Smith', the second for entity 'Jones' and so on. Similar tables are shown for the entity types ORDER and LINE_ITEM. The table ORDER_LINE_ITEM has special significance which will be discussed in a moment.

CUSTOMER TABLE

name	credit_status	business-type	etc
Smith	Excellent	Retail	—
Jones	Good	Wholesale	—
Brown	Fair	Multiple	—

ORDER TABLE

number	date	cust_name	etc
100	01/02/91	Jones	—
101	04/12/90	Smith	—
102	15/01/90	Jones	—

ORDER_LINE_ITEM TABLE

order_num	lintm_name	quantity	etc
100	Axe	15	—
100	Spade	10	—
101	Shovel	12	—
102	Spade	50	—

LINE_ITEM TABLE

name	unit_price	stock	etc
Axe	£15	400	—
Spade	£34	200	—
Shovel	£3	600	—

Figure 3.4 Relational Tables

It is important to note that the actual *position* in the table of rows and columns is of no importance. If the position of rows and/or columns were changed in any of the tables

44   *Data models*

there would be no change to the information content or accessibility of data. It can be stated that access to data in a database constructed according to the relational model has no dependence on positional information whatsoever. Another important point is that the tables must be flat, that is, repeating columns are not allowed in the model. The reasoning behind both of these statements will be presented in Part 2.

Relationships in the relational model are represented by the use of primary keys as illustrated in bold faced type in Figure 3.4. The entity types, CUSTOMER and ORDER, have the primary key attributes 'name' for customers and 'number' for orders respectively. In order to represent the relationship 'Customer *places* order', the primary key attribute values from the CUSTOMER table are embedded in the ORDER table in its 'cust__name' column to establish a cross reference. 'Customer places order' is a 1:m relationship and the method shown of representing such relationships is always appropriate to this proportion. The relationship between orders and line items, on the other hand, is m:n. Any order can contain many different line items and any line item can occur in many different orders. This relationship can only be expressed by the use of a separate table. In the example, the table ORD__LINE__ITEM serves this purpose having both the order and line item primary keys embedded in it to establish the cross reference. Note that the attribute 'quantity' is also represented in this table as a column. This is because it can only occur when there is also an occurrence of the order to line item relationship.

It would have been possible to represent the 1:m 'customer *places* order' relationship with a separate cross reference table having the customer and order primary keys embedded within it, but this would be much less economical than the solution shown.

Although operators have not been discussed for the earlier data models overviewed, a few words are said about the relational operators because the model is, after all, the book's prime topic.

The relational model includes a definition of certain fundamental operations which can be carried out with a relational database. These are incorporated into the international standard for a relational database language providing both DDL and DML capabilities, the SQL language. SQL will be described in detail in Part 4. Meanwhile, to illustrate how access is made to a relational database, three of the most significant operations supported by it are described, *selection, projection* and *join*. The syntax of SQL is not explained at this stage, since SQL is 'English like' enough to be followed intuitively. Use of interactive SQL at a terminal is assumed in the examples which follow and these examples are based on the tables in Figure 3.5.

Selection

Suppose that one wished to obtain all information about the customer entity 'Smith' as shown in the CUSTOMER table of Figure 3.3. A SQL select statement could be constructed as follows:

select*
from customer
where name = 'Smith';

The asterisk indicates that all attribute values for the row identified by the 'where' clause are to be returned and 'name' in the 'where' clause is the primary key column of the CUSTOMER table. The query would result in the system returning the following

The relational model 45

information to the user's screen.

name	credit_status	business_type
Smith	Excellent	Retail

Note that the same information would be obtained even if the position of columns, or of the row containing Smith's details, were different in the table. The order in which columns are retrieved can, however, be controlled in the SQL query, for example:

select business_type, name, credit_status
from customer
where name = 'Smith';

where 'business_type', 'name' and 'cedit_status' are column names in the CUSTOMER table, would return:

business type	name	credit status
Retail	Smith	Excellent

Projection

If only certain attribute values were wanted, that is, if only certain columns were to be *'projected'*, the unwanted attribute names would be left out of the list in the query. Thus:

select name, credit_status
from customer
where name = 'Smith';

would return:

name	credit status
Smith	Excellent

Join

A join operation is one of the SQL operations which allows a query to span across two or more tables as in the following example:

select cust_name, number, lintm_name, quantity, unit_price
from order, order_line_item, line_item
where number = order_num
and lntm_name = name
order by cust_name;

where all tables concerned in the join are named in the FROM clause and the columns over which the join has to take place are named in the WHERE clause. The ORDER BY clause ensures that the rows are returned in ascending order of customer names.

The query will return attribute values from all the three tables named as follows:

46   *Data models*

cust_name	number	lintm_name	quantity	unit_price
Jones	100	Axe	15	£15
Jones	100	Spade	10	£34
Jones	102	Spade	50	£34
Smith	101	Shovel	12	£3

3.2.5   The Entity-Relationship (E-R) Model

At the same simple level of treatment just applied to the relational model, the E-R model differs from it in only one significant respect. In the E-R model, all relationships *must* be represented by a separate table. The prime reason advanced by the model's originator (Chen) for this departure was to improve the semantics of data in his model. He also demonstrated that his model was more general than those, like the relational and network models, which preceded it in that they could both be derived from it. There has been no cogent commercial imperative for the widespread implementation of Chen's model as commercial DBMSs and very few instances if such implementations exist. The other aspects of the model, improved data semantics and extended generality, however, have had significant impact on the industry at large. In his original and subsequent work on his model, Chen introduced a graphical notation for the representation of entity types, associative entity types and relationships. This simple notation, reflecting the model's generality and relative semantic richness, and subject to some elaboration and variation by others over the years, forms the basis for most information modelling notations currently in use in modern methods of analysis and design. This notation will be described in detail in Chapter 4.

3.2.6   Comparison of the Relational Model with Earlier Models

The first thing that may strike the reader about the models just described is how simple the relational model is compared with those which preceeded it. This is because of the level of abstraction it achieves from the underlying complexities of computer storage structures. The hierarchic, network and inverted list models all to some degree or other reflect the underlying logical storage structures, described in Chapter 2. The relational model, on the other hand, concerns itself solely with the representation of information and was thus the first truly semantic data model to be defined. It does not concern itself at all with the storage structures needed in a computer to support it. The result is that relational DBMSs (RDBMSs) are exceptionally easy to use in comparison with their predecessors. Most people are thoroughly familiar with tables and use them in their everyday lives. At a simplistic level, relational databases are as easy to understand as the simple card filing system which was used in Chapter 2 to introduce the notion of data structure. This is not to say that the process of analysing, designing and maintaining a relational database are all *that* simple, but they are much more so than the same processes when used with the earlier models.

Another less obvious but even more important point has to do with the way data are accessed in the models. Because the earlier models reflect underlying computer storage structures, access to data within databases based upon them must always entail a degree of 'navigation' involving decision taking. For example, in finding data within a

CODASYL style database, one has to use operations like 'get next', 'get before', etc. in searching one's way through set structures and one has to make decisions based upon what is found in order to decide what to do next. This means that the language used must be a procedural language such as COBOL, Fortran or Ada. This should be compared with the relational model's non-procedural, declarative SQL language, where a single statement, with no decision branches, can perform a retrieval (or update, deletion, insertion) operation which would entail many statements with many decision branches in a procedural language. Note that this does not mean that procedural languages cannot be used with relational databases, but, where they are so used, they access the database by the use of *embedded SQL* statements within the native code. The SQL, non-procedural approach is made possible because no positional information is required in accessing data in a relational database.

In a much quoted anology, getting to data in a 'positional' style, formatted database compared with getting them in a relational database is like driving a car to an airport as compared to taking a cab to get there. In the first case, a map is needed by the traveller which must be consulted in order to navigate to the airport, even if the map has been committed to the driver's memory. In the second case, the traveller simply asks the cab driver to take him to the airport and, in due course, he arrives there. The traveller needs no map in this case. To stretch this analogy a little further, a program which has to navigate to its data must have a map to get there. If the map changes, that is if the structure of the data changes, then the program has to change. This means that the logic of the program is strongly coupled to the structure of the database. Because the relational model does not use positional information, this strong coupling is avoided and it is possible, with only a few restrictions and provided that the database has been properly designed, to change and extend the database to cater for new user requirements without necessitating change to programs already accessing it. Thus databases following the relational model are intrinsically more flexible to change and extension than those following the earlier models.

3.3 Semantic Data Models

3.3.1 The ANSI-SPARC Architecture

In 1975 the database management systems study group of the ANSI/SPARC committee published a report proposing a three level architecture for DBMSs. This is illustrated in Figure 3.5.

The gist of the proposal was that DBMSs should support three views of the database. *External schemata* would provide user views of the database tailored to individual needs. A *conceptual schema* would give a complete and explicit description of the entire information content of the database and would also serve as a link between the external schemata and an *internal schema* which would concern itself with the way data were physically stored in the computer. The hub of the architecture is the conceptual schema which, as stated, had, as its prime role to serve as a complete and explicit description of the information content of the database. This is the same as saying that it must be a semantic data model.

48   Data models

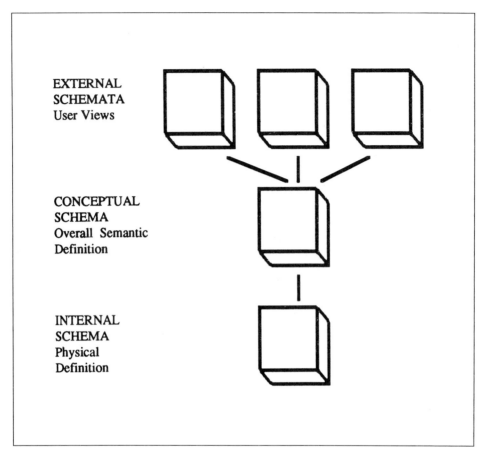

Figure 3.5 The ANSI/SPARC three level model

The proposal aroused, and continues to arouse, much debate and controversy, but has yet to see full practical implementation in DBMSs. This is because it has proved difficult in practice to realise how the second role of the conceptual schema, that of serving as a link between the external and internal schemata, can be achieved. For this reason attention has focussed on the first role of the conceptual schema, and this in turn has focussed attention on the role of the semantic data modelling in general. It could be argued that the most important impact of the ANSI/SPARC proposal has been to bring about an increased awareness of semantic data modelling and its importance in the construction of organisational information models.

3.3.2   Semantic Data Model Objects

When divorced from the ANSI/SPARC proposal considerations, the role of the conceptual schema, that is, of semantic data models, moves away from concern with DBMS implementations to a more general concern about how one goes about modelling the information requirements of an organisation, irrespective of how these will eventually be implemented. That is, it is principally concerned with how one goes about analysing these requirements and representing them in some written or electronic form so that they can be discussed and agreed with the user community.

The basic objects of a semantic data model have, in fact, already been discussed in Chapter 2, where the notions of entity types, attributes relationships, associative object types and subtypes/supertypes were introduced. In Chapter 4, a widely used graphical and textual notation which can be used to represent these semantic data model objects will be described.

3.3.3 Information Models

The objects of a semantic data model are used to assist the analyst in defining an information model representing the information requirements of an organisation. This distinction between an information model and a semantic data model may seem to be pedantic, but the terminology in the industry is very confusing. Information models are referred to variously as data models, semantic data models, database models and entity relationship models. A semantic data model contains no information except about itself. An information model constructed using the objects of a semantic data model contains information specific to an organisation. In effect, the semantic data model provides a *method* for construction of an information model.

The reader may question whether one should bother with using semantic data model objects to construct the information model in the first place. Why not go straight to the relational model and construct an information model from it? Or, for that matter, why not skip the information model and go straight to the relational database design? The answers to these questions are pragmatic.

Firstly, the information model is of interest not just to the analyst but also to his users. Properly documented, it presents a concise but comprehensive statement of the user community's information requirements and as such is the major output from the data analysis process and can be discussed with users to check that their requirements are actually being met. To enable such discussion, it must be as semantically rich as possible, it must be able to convey as much meaning as possible to users. In the next Chapter, it will be shown how the objects of the above model can be represented graphically (a picture is worth a thousand words) in an *Entity Relationship Diagram* (ERD) with supplementary detail provided in structured textual form in a *data dictionary*.

Secondly, the semantic data model used in information modelling, with richer semantic capabilities than the relational, is a very useful tool for the analyst, promoting method, clarity, precision and accuracy in the analysis and recording of user needs.

4

Introduction to Modern Methods of Analysis and Design

4.1 Introduction

A complete database system will consist of the database schema and the applications software which uses it. The schema implements the *data requirements* of the enterprise for which a system is being developed. The applications implement the *functional requirements* of the enterprise. This leads to a chicken and egg situation. Do we analyse the data requirements first and then the functional requirements, or do we analyse the functional requirements first and then the data requirements? There is no black and white answer, of course. Both forms of analysis are required and to some degree or other must be carried out concurrently, but data analysis will be stressed during the early development stages of a database system. Functional and data analysis techniques are both supported by the so called *modern methods of analysis and design* which have been introduced and which have come into widespread use over the last decade or so.

Increasingly, the analyst/designer who is involved with relational database development work will be constrained to work within the framework of some set of these modern analysis and design methods which have been adopted by the organisation to which he or she belongs, or is consulting to. Such methods are usually supported by the use of commercially available CASE (Computer Aided Systems Engineering) tools. In this chapter, the most mature and widely used of these methods are overviewed. This overview is intended to serve as background information for later chapters and also to introduce some useful graphical and textual notations which will be used extensively during the course of this book.

4.2 Background

The impetus for the development of modern methods of analysis and design and the CASE tools which support them came from an increasing perception in the industry that the technical problems of getting medium to large scale software development projects up and running within the estimated budget and timescales and according to the original requirements specified had to be addressed at the *earliest* stages of the project, that is, during the analysis and design phases. The reason for this is illustrated in Figure 4.1.

Studies made by various researchers during the nineteen-seventies showed that the highest proportion of systems errors were introduced during the early analysis and design phases. Typical proportions of errors are shown in Figure 4.1, for the analysis and design phases as compared with the detailed coding phase. The studies showed that whereas the majority of coding errors were cleared up before acceptance trials of a system began, close to half the errors made during analysis and design did not become apparent until acceptance trials were being conducted. These late discovered errors were, of course, by far the most expensive to correct, since they revealed fundamental misunderstandings, both about the enterprise problems the system was created to solve, and the overall technical approach to their solution.

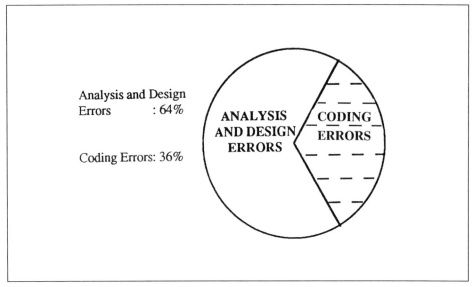

Figure 4.1 Most errors created during early phases

By the middle nineteen-seventies, the coding phase of development has already been improved with the widespread promulgation and acceptance of *structured programming* techniques. The studies described above resulted in attention being focussed on complementary methods of *structured design* and, later, on methods of *structured analysis*, both of which have come into widespread use during the nineteen-eighties. The industry has also seen the introduction of *object oriented programming* techniques and languages in their support, followed by the introduction of *object oriented design*.

Mature and well established CASE tools in support of structured analysis and design methods have been available for a considerable time and are beginning to emerge for object oriented design. The problems that all modern methods of analysis and design set out to solve are essentially the same and are discussed in the following paragraphs.

Poor inter-human communication between developer and user: Bad communication between the developers of a system and its potential users is the major reason for the failure of software projects. The production of a formal specification of the users' requirements of the system which is concise, understandable by both developers and users, and which can be related both backwards into the users' original less formally expressed requirements and forwards into the developers' design, is fundamental to the ultimate success of complex systems. Modern methods of analysis enure that such a document is the prime output from the analysis phase. Lack of any formal means to record the users' requirements means that they may easily be lost sight of as the development progresses. It becomes difficult, if not impossible, particularly where formal contract work has been undertaken, to demonstrate that the system designed is actually compliant with the original requirements. This problem is exacerbated by the fact that it is normal and inevitable that the requirements change during the course of any large software development.

Poor communications within the development team: The definition of clear phases in the analysis and design process together with clear specification of the outputs to be achieved from these phases, is essential to effective management planning and to communications within the development team. Just as important is a commonly shared understanding and acceptance amongst the development team of the technical *methods* to be used in achieving these outputs. This greatly reduces the possibility of technical misunderstandings. It is far less important that individuals in a team follow some 'best' method, rather than that all follow the *same* method from the point of view of effective communications amongst them. Communication between team members is also greatly improved if concise, graphical means are used to the maximum extent possible to record analysis and design decisions. These decisions otherwise tend to get lost in the 'paper explosion' which invariably occurs as the project progresses. The essence of modern methods of analysis and design is support for clearly defined project phases, with clearly defined methods for achieving their outputs, and the use of graphical notations to the maximum extent possible in the construction of these outputs.

Poor quality of the design structure: Simple minded, unmethodical approaches to overall analysis and design, based on the analysis/designer's intuition alone or some vague, 'top down' decomposition of the problem, usually lead to over complex interfaces between the resulting system modules, thus greatly increasing the cost and risk in developing and maintaining them. Modern design methods are aimed at constructing system modules which have the properties of being as loosely coupled as possible with each other whilst being internally cohesive, thus minimising the complexity of the interfaces between them. Such methods proceed in general by building a series of models of the system to be implemented, each model produced serving as input to the construction of the next. The earliest models are at the highest level of abstraction of the problem with successive models introducing more detail as needed. The final model output from the process is a specification from which programmers can begin the detailed coding of the system. Each model is the deliverable from some specific phase or sub-phase of the develpment activity and each concentrates on the issues important to its phase. The components of the deliverables are some form of graphical representation of the system with accompanying test. The textual part of the model, which may itself be structured, serves to clarify the graphical model and to supplement it with more detail.

The graphical and textual constructs supported by a given method or set of methods are the *tools* provided to the analyst/designers to assist them in their tasks. These may be available in automated form as a CASE tool. A well documented (and/or well taught) method will also provide the analyst/designer with a set of detailed guidelines, sometimes referred to as *heuristics* (rules of thumb) usually supplemented by quality assurance rules, on how to go about the task of producing the model for a specific development phase. It is important to realise that an understanding of these guidelines is necessary before the method can be used. Automatic tool support for various analysis and design methods

54   *Introduction to modern methods of analysis and design*

is widely available, but the user documentation for these CASE tools and the training provided with them is likely to concern itself primarily with the mechanics of their use rather than with the method of analysis and design to be followed with their help. For this knowledge, supplementary reading and/or training is required and this is also widely available, whether from the tool vendor or from consulting organisations.

This chapter deals first in some detail with *structured analysis* and *structured design*, the most mature of the current methodologies. This is followed by a brief discussion of *object oriented design*. It has to be stressed that all that can be achieved in one short chapter covering these complex topics is to give an outline understanding of them. A detailed cover of modern methods of analysis and design is well beyond the scope of the book. However, a broad understanding at least of them is required for an understanding of how the specialist discipline of relational database systems analysis and design fits within their framework, and this is why the chapter has been included.

For readers who wish to obtain an in depth knowledge of the structured methods described in this chapter, a number of standard books and state of the art papers are listed in the Bibliography and Reference section The original widely available work on structured design was by Yourdon and Constantine in 1975[7]. This was followed up by a book on structured analysis De Marco in 1975[8]. Structured analysis and design was elaborated to cover real time systems by Ward and Mellor[9] in 1985. Other relevant books have been written by Hatley and Pirbhai[10], Page-Jones[11], Yourdon[12] and by Gane and Sarson[13]. Many courses on the topics are available from consulting and training organisations and from the vendors of CASE tools. Object oriented design is covered by references[14], [15] and [16].

The overviews of strucured analysis and design given here follow in general the precepts given by Yourdon, De Marco and Ward and Mellor, and the graphical and textual notations used also follow in general those used by them. It is the notation supported by the Team*work*™ CASE tool kit marketed by Cadre Technology.

It is emphasised that these methods are not formal in the mathematical sense. They should not be regarded as religions whose precepts must be accepted as dogma by their users. They are there to assist and guide the intelligent analyst/designer who will adapt them as necessary to the specific needs of his or her task. They are not a substitute for intelligence on the analyst/designer's part, but only supplementary to it.

4.3   Structured Analysis (SA)

The product of SA is described variously as a logical or *essential model*. The term 'essential model' will be used in what follows. The essential model is a statement of *what* the system has to do not *how* it has to do it. The essential model's purpose is to model the requirements the system has to satisfy. It is free of implementational detail. It assumes 'perfect technology' that is, it assumes that all the processing power and storage capacity required to implement the system will be readily available.

It is comparatively rare these days for an analyst to be employed in the development of an entirely new system. It is much more likely that the system to be developed will be based, at least in part, on an existing system. This system may be manual, automated, or some mixture of both. In this case a description of the current system must first be written down if such a description is not already available. (If available, it will usually require bringing up to date). The current system must then be abstracted into an essential model removing all physical detail and simply stating what the current system does, not how it does it. This essential model can then be elaborated to include any enhancements to current facilities required, new facilities to be included and facilities to be removed.

The essential model has two components, an *environmental model* which defines the boundary between the system and the external world with which it interacts and a *behavioural model* which defines the system's behaviour, that is, what the system has to do. Both these models are graphical in nature and both are supported by textual data in a *data dictionary*. The behavioural model is further supported by textual detail in *process specifications*.

The Environmental Model

The environmental model is represented by a *context diagram*. This diagram has three components: a single, *transform 'bubble'* representing the system and containing a very high level statement on what it has to do; *terminators*, represented as rectangles, which correspond to the ultimate sources and sinks for data entering or leaving the system; *data flows*, arrowed lines connecting the terminators to the system bubble and labelled with names for the data flowing between the system bubble and its terminators. This data is described in detail in the data dictionary. Description of the data dictionary will be postponed until the behavioural model is discussed. A simple example of an environmental model is shown in Figure 4.2.

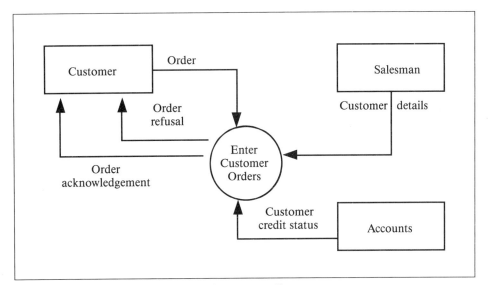

Figure 4.2 Environmental model – the context diagram

The system illustrated has to register and acknowledge customer orders. The sinks and sources for the net data which flows in and out of the system are shown as terminators and the data flows between them and the system are also shown. The customer originates orders and receives acknowledgements for them when they are accepted by the system. Details about customers, their names, addresses etc, are fed into the system by salesmen and the accounts department keeps the system informed about the credit status of customers. Note that the context diagram shows the *ultimate* sinks and sources for data. Data about orders, and their acknowledgement are shown going to and from the customer terminator, not to some item of terminal equipment. Note also that the scope of the environment model covers everything that the system has to do without reference as to how it will eventually be implemented. For example, some functions included within the system boundary may, in the event, be performed by people rather than by equipment.

The Behavioural Model

The behavioural model enables the analyst to take three complementary views of the system. These views are illustrated conceptually in Figure 4.3. An *information model* is used to model the data requirements of the system. The graphical component of this is frequently referred to as an *Entity-Relationship Diagram* (ERD). Complementing this information model there is a *data transform model*, which models the essential functionality which has to be delivered by the system. The graphical component of this is referred to as a *Data Flow Diagram* (DFD), A *dynamics model*, the graphical component of which is referred to as a *State Transition Diagram* (STD), models the behaviour of the system over time and hence its reponse to external events. Note that the dynamics model was introduced for the specific purpose of assisting in the analysis of real time systems. The ERD and DFD of the information and data transform models are supplemented by structured textual detail in the *data dictionary*.

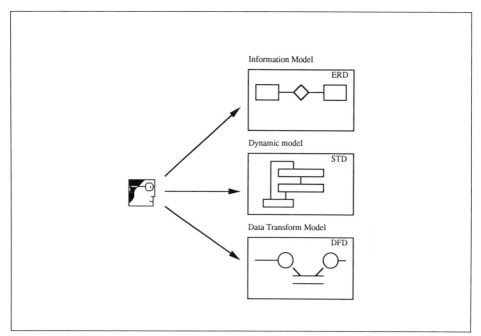

Figure 4.3 The behavioural model – three complementary views of the system

The Data Transform Model

The data transform model deals with the system's data inputs and outputs and the transformations which take place between them. The basic graphical constructs of a DFD are shown in Figure 4.4. *Data transforms*, as their name implies transform inputs of data into outputs of data. Labelled *data flows* define these inputs and outputs. Named *data stores* model data which must be brought to a state of rest within the system in order to accommodate time delays between data transformations. *Terminators* have already been discussed. (At this point it should be clear that a context diagram is simply a very high level DFD.)

The graphical depiction of data flows and data stores is supplemented with textual detail in the data dictionary. Data transforms representing a data transformation of some complexity may be decomposed into lower level DFDs. The transforms within this DFD may be further decomposed into further lower level DFDs and so forth.

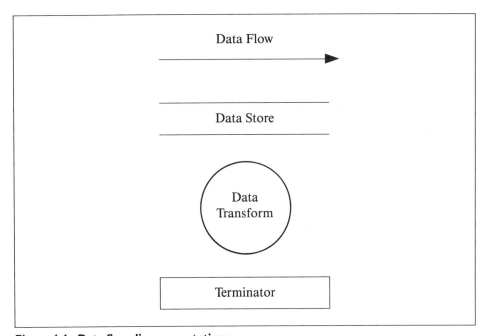

Figure 4.4 Data flow diagram notations

A simplified example of a DFD based on the context diagram of Figure 4.1 is given in Figure 4.5. Data flow diagrams are *not* flowcharts. They do not explicitly show the sequence in which the transformations take place, although this can usually be inferred from the general flow of data through them.

The Information Model

The information model consists of an *entity relationship diagram* (ERD) and a *data dictionary*. Information models are of great importance in database development work.

58 Introduction to modern methods of analysis and design

The graphical symbols and textual notations used in their construction are gone into in detail here as they will be used very frequently in the course of this book.

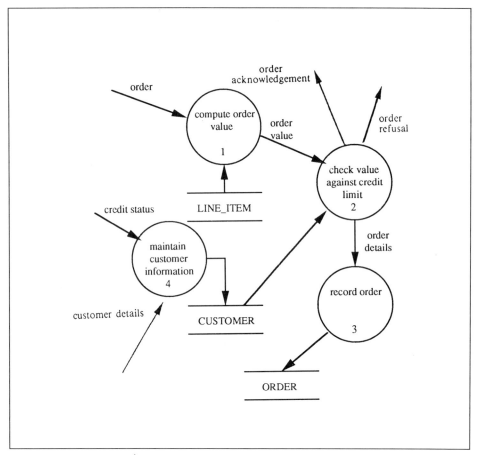

Figure 4.5 Data flow diagram

Graphic notation: An ERD is constructed using a number of simple graphical symbols each of which correspond to one of the objects of the semantic data model which were described in Chapter 2.

Using this notation an entity type (usually referred to as an *object type* in structured analysis terminology), is represented by a named box and a relationship by a named diamond. By convention, entity type names are given as single nouns in upper case letters and relationship names as verbs in lower case letters. A relationship diamond is connected by lines to its participating entity types. The proportion of a relationship is shown by the appropriate use of the symbols '1' and 'm'. The insistence of a relationship is shown by attaching the symbol 'c' to the line pointing to an entity type whose occurrences must all participate in the relationship. Figure 4.6 illustrates how this graphical notation is used to represent the entity types 'order' and 'line_item' and the m:n relationship 'consists of' between them.

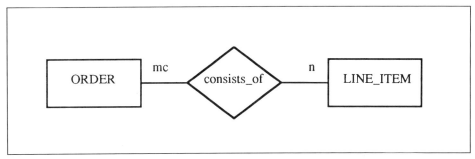

Figure 4.6 Entity types and an m:n relationship

Note that the occurrence of an order means an obligatory occurrence of the relationship, since no order can exist which does not contain line items. Specific occurrences of line items, on the other hand, need not be on order.

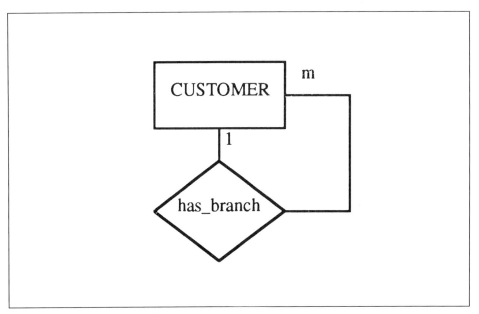

Figure 4.7 Loop relationship

The notation for a loop relationship is illustrated in Figure 4.7. The assumption is that a customer can have a single 'head office' which controls a number of branches and hence that the relationship is 1:m. Participation in this relationship is non-obligatory, since it is possible for some customers not to have the head office and branch relationship.

Subtypes and supertypes are indicated by the use of an unnamed diamond, to which their boxes are attached. The supertype is indicated by a bar across the line connecting to it. The bar may be supplemented by or replaced by the legend 'is a'. This is illustrated in Figure 4.8.

60 *Introduction to modern methods of analysis and design*

The entity type 'customer' is shown as being a supertype of the subtypes 'cash_customer' and 'credit_customer'. Proportion and insistency are not shown, since subtypes and supertypes are not the same semantic concept as a relationship.

The ERD corresponding to the DFD of Figure 4.5 is shown in Figure 4.9. Note how the two views of the system reinforce each other. The analysis in this very simplified example might have started with the context diagram, progressed through the ERD and have been completed with the DFD. However the analysis is conducted, it is important that the ERDs and DFDs be *balanced*. That is, the object types shown in the ERD must have corresponding named stores in the DFDs.

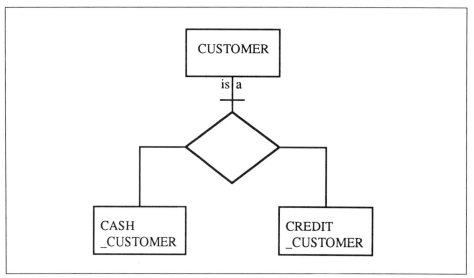

Figure 4.8 Supertype and subtypes

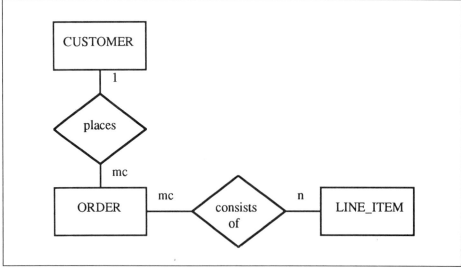

Figure 4.9 Entity relationship diagram

Data dictionary: The Data dictionary is a repository holding detail about the data conveyed in data flows or staticised in data stores in the DFDs of the data transform model and for the entity types and relationships identified in the information model. The syntax for data dictionary entries is now reviewed in some detail, because use of this notation will be made in later chapters.

The notation used in the data dictionary is as follows:

Equals Sign (=)		Used in the meaning of 'is defined as'.
Plus Sign (+)		Used as a delimiter between item names in a data dictionary entry.
Braces ({})		Used to indicate a repeating item.

Note. Braces can be qualified to show the bounds of the iterations possible:

{} means zero or more.

1{} means one or more.

{}3 means from zero to three.

2{}4 means from two to four inclusive.

4{}4 means four exactly.

Up Bar (x|y|z)	Used to indicate an Exclusive OR function amongst items.
Brackets (( ))	Used to indicate an optional item.
Quotes ("")	Used to indicate literals.
Asterisks (* *)	Used to delimit comments.
At Sign @	Used to indicate identifying attributes.
Double Period (..)	Used to indicate a range.
Period (.)	Used to indicate end of dictionary entry.

The following examples illustrate the use of the above notation:

Time = hours + minutes + seconds *GMT*.

Customer   = @identity_code + name + credit_status + 2{address}6 + superior_branch_identity_code.

Order = @order_number + date_of_order + promised_delivery_date + standard _discount | special_discount.

Constants = "12" + "ABC" + "48" + {(others)}.

Within a data dictionary entry one or more of the items listed may by further definable. For example, the entry 'hours' in the first of the above examples might itself have the entry in the dictionary:

hours = 0..24.

and 'credit_status' in the second example might have the corresponding entry...

credit_status = "Excellent"|"Good"|"Fair"|"Bad".

In many of the examples given in this book, a slightly abbreviated form of the above notation will be used. 'Customer', as in the above example, would be written simply as:

CUSTOMER(@identity_code + name + credit_status + 2{address}6   + superior_branch_identity_code)

The Dynamic model

The third sub-model of the behavioural model, the dynamic model, is represented by a *state transition diagram* (STD) or a series of such. The simple graphical symbols of an STD are shown in Figure 4.10. A rectangle represents some state of the system. The arrowed line indicates that a transition is taking place from one state to another. Against this line the condition which causes the transition to take place and the actions the system must take when the transition occurs are listed.

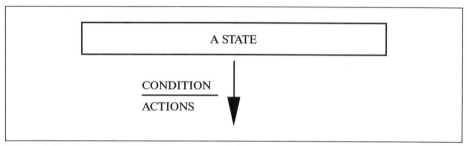

Figure 4.10 State transition diagram symbols

A simple example of an STD using this notation is given in Figure 4.11. Here, a word processing system can be in two states with respect to the current typeface, bold text mode or plain text mode. The user can toggle a key on his keyboard to switch from one mode to the other. The condition in the figure is that the switch has been toggled. The action to be taken depends on the current state of the system, if it is in bold text mode it will be changed to plain text mode and vice versa.

The main relevance of STDs in structured analysis is in the analysis of real time control systems such as industrial process control and of the embedded real time command and control systems which are common in military applications. They are also very useful for modelling the detail of MMI (Man Machine Interaction). They highlight what actions must be performed by the system in response to specific events and conditions whether occurring in the real world or generated within the system itself. The information obtained from an STD, the actions which must be performed by the system, can be introduced into the DFDs for a system by the use of special notations called *control specifications (c-specs)* (or *control transforms*) and *control flows*.

Process Specfications

Process specifications (p-specs), also known as *mini-specs*, are textual description of the processes named in the transform bubbles at the lowest level of DFDs. Their purpose is to allow the analyst to give a precise and reasonably detailed description of what the transform has to achieve. Note again that the description of *what* has to be achieved, not *how* it is to be achieved. These descriptions may simply be written in plain text, but it is preferable that they be given in a more structured form. The most popular approach to writing p-specs is to use a form of structured English which provides a compromise between ease of reading and rigour. (Other possibilities include the use of flowcharts or decision tables. But remember that the essential model is, inter alia, a document for communication with suitably indoctrinated end users or their agents.)

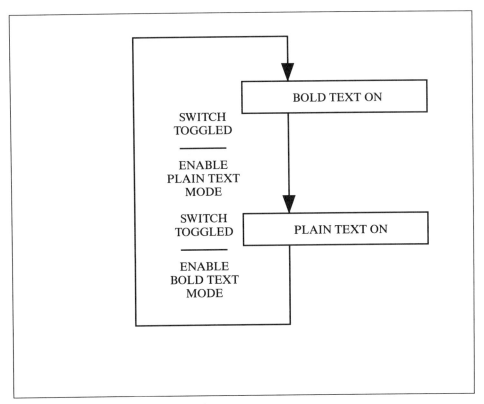

Figure 4.11 State transition diagram

Structured English tries to eliminate imprecision and ambiguity from the p-specs by:

- Confining itself to imperative verbs.

- Eliminating adjectives and adverbs.

- Using reserved words and word sequences like **if...then...else** to indicate sequential logic.

- Using reserved words like **insert, retrieve, update** and **delete** to access data stores by the names given them in the data dictionary.

- Using reserved words like **get** and **put** to indicate movement of data into and out of the transform.

64   *Introduction to modern methods of analysis and design*

For example, the transform 'Compute Order Value' shown in Figure 4.5 might be described by the p-spec:

Compute Order Value

In : order
Out : order value

get order
identify line item names, prices and quantities

retrieve LINE__ITEM prices
calculate total value of order

put order value

The p-spec must be kept brief and to the point. If it exceeds a page, then it is either too verbose or the transform needs further decomposition. Note that structured English is *not* meant to be pseudo code. It is simply a concise and unambiguous statement of what has to be done.

Essential modelling strategies

The description of essential modelling given above has been for the most part simply a description of the tools to be used, together with some (necessarily trivial) examples of their use. Such a description serves to introduce the general idea of the method, but in no way should be regarded as a full description of it. Structured analysis has been with us for some considerable time. A comprehensive body of practical experience has been built up in its use and this has lead to refinement of the method over time. A person or organisation using the structured analysis method for the first time would be foolhardy not to tap into this experience. Some of it is communciated in the standard works on the topic which were referenced at the beginning of the chapter, but there is no real substitute for giving development staff formal training in the method from a consulting/training organisation with good experience in its actual application, or moving staff already experienced in the method into start up projects. The most common structured analysis strategies in use are:

- Top Down Decomposition
- Data Flow/Data Store Driven Analysis
- Event Driven Analysis
- Information Model Driven Analysis

Top down decomposition: In this approach to analysis the requirements to be satisfied are grouped together, to some extent intuitively and to some extent by an examination of the inputs and outputs to the system (as provided in the context diagram), into a small number of broad functional areas which the system has to provide. Each of these functions is then decomposed into smaller, sub-functions and so forth until the problem is broken down to the point where each function to be provided by the system is described in sufficient detail. The problem with this approach is that it relies very heavily on the experience and intuition of the analyst or analyst team in getting good functional partitioning at the initial top level. If this is not achieved, then the interfaces between the lower level functions in the model can become very complex indeed with later adverse impact on the design. Top down decomposition as an approach to systems analysis should be used only as a last resort.

Data flow driven: In this approach, the emphasis of the initial analysis is on the inputs to and the outputs from the system as expressed in the data flows of the context diagram, and on the identification of intermediate data products (data flows and data stores) required, before identifying the transforms. This is a sound approach, resulting in a good, loosely coupled partitioning of the system. It is to be preferred for the analysis of typical traditional commercial systems with no severe real time control problems to be addressed and where there is no requirement for a database, as defined in Chapter 1, to be provided in the final system.

Event driven: This is the most appropriate approach for systems in the embedded real time and process control categories, the types of system which will require extensive use of STDs. The partitioning into transforms reflects the data and control responses to events external to the system boundary as defined in the context diagram. These events must be completely listed as the starting point for the analysis.

Information model driven: This is the analysis approach which is most appropriate (one is tempted to say mandatory) for systems which will be built round a database.

A single strategy is very unlikely to be sufficient for the needs of analysts engaged in a complex system development. One strategy, however, will be the dominant one and the others will be used to supplement it as necessary.

(*Note*: A logical extension of the information model driven analysis approach is *object oriented systems analysis*, as described by Schlaer and Mellor in [17]. This has its roots in the notions of information modelling which were discussed in Chapter 2 and makes extensive use of graphical symbols and textual notations which are similar to (but not completely identical with) those which have been described for structured analysis earlier in this chapter. The method proceeds in three, broad steps.

The information modelling stage: The first step in object oriented analysis is the production of an information model; that is, an ERD and a series of object descriptions (similar to data dictionary entries) which describe all the object (entity) types, their attributes and the relationships of relevance to the system to be developed.

The life cycle definition stage: The next step is to define the states which occurrences of these objects can assume over time. These states can be modelled using STDs, although other techniques are possible.

The process modelling stage: The final step is to examine the processes implicit in the actions defined in the state model and make them explicit in DFDs.)

4.4 Structured Design

The process of structured design starts from a completed essential model. It proceeds through three successive models each incorporating more detail of the implementation technologies which are to be used. The final output from structured design is a series of *structure charts* from which the detailed coding of the system can be started.

Figure 4.12 shows the three stages of structured design. Older variants of structured design may omit the first two models, although the function they serve in the design process must be implemented in some fashion.

The Processor Environment Model

The first stage in structured design is the production of a *processor environment model* (PEM), which uses the same graphical and textual constructs as the essential model. This is a restructuring of the essential model to take into account the actual hardware and people configuration which will be used to support the system.

In the simplest case where the system will be implemented entirely in computer hardware and software and where a single computer, or a closely coupled multi-processor/clustered system is to be used which can be treated as a single computer from the point of view of the software implementation, there is no work to be done. The PEM is the same as the essential model.

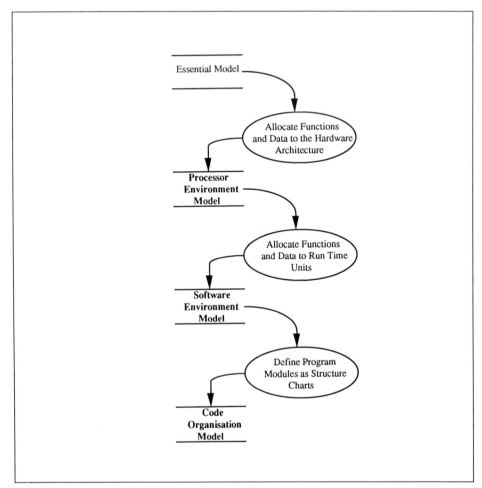

Figure 4.12 The models of structured design

Frequently, however, the system will be implemented over a complex of loosely coupled computers of varying power and, possibly, from various manufacturers. This is true of many military real time embedded and commercial control systems and of many large on line commercial systems. People, that is functions to be performed by people, may also lie within the system boundary. In this case the transforms of the essential model must be allocated to specific people/departments as well as to computing equipment. The analyst must be concerned to match the transforms and data stores of the essential model to the capabilities of the hardware such as speed, main and backing memory size, the physical location of equipment and interfacing capabilities between computers in the complex. In military systems and industrial control systems, issues of ruggedness of the equipment and of security will also have to be taken into consideration.

The analyst will minimise distortion to the essential model during allocation of its transforms. Care must be taken to avoid, as far as possible, the 'splitting' of transforms across two or more processors and to minimise the number of data and/or control flows which cross processor boundaries.

The Software Environment Model

Having allocated the transforms and data stores of the essential model to individual processors in the PEM, the next step is to allocate them to the run time software environment provided with the processors. This environment in most cases will be provided by an operating system which supports concurrent processing. Thus the main task at this stage is to allocate the essential model transforms and data stores to *run time units*, units of software which can be run concurrently. The SEM is also concerned with the identification of interrupt and exception handlers, with the definition of buffer storage areas and with interfaces to the operating system software, such as device handlers, file handlers and schedulers and to the database management system if present. In the absence of an operating system, as in the case of specialised control applications, such basic mechanisms as device handlers, interrupt handlers and schedulers may have to be added. The man machine interface if appropriate, will also be modelled in detail at this stage (using STDs) and supplemented, if necessary, by mock ups of forms, etc. The notation used remains as for the essential and processor environment models.

For example, returning to Figure 4.5, the transforms 'compute order value' and 'check value against credit limit' taken together could be a single run time unit, 'record order' could be another and 'maintain customer information' yet another. Having made these decisions, the designer would now have to include a buffer store to hold 'order details' whilst they awaited processing by the separate 'order entry' run time unit.

The Code Organisation Model – Structure Charts

The production of the code organisation model is the final stage of the structured design process. The PEM mapped the essential model onto the processor architecture and the SEM mapped it into run time units within the software architecture provided with each processor. The remaining step is to map each run time unit into its component software modules. In fact this step is what was originally known as structured design. The PEM and SEM can be regarded as a technical bridging between the newer technique of structured analysis and the older technique of structured design.

68 *Introduction to modern methods of analysis and design*

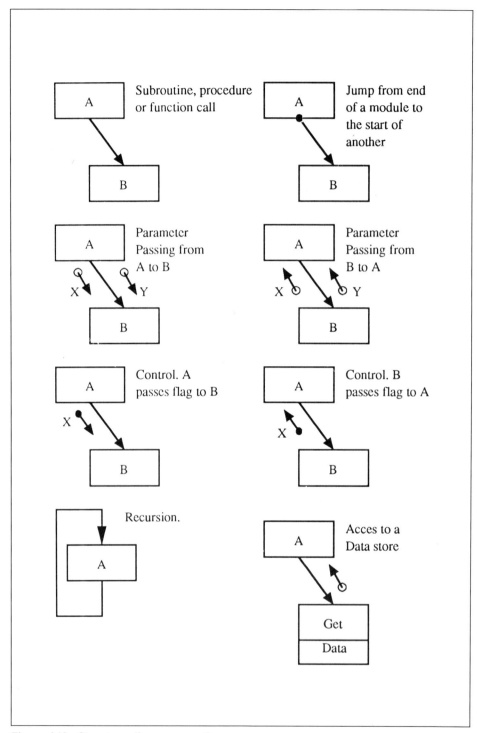

Figure 4.13 Structure diagram notations

The various models so far discussed have been based on graphic symbols and textual notations which were developed to support structured analysis. The completed models were represented as DFDs. DFDs cannot model the sequential nature of software within a run time unit, although, as we have seen, they can be used to model concurrency. We need to map from the DFDs to a notation which models the sequential and modular nature of run time units and which provides a natural bridge to the actual writing of program code. This notation ante-dates DFDs (because structured design ante-dates structured analysis) and is referred to as the *structure chart*.

Structure charts use a somewhat richer set of graphic symbols than DFDs, reflecting the fact that they are much closer to the program detail. Some typical elements of the notation, as used in the Yourdon SD method, are shown in Figure 4.13 with explanatory notes.

As always, the notation for structure charts is simply a tool for their construction. Possession of this tool, whether or not it is automated by some CASE product, does not mean possession of a method for its use. The structured design method has clearly defined objectives and alternative strategic approaches together with a well established body of heuristics. It also, inevitably, has developed a special jargon of its own. These topics can only be touched upon in the following paragraphs, but are covered in great detail by the references given at the beginning of this chapter.

The objective of structured design is to produce a system where the program modules at the detailed design level are cohesive, loosely coupled and do not have pathological connections between them. The quality of a software design can be measured by the extent to which it meets this objective.

Cohesion has to do with the internal 'togetherness' of a program module in accomplishing a task. All of the internal logic of a module should be strongly associated together in accomplishing a single task. Modules should perform the same task each time they are activated. The best cohesion occurs when a module performs *one* and *only one function* for the other modules which may call on its services. Bad cohesion can occur for a variety of reasons. Simple carelessness, or a desire to partition the later programming work in some way which is unrelated to the design task, may lead to grouping of completely unrelated functions into a single module. Loose thinking can lead to certain functions which *sound* similar to each other, but are not really so, being grouped together into a single module; for example, input routines for different input devices. An over bureaucratic obsession with keeping all modules close to a certain standard size can result in a module being 'filled out' with functions unrelated to its main purpose or to each other in order to meet its 'quota' of instructions.

Loose coupling means keeping the interfaces between program modules to the minimum and keeping these as straightforward and simple as possible. Each module should present a simple and clear interface to other modules which isolates them completely from its internal workings (the 'black box' principle). Modules should be arranged in a hierarchy where a module at one layer of the hierarchy makes use of the services of the modules at lower layers. Control passes down the hierarchy; never up without very good reason; that is, modules at a lower level never call on the services of modules at a higher level. Higher level modules perform the major tasks and make the major decisions in performing a task, delegating the minor tasks and decisions to subordinate modules at a lower level in a fashion analogous to management hierarchies in human organisations. Good, loose coupling is perhaps best clarified by examples of what is meant by bad couplings as in Figure 4.14.

70 *Introduction to modern methods of analysis and design*

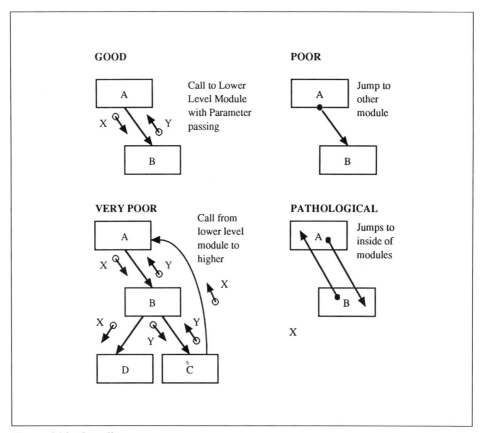

Figure 4.14 Coupling

In the first example the higher level module calls the lower level module, which could be a sub-routine, function or procedure, and communication is by the exchange of parameters. Neither module knows anything about the internal logic of the other. This means that either module can be modified without entailing need for modification of the other, provided that the parameter passing interface itself remains unchanged. The second example, where the higher module makes an unconditional jump to some defined entry point in the lower module is acceptable where a simple sequence of processes needs to be carried out to complete a task, but cannot be combined into one module without making it of an unacceptable size. The weakness lies in the fact that in the absence of parameter passing, the modules will have to communicate via some shared data area thus tightening the coupling between them. Calling a higher level module from a lower level one is to be avoided if at all possible, because it means that low level modules are controlling higher level modules; that is, major decisions are being taken at the lower levels in the hierarchy. It also makes it difficult to set up orderly testing of the modules. Jumping from the internal logic of one module to the internal logic of another means that the modules are very tightly coupled and that changes to one are very likely to have a ripple effect in causing changes to others.

The objectives of structured design are very clear. To assist in meeting those objectives, a number of *design strategies* have been evolved. No single strategy is likely to be sufficient for the purpose of a complex system, but one, dominant strategy is likely to be evident. This will drive the design, being supplemented by the less dominant strategies as necessary in a similar manner to the essential modelling strategies discussed earlier.

Before discussing design strategies, some further structured design ideas must be introduced. Structured design admits of the existence of only five types of design module, namely, *afferent modules, efferent modules, transform modules, access modules* and *coordinating modules*. These are illustrated, with explanatory notes, in Figure 4.15.

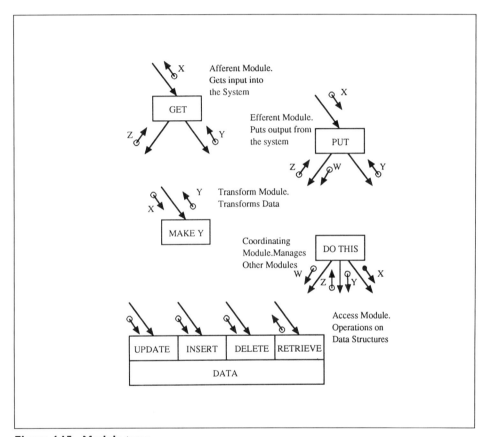

Figure 4.15 Module type

Afferent modules are those which do input to the system. They will be at a low level in the hierarchy, passing information upwards through it to higher level modules. Efferent modules are those which do output from the system, calling on the services of lower level modules to do the detailed work. Transform modules are those which process data, transforming them from some form into another. Co-ordinating modules are those which coordinate the work of subordinate modules. Access modules are those which provide access to data for higher level modules, whilst concealing the detail of how this is done from them.

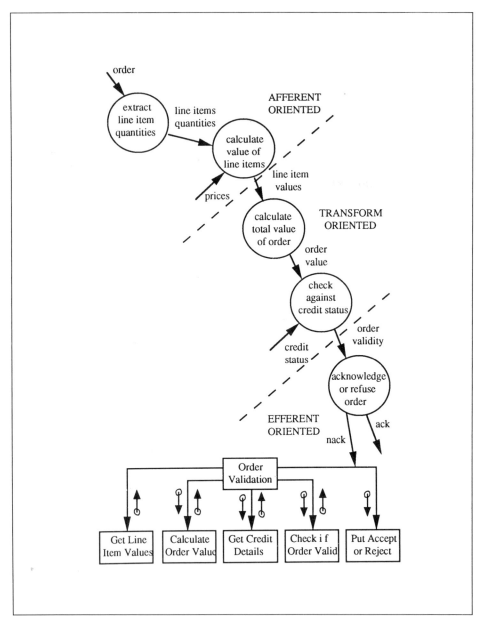

Figure 4.16 Transform centred design

The two most common structured design strategies are *transform centred* and *transaction centred*.

Transform centred design: This strategy is appropriate where input data are subject to a progressive series of transformations, as reflected in the DFD, before being output. It will usually be possible under these circumstances to partition the DFD into an afferent

Object oriented design 73

part, a central transform part and an efferent part and to put a coordinating module in charge of these. For example, a series of transforms (forming a run time unit) may: input order details; extract line item identities and the quantities of each requested in the order, get the individual prices for the line item types in the order; calculate the total value of the order, check this value against the customer's credit status; acknowledge or refuse receipt of the order. This example is shown in Figure 4.16, together with the initial, top level structure chart which might be derived from it. The main flow of the data through the DFD is examined and the transforms grouped into afferent, central transform and afferent parts. This partitioning is now modelled with a coordinating module as shown. The figure shows only the first two layers of the hierarchy of modules which could be designed. Further modules will be required to perform services for the modules at the second layer. For example, the 'Get Line Item Values' module will require service modules to obtain order details, extract details of the line items contained in an order, obtain prices for these line items from the database and calculate the total value for each line item in the order.

Transaction centred design: This strategy is appropriate where a single data flow can give rise to a number of different transforms being required. For example, a data flow input to the system from an airline booking clerk could give rise to the different transactions (represented in a DFD as transform bubbles) 'query seat availability', 'make booking', 'cancel booking' and so forth. A coordinating module would be appointed to control the work of individual modules which: input and identify the type of transactions; retrieve data from the booking database; make a seat booking; delete a seat booking; and so forth.

The internal workings of each module in a structure chart are defined using *pseudo code*, which itself will be designed in part from an examination of the structured English process specs associated with related transform bubbles which detail what the module has to do.

4.5 Object Oriented Design

4.5.1 Action versus Data Structure Driven Design

Earlier in this chapter, two of the most common structured analysis strategies were introduced as:

- Data Flow/Data Store Driven Analysis

- Information Model Driven Analysis

and object oriented analysis[17] was discussed briefly as the logical extension to the second of these. In a similiar fashion, the question has been raised as to whether systems design should be driven by the actions (functions, processes) a system has to perform, or by the data structure objects it has to support.

The second approach to system design has gained favour in recent years. The earliest software design method based on it was JSD (Jackson Structured Design[18]). A more

74 *Introduction to modern methods of analysis and design*

recent method which has gained particular favour in the defence industry is generally referred to as *object oriented design* (OOD), although, for reasons which will be given shortly, it might be better referred to as *object based design*.

The underlying motivation for object oriented design lies in the fact that during the life cycle of a software system, including its extended maintenance phase, the data objects processed are less likely to be volatile than the processes which are applied to them. To take one example, an inventory system might deal with the products a company makes, the parts they are made up from, the suppliers of these parts and so forth. Its initial purpose might simply be to keep an up-to-date record of the parts and products held in stock. But later, the system might be enhanced to do more sophisticated things like automatically re-ordering parts from suppliers when stocks are becoming too low and keeping statistics on the quality of parts received from various suppliers. The function of the system is extended, but the data objects supported remain essentially the same. Thus, a system structured around data objects will be more resilient to change than one which is structured around the functionality it has to deliver. The case for this is well argued by Meyer [14].

Just as structured design methods evolved from structured programming, object oriented design methods have evolved from object oriented programming (OOP). A number of well established object oriented programming languages exist, including Simula[19], Smalltalk[20] and Eiffel[14]. Extended versions of conventional languages such as C[21], Fortran and LISP have also been developed to give them an object orientation. OOP will be looked into in some detail when *object oriented databases* are discussed in Appendix A. Meanwhile, the general concept is introduced.

The essence of OOP lies in the way that data and the procedures that manipulate them are brought together into a single entity called an *object*. In conventional programming languages, data and the routines that manipulate them are seen as distinct things. A system works by invoking routines (procedures, functions, subroutines, etc.) and giving them data to work on. In object oriented languages, data and procedures are encapsulated together into objects. An object is a data structure together with descriptions of the way it can be manipulated. Data are manipulated by one object sending a *message* to another object which contains them. The message includes identification of the manipulation required and the object then determines how to manipulate itself depending on the content of the message. The point is that the requestor of a manipulation is unaware of the mechanism by which the manipulation is carried out. This means that this mechanism, which is internal to the object could be changed or extended without the requestor object itself having to be changed. This leads to good loose coupling of the program modules.

The essence of OOD as compared with SD follows this object principle in that whereas the 'structured' designer sees the system modules in terms of processes which are applied to data, the 'object oriented' designer sees the system modules in terms of objects which contain a description of the services they provide. In the first case, processes are all important to the design structure and data are simply something to be tacked on to it; in the second case, data objects are all important to the design structure and processes are seen as simply the services provided in relation to the data.

OOD shares the same objectives as SD, including good cohesion and loose coupling of modules and the avoidance of pathological connections between them. It also stresses re-usability of modules. It borrows the 'object' principle from OOP and also many complementary ideas which are fundamental to OOP including:

Classes, objects and abstract data types 75

- Classes, Objects and Abstract Data Types
- Genericity and Overloading
- Inheritance

In this section these fundamental concepts and some other commonly used OOD terms are explained. In order for a design following these OOD principles to be implemented in programs, the language and compiler used must be capable of supporting them. This topic of language support is returned to in Section 4.5.5.

(*Note:* In fact, some modern languages like Ada directly support, or can be used to support only some OOP features like classes, genericity and overloading, but not inheritance. Since the concept of inheritance is absolutely fundamental to OOP, it would be better to refer to some of these so called object oriented methods as object *based*. Most currently available OOD methods are specifically tailored to the requirements of the Ada language.)

It must be stated that as yet there is no widely accepted standard method for OOD. A number of different methods have been developed under the OOD banner and proprietary CASE tools are emerging in support of some of them. However, the basic principles discussed in these paragraphs are generally accepted as the common basis for such methods.

4.5.2 Classes, Objects and Abstract Data types

When discussing systems structured on the basis of the objects they deal with, we are more interested from a design point of view in *classes* of objects than specific occurrences of them. For example, if we have an object 'employee', we are interested in employees as a class and the permissible operations common to that class and not in some individual occurrences of an employee. The term *object* in OOD terminology is reserved to mean occurrences of a class and as such is a program run time, rather than a design, consideration. Thus, OOD deals with classes of things rather than occurrences of them. Of course, we need to think about occurrences of classes during the design process, but the design produced deals only with classes.

(*Note:* This distinction between the type of thing we are interested in and occurrences of it was also made when entity types and occurrences of them were discussed in Chapter 2 in the context of an analyst's view of data. The terminology used varies, but the underlying idea is the same).

Classes in OOD can be represented by *abstract data types* (ADTs). An abstract data type describes a class in terms of the operations which can be carried out on the underlying data it represents, together with the properties of these operations which a user of them needs to know. It exploits the principle of *information hiding*. This simply means that in a well designed system, a module is seen by other modules only through the interface provided by that module. The manner in which the underlying data is structured and the actual mechanisms for manipulating it are not made visible in the abstract data type. All that is 'on view' is the name of the class it represents and information about the interfaces it provides to other modules. Thus, an object oriented design can be thought of as a collection of abstract data types structured in some way in relationship to each other.

A number of proprietary and non proprietary design methods have been evolved under the OOD banner, each of which uses its own notation. These notations vary from those provided by an enhanced version of the structured design notation which was described earlier, through Buhr's Ada Structure graphs and Booch's Boochgrams to HOOD™. Of these, only the first and the last are divorced from Ada considerations.

An example of a class is shown in Figure 4.17, which uses a simplified version of the HOOD notation. (HOOD stands for Hierarchical Object Oriented Design. It is an OOD method developed for the European Space Agency). In this example the class name is 'account', meaning a bank account. The operations which other classes can carry out on 'account' are 'open account', 'close account', 'make deposit' (to account) and so forth. A class can call on the services of other classes in order to do its job as shown by the arrowed line. The body part of this class notation symbolises the implementation of the provided interfaces and the actual underlying implementation of the data structure for the class 'account'.

The body can be used to hold *child* classes of a *parent* class as shown in Figure 4.18. The parent class 'account' can call on the services of the child 'account list' and 'account details' classes, to assist it in carrying out its various operations on the account data object. All of the operations provided by 'account' will require to find an account instance, then access details of that account for various purposes. Note that the child classes are visible only to their parent unless they are made explicitly available as operations interfaces to other classes by the parent.

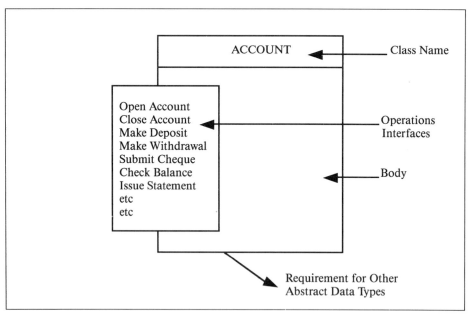

Figure 4.17 An abstract data type

Classes can be defined within an hierarchical relationship where senior classes call on the services of more junior classes. In Figure 4.19 the senior class is said to be a *client* of the junior class; the junior class is said to be a *server* (or *supplier*) to the senior class.

In the example, a client class 'scheduler' uses the services of a server class 'process manager'. The 'scheduler' class uses 'process manager' to determine which processes

Genericity and overloading 77

in a shared resource operating system environment are free to run. On the basis of this information, it decides which of the free processes should be the next to run, whether a running process should be suspended and so forth.

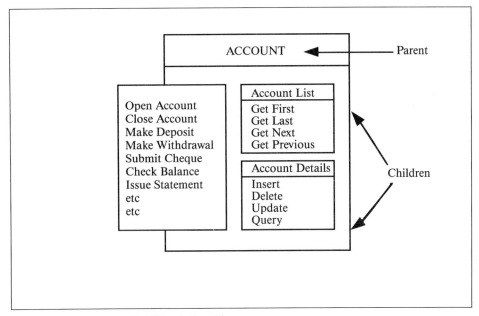

Figure 4.18 Parent and child relationship

Operations which create new run time objects, that is, new occurrences of a class, are called *constructors* and those which destroy them, *destructors*. Operations which change the values of and object's attributes are called *transformers*, those which leave them unchanged, *accessors*. In Figure 4.18, the 'open account' operation is a constructor, 'close account' is a destructor, 'make deposit' is a transformer and 'check balance' is an accessor. The first creates a new account object, the second deletes an account object, the third increases the value of the credit attribute of an account object and the last returns the value of the balance of an account object without affecting any of its attribute values. (*Note:* The OOD notions of constructor, destructor, transformer and accessor correspond respectively to the database operations insert, delete, update and query which were discussed in Chaper 1.)

4.5.3 Genericity and Overloading

A class is said to be *generic* where the same algorithm can be executed using the same underlying data structure but on different data types embedded within that structure. Consider again the 'account' class illustrated in Figure 4.18. Were this only to allow operations on sterling bank accounts, for example, then it would not be generic. If, on the other hand, it permitted a client class to decide whether it wants the operations to be on sterling accounts, dollar accounts or deutschmark accounts, it would be generic.

78 Introduction to modern methods of analysis and design

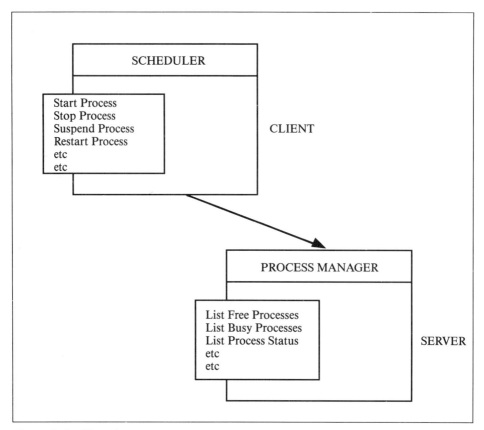

Figure 4.19 Class hierarchy

The permissible operations on each of these data types are the same, only the data type involved differs. When implemented as program code, generic classes become code 'templates' and these templates are compiled into the appropriate code to handle the data type specified by an occurrence of a client object class. Genericity supports re-usability in that it allows system modules to be defined in a general purpose way, making them more suitable for 'putting on the shelf' for later reuse by other systems.

Overloading is a complementary concept to genericity and again is aimed at promoting re-usability. It can be defined as the ability to assign more than one meaning to the name of an operation appearing in a programmed system. Returning to the 'account' class example again, suppose that we wanted it to represent not just bank accounts but also building society accounts and post office savings accounts. The permissible set of operations on each of these types of account is the same, but the manner in which data about them are structured and the manner in which the various permissible operations on them are implemented is likely to be such that an attempt at a generic design would lead eventually to a very complex code. In this case the class 'account' might be defined with the names of its operations overloaded. In implementing the class, different routines would be written to cater for each of the account types against each permissible operation.

4.5.4 Inheritance

The concept of *inheritance* is applied where two or more classes can be constructed as 'subtypes' of some existing 'supertype' class. Suppose that a 'customer' class was available representing the external customers of an organisation. Now suppose that the organisation decided to sell its goods to its own staff at special discounts. The 'staff customer' class would have many attributes and operations in common with the original 'customer' class, but would also have some which were different. In this situation, the choice would normally be between redesigning (and rewriting) the 'customer' class to accommodate the extra requirements of the 'staff customer' class, or designing (and writing) a new 'staff customer' class from scratch. The first approach is very unattractive since it means 'opening up' design/code which is in a stable working condition. It may not even be permitted if a strong policy of configuration management is in force, and the working design/code have been baselined. The second approach is also unattractive since it would mean redoing work which has already been done. In OOD/OOP, the solution would be to have the new, 'staff customer' class *inherit* the attributes and/or operations of the existing 'customer' class. The inheritance principle is illustrated in Figure 4.20.

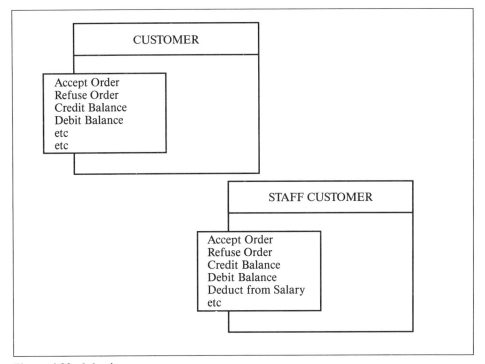

Figure 4.20 Inheritance

In this example, the new 'staff customer' class inherits all the operations from 'customer' and adds those special to itself. It is an *heir* to the *ancestor* 'customer' class. For example, the operation 'deduct from salary' is applicable to a staff customer, but not to an external

80 *Introduction to modern methods of analysis and design*

customer. The effect of inheritance is to increase the re-usability of existing modules by extending what they can do without having to change the existing design/code. The concept of inheritance as outlined in Figure 4.20, enables new modules to be built, with minimum extra work by inheriting the design/code of established modules.

4.5.5 Concluding Remarks

OOD is extremely bound in with the language in use and the support that language gives for concepts such as abstract data types, genericity, overloading and inheritance. Object oriented languages such as Simula and Smalltalk are designed to support these and other OOD concepts. Other modern languages such as Ada and Modula-2 support some but not all of them. Older languages such as Cobol and Basic simply do not support the concepts at all.

A further problem with implementation of the OOD approach lies in the fact that it has yet to acquire a widely accepted, systems analysis 'back end'.

Part 2
Relational Database Theory

The second part of this book concerns itself with the theoretical considerations which lie behind the relational model. Unlike the earlier database models which were overviewed in Part 1, the relational model was subject to definition prior to the implementation of the RDBMSs which follow its precepts. E.F. Codd, who defined the relational model, framed his definition within the mathematical theory of relations. He did not allow his model to be distorted by consideration of existing computer storage structures. He was thus able to define a model which was both truly aimed at satisfying the needs for information storage of the user community and subject to some of the rigour of mathematical proof.

Since Codd's original papers were published some twenty years ago, the basic theory he expounded in them has been elaborated on and clarified to a degree by Codd himself and by others, but still stands up very well to scrutiny at this time. In the following chapters only the theory which is appropriate to an understanding of the use currently available RDBMSs is covered, as this will be of prime interest to practising analysts and programmers.

Part 2 contains four chapters. Chapter 5 introduces the relational model, beginning with a discussion of the background to it and introducing the concept of relational tables. It goes on to show how these can be used to provide a tabular representation of entity, attribute and relationship types and their occurrences. The initial constraint which must be placed on their use in the model, the so called First Normal Form (1NF) is then discussed. Chapter 6 introduces the basic operators of the relational model. Chapter 7 introduces the basic integrity rules of the relational model, the entity and referential integrity rules. Chapter 8 discusses some important constraints which must be applied in designing a relational database schema in order to ensure that it is free from update, delete and insertion anomalies. These are so called 'further normal forms' of the relational model. Chapters 5 and 6, in particular, require of their reader a very elementary knowledge of set theory.

5

Tables, Relations and First Normal Form (1NF)

5.1 Background

The relational model was defined by E.C. Codd in a series of papers published in the early nineteen-seventies, [22], [23] and [24]. The model appealed to the computer science community because of its mathematical basis and to the computing industry at large because of the simple way in which it represented information by the well understood convention of tables of values. It was, however, at a higher level of abstraction from the basic computer physical and logical storage structures described in Part 1 than earlier database models. However convenient this might be for the representation of information, a price has to be exacted for the implementation of such abstraction in terms of computer performance (processing and disk I/O times) which could only be paid for by provision of the necessary computer power. This was a very expensive commodity at the time of Codd's original papers.

Commercially available RDBMS products based on Codd's relational model did not appear until the late seventies and sales of these in high volumes did not really take off until the early eighties when the impact of improved hardware chip technology caused a dramatic improvement in computer price to performance ratios. The increased concern with ever rising software development costs was also a major factor in the acceptance of RDBMSs, since they introduced so called 4GL (Fourth Generation Language) or 'application generation' facilities which helped to reduce the costs of developing the many types of software application which made use of relational databases.

The earlier RDBMS products were developed by independent software houses, ORACLE and ASK Ingres (formerly Relational Technology) being the most prominent, and were marketed from the late seventies. The major computer manufacturers did not introduce their RDBMS products until the early eighties, two key products being IBM's DB2 and DEC's RdB. Currently, RDBMS products outsell all other DBMSs in the mini and mainframe market places and database technology is rapidly becoming synonymous with relational database technology. Codd, therefore, could be said to have founded a major new sector within the computer industry.

5.2 Relational Tables

In Chapter 3 the table was shown to be the basic object of the relational model. Relational model tables conform to the intuitive notion of tables with columns of values and a header name for each column with which we are all familiar. However, they also have some important mathematical properties when they are considered in the context of the model.

84 Tables, relations and first normal form (1NF)

Before going on to examine these properties, it will be useful to introduce the terminology which has become associated with this special kind of table. This terminology is illustrated in Figure 5.1.

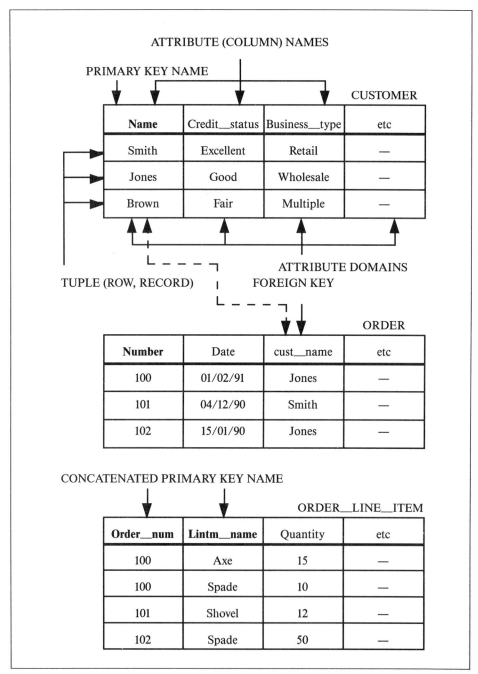

Figure 5.1 Table terminology

Looking at the CUSTOMER table first, this, of course represents entities of the type 'customer'. The table has two distinct parts, a *header* part and a *body* part. The body part consists of a number of rows or *tuples* as illustrated. A tuple corresponds to the conventional file storage notion of a record containing a number of fields, but where each record has the same number of maximum fixed length fields. Each tuple corresponds to an occurrence of a 'customer' entity. The intersection of a tuple with each column of the table (corresponding to the fields of a record) holds an *attribute value* for that entity. Each column in the body part of the table holds attribute values corresponding to only one type of attribute. The list of values which attributes in one column can take is referred to as the *domain* of that attribute. The terms column and domain have become synonymous in the relational database literature.

Turning to the header part of the table, this contains an *attribute name* for each column. Each attribute name must be unique within a table. In the CUSTOMER table the attribute name 'name' identifies an attribute which is a *primary key attribute,* or, briefly, a *primary key.* (A Primary key corresponds in meaning to an identifier attribute as described in Chapter 2 where semantic data model objects were discussed.) Note that in the figure this and other primary keys are shown in bold faced type, a convention which will be maintained in the rest of this book.

Returning to the body of a table, the values of a primary key attribute must each be unique within the domain of that attribute. Thus the values contained in the 'name' column of the CUSTOMER table must all be unique. Otherwise 'name' would not be a primary key. Primary key values are used to identify uniquely each tuple within a table, that is, they uniquely identify each occurrence of the entity type which the table represents. In Figure 5.1, for example, 'Smith' uniquely identifies a customer entity and '100' uniquely identifies an order entity.

In the figure the values of the primary key attribute 'name' from the CUSTOMER table are used to associate tuples in that table with related tuples in the ORDER table. For example, order numbers 100 and 102 are shown as having been placed by customer 'Jones'. A primary key for one table is known as a *foreign key* in the table into which it is embedded for the purpose of identifying relationship occurrences. The ORDER_LINE_ITEM table is shown as requiring two columns containing foreign keys in order to construct a primary key. Where more than one attribute column is needed to establish unique identification for tuples within a table, the resulting primary key is referred to as a *concatenated primary key*.

5.3 Table Headers and Bodies

The header and body parts of tables in the relational model serve different purposes and have somewhat different mathematical properties. The table header is a simple mathematical *set.* The table body is a special kind of mathematical set known as a *relation.* The term 'relational model', in fact, reflects the presence of mathematical relations in the tables of the relational model.

Throughout this book the importance of distinguishing between types and occurrences of things has been stressed. The header part of a relational model table defines a *type* of entity or relationship and the body of the table contains *occurrences* of that entity type or relationship.

86 *Tables, relations and first normal form (1NF)*

The relational model was originally defined by Codd (in references [22], [23] and [24]) in terms of mathematical relations. The more intuitive notion of a table was added in the practical implementation of his original concept. Thus most of the basic theory revolves around mathematical relations and these are discussed next.

5.4 Mathematical Relations, the Table Body

The definition of a mathematical relation given by Codd [22] is:

Given sets S1, S2, ..., Sn (not necessarily distinct), with corresponding value domains D1, D2, ..., Dn, R is a relation on these sets if it is a set of n-tuples each of which has its first element from D1, its next from D2 and so forth.

A relation can be easily understood and represented as an un-headed table of values, thus:

$$\{D1.1, D2.1, ..., Dn.1$$
$$D1.2, D2.2, ...Dn.2$$
$$............................$$
$$............................$$
$$D1.y, D2.y, ..., Dn.y\}$$

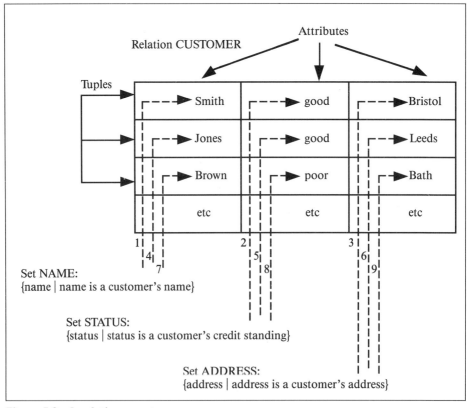

Figure 5.2 A relation on sets

Mathematical relations 87

where each row of the table corresponds to an element (n-tuple) of R, each column to a selection from the domain of values contained by sets S1, S2, ..., Sn, respectively, and where y is an integer corresponding to the number of n-tuples in R (rows in the table).

Figure 5.2 is intended both to assist with an understanding of the above definition, by clarifying how a relation can be represented in the form of an un-headed table, and to show how its *n*-tuples can represent occurrences of an entity type, in this case the entity type CUSTOMER.

In the bottom half of the figure three sets NAME, STATUS and ADDRESS are defined.

For readers who may be unfamiliar with the notation used, the first definition given should be read as 'the set of *all* name *such that* name is a customer name.' The vertical bar means 'such that'. The braces merely delimit the definitions. The other definitions follow suit.

The domain of set NAME is all the permissible values for the customer attribute 'name'. In constructing the relation CUSTOMER, three values each have been taken in turn, in the numbered sequence shown, from the value domains of sets X, Y and Z. Each triplet of values so obtained makes up a tuple of the relation and corresponds to a row of an un-headed table. (Note that *n*-tuple is the correct term, but it is conventional and convenient to leave off the 'n'.)

Each column of the tabular representation of the relation contains attribute values of the same attribute type and the collection of attribute values in a tuple (row) represent an occurrence of information associated with an occurrence of the entity type 'customer'.

The number of tuples in a relation is referred to as its *cardinality*. The number of 'columns', that is the number of attributes expressed in a relation is called its *degree*. It is possible to derive more than one attribute from the domain of a single set as illustrated in Figure 5.3.

In this figure it has been recognised that a customer can have more than one address, for example an 'invoicing' address and a 'ship to' address. To express this, two attributes are needed, one for the shipping address and one for the invoicing address and an extra column has been introduced to cater for this as compared with the Figure 5.2 example. However, the number of sets from which the relation is derived remains the same, since both 'ship to' and 'invoice to' address attributes take their values from set Z.

Since a relation is a set, it follows that the order of its members, its tuples, is immaterial. At first sight it might appear that the order of the attribute columns in a tabular representation of a relation matters, since the relations illustrated in Figures 5.2 and 5.3 were obtained from the domains of sets, X, Y and Z in strict order as shown. But all that is really being shown in the figures is, that a decision having been made on an initial order of copying values from the domain of the sets, then that order is then kept to. In Figure 5.2, it would have been possible to copy values from sets Z, X and Y in order, rather than X, Y and Z. The attribute columns would now be in a different order, but the information content of the relation would remain exactly the same. Thus, the order of columns in the tabular representation of a relation is also immaterial in respect of the information it conveys.

In passing it should be noted that, as Codd pointed out in [22], a mathematical *relationship* (not to be confused with the same term as defined earlier in the context of semantic data modelling) is the domain unordered counterpart of a relation. Thus although the term 'relation' is always used in discussing the relational model, it does

88 Tables, relations and first normal form (1NF)

strictly mean the special class of relation in which the order of columns of its tabular representation has no significance.

It also follows from the fact that a relation is a set that all of its tuples must be unique. (All elements of a mathematical set are unique.) What this means is that some attribute value, or combination of attribute values, within a tuple must make the tuple unique from all others in the relation. This, of course corresponds exactly to the notion of a primary key which was discussed earlier. If more than one attribute is required to establish a key, the key is referred to as a concatenated key. In Figures 5.2 and 5.3, the assumption was that each occurrence of the attribute 'customer_name' was unique in value and that it was, therefore, the key attribute in the relation CUSTOMER. Note that it is possible for a relation to have more than one attribute, or combination of attributes which could serve as a key. In this case the choices available are referred to as *candidate keys*. The chosen key is the primary key.

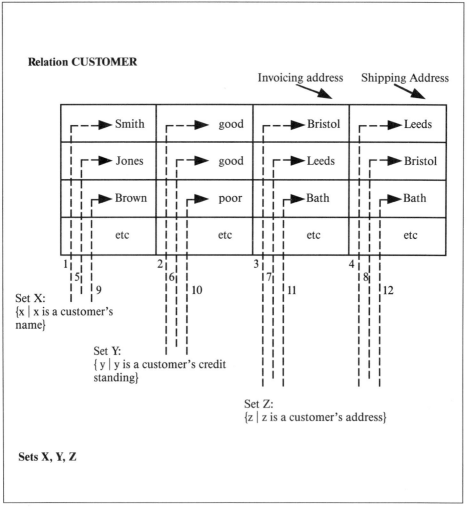

Figure 5.3 Different attributes from the same domain

5.5 The Table Header

The representation used for a relation has been an un-headed table, but this representation suffers from a major semantic deficiency in that it does not allow for the *naming* of columns. Without column names the position of the columns is critical from the point of view of access to data within the relation, if the columns have no identifying name then they can only be identified by position. If attributes of a tuple have to be found by their position in the tuple then the data being accessed cannot be completely de-coupled from the logic of the accessing programs and this de-coupling is a prime objective of the relational model. Thus a header set giving unique attribute names is required in addition to the relation. This, named header set then also constitutes a definition of the table.

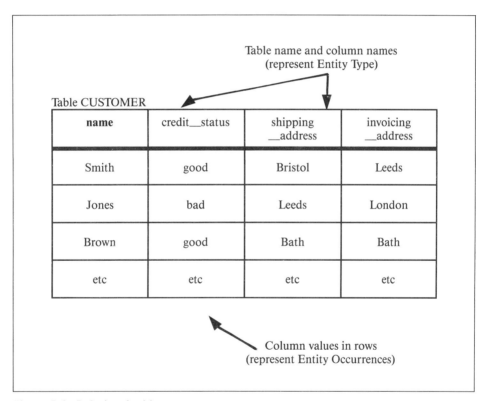

Figure 5.4 Relational table

The header part of the table is a simple mathematical set whose name is given by the table name and, being a set, has the properties that each of its members, the attribute names, must be unique and that the order of these attribute names is immaterial. The specific table header illustrated in Figure 5.4 can be written, using the data dictionary notation described in Chapter 4, as:

CUSTOMER (@ name + credit__status + shipping__address + invoicing__address)

90   *Tables, relations and first normal form (1NF)*

This notation, will be used from now on in this book to represent a table definition.

It is quite common for 'table' and 'relation' to be used interchangeably to mean the same thing. This, perhaps, is of little consequence in the literature about relational databases in general, but can be confusing when discussing the theory. A table and a relation are quite different things. The header and body portions of the table serve different, although complementary, purposes and the operators associated with them are different. Operators associated with header part relate to *data definition language* (DDL) operations and those for the body to *data manipulation language* operations (DML). The contents of the header part of a table, once defined using the DDL, do not vary over time unless the basic structure of a database is being altered. The contents of the body part of the table, on the other hand, are time variant depending on the operations carried out by programs on it using the DML.

5.6   First Normal Form

Consider the table as illustrated in Figure 5.5. In this example it is again recognised that a customer can have many addresses, but in this case the information required is simply a list of all the locations the customer operates from. To represent this a repeating column for the 'address' attribute has been introduced into the table.

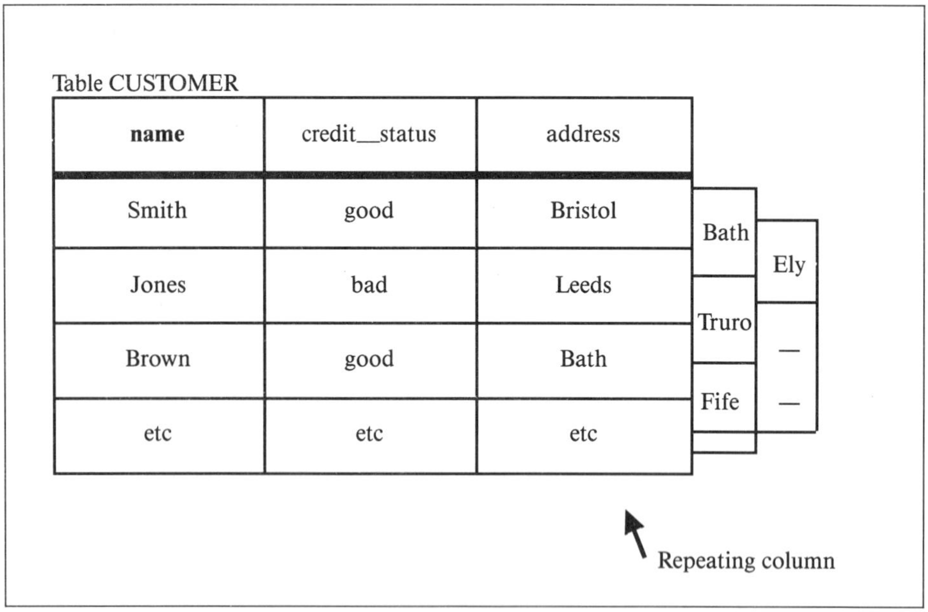

Table CUSTOMER

name	credit_status	address			
Smith	good	Bristol	Bath		Ely
Jones	bad	Leeds		Truro	
Brown	good	Bath		Fife	—
etc	etc	etc			—

Repeating column

Figure 5.5   Repeating columns

This table is obviously a more complex object than that shown earlier, being three rather than two dimensional. It is more complex both from the point of view of representation, whether on paper or in a computer and, more importantly from the point of view of the relational model, because it will require much more complex operators to access data within it than the 'flat' tables shown earlier. Thus, in order to simplify the operators of the relational model and to simplify the model in general, *repeating columns are not allowed in its tables.*

Figure 5.6 shows the effect of 'flattening' the CUSTOMER table and thus removing the repeating columns. Such a 'flat' table is said to be in *first normal form* (1NF for short). However, it suffers from major problems. Firstly, it contains redundant information, for example, the fact that 'Smith's' credit status is 'good' is repeated several times. This will lead to update difficulties when Smith's credit status changes, since many occurrences of his credit status will have to be found and updated when it does. The same problem exists for the other customers. Secondly, the 'name' attribute can no longer serve as a primary key, since the same value for it can now occur many times in different rows of the table. To obtain a key for the table, the 'name' and 'address' attributes must be concatenated and this is clearly not what would be required by a user.

Table CUSTOMER

name	address	credit__status
Jones	Leeds	bad
Jones	Truro	bad
Smith	Bristol	good
Smith	Bath	good
Smith	Ely	good
Brown	Bath	good
Brown	Fife	good

Figure 5.6   Flat table — first normal form

In Chapter 8, it will be shown how these design anomalies, amongst others, can be removed by the application of the so called *further normal forms.*

Another way of expressing the concept of 1NF is to say that all attribute values must be *atomic.* They must be un-decomposable. In the Figure 5.5 example values for the attribute 'address' were not atomic but, rather, lists of values. Note that the term 'atomic' actually means *semantically atomic* when used in reference to the relational model. For example, the address value 'Bristol' could, of course, be decomposed into its individual letters, but would lose all its meaning in the process. The essential point is that at the junction of each row and column of a table, one and only one attribute value should be present.

5.7 Relationships

Earlier we saw that relationships are represented in the relational model by the use of primary keys for cross referencing between the tables which represent the related entity types. Figure 5.7 shows a further two examples of this.

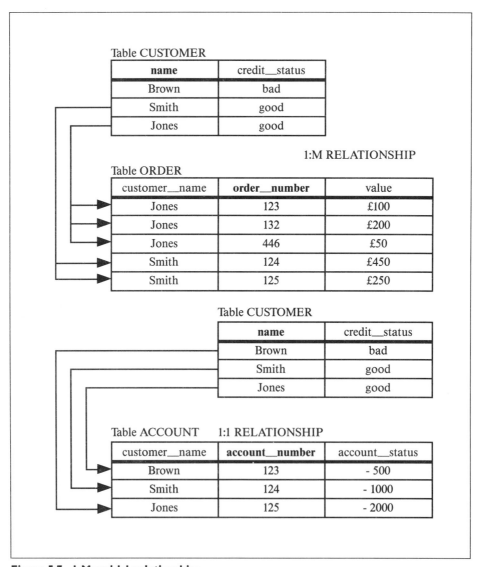

Figure 5.7 1:M and 1:1 relationships

In the top half of the figure a 1:m relationship between the entity type CUSTOMER and the entity type ORDER is shown. To represent occurrences of this relationship, firstly the name, or some equivalent name for the primary key attribute of the CUSTOMER table is introduced into the ORDER table. Then for each tuple of the body of the ORDER table the appropriate primary key value from the CUSTOMER table can be inserted, thus matching occurrences of customers in CUSTOMER with related occurrences of orders in ORDER. It is always possible to represent a 1:m relationship in this way, that is, by taking the primary key attribute(s) from the table on the 'one' side of the relationship and embedding it (or in the case of a concatenated key, them) into the table on the 'many' side of the relationship.

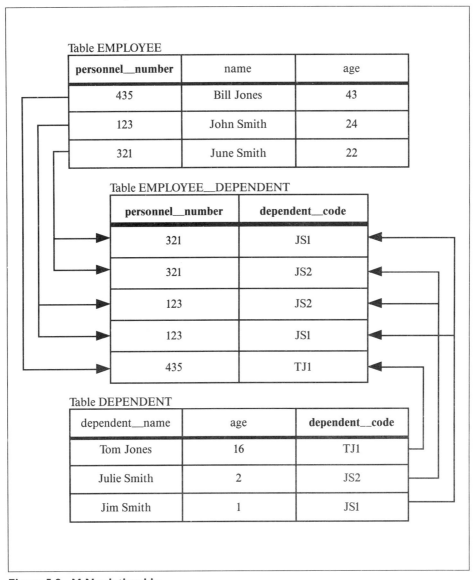

Figure 5.8   M:N relationship

94   *Tables, relations and first normal form (1NF)*

The bottom half of the figure shows a 1:1 relationship between the entity types CUSTOMER and ACCOUNT. The same technique has been used as for the previous example, but note that in this case the embedded primary key attribute could have been taken from either side of the relationship. That is, it would have been just as valid to embed the 'account__number' key attribute from the ACCOUNT table in the CUSTOMER table as to take the key attribute as shown from the CUSTOMER table and embed it in the ACCOUNT table. It is always possible to represent a 1:1 relationship in this way, that is, by taking the key attribute(s) from a table on one or the other side of the relationship and embedding it (or them) into the other table.

Figure 5.8 shows how the more complex case of a m:n relationship is handled. The example in this case is the m:n relationship between the entity type EMPLOYEE and the entity type EMPLOYEE__DEPENDENT. (Employees are assumed to be able to inter-marry.) Employees John and June Smith are married and have children Julie and Jim. A separate table has to be formed to represent the relationship, using the key attributes from both the related tables. It is always possible to represent an m:n relationship in this way.

If only for reasons of symmetry, the reader may feel that this relationship could be represented by treating the m:n relationship as two 1:m relationships and embedding the key attribute from the EMPLOYEE table in the DEPENDENT table and vice versa. However, if this is done, it becomes impossible to maintain the integrity of the keys for each table without making the tables three dimensional and violating 1NF.

If the reader is unconvinced of this, a few moments with pencil and paper will prove the point.

As stated earlier, key attributes are referred to as foreign keys when they are used in any of the above ways outside their 'native' table. Note that they do not necessarily form part of the key for the table they have 'migrated' to. In Figure 5.7, 'customer__name' is a primary key in the CUSTOMER table and a foreign key in the ORDER table, but does not form part of the ORDER table key. When used in the ACCOUNT table, however, it becomes a candidate key for that table, although it is unlikely to be chosen as a primary. But in Figure 5.8 'personnel__number', the primary key for the EMPLOYEE table and 'dependent__code', primary key in the DEPENDENT table are both foreign keys in the EMPLOYEE__DEPENDENT table and are concatenated together to form its primary key.

6

The Relational Model Operators

6.1 Introduction

In his original paper on the relational model [22], Codd introduced eight basic operators which could be used to manipulate data within the body (relation) parts of tables of a relational database. Four of these, *union, intersection, difference* and *Cartesian product* are traditional set operations, albeit modified to take note of the fact that their operands are relations which, as has been seen, are special kinds of sets. The other four are the special relational operators *restrictions, projection, join* and *division*. Note that all of these were referred to as basic operators, not primitive operators. The join, intersection and division operations can be derived from the other five, but it is very convenient to have them as separate operators.

Codd did not advance the above operators as the only ones which might be used in the relational model. They provide the basis for a very minimal DML only and take no account of DDL requirements. Codd did, however, advance them as the fundamental operators of the relational model in the sense that if they were implemented in a DML, then there could be no possible restriction on access operations with respect to a database consisting of the flat tables described in Chapter 5. It should be noted that his paper was written against the background of earlier database models where such access restrictions were very common and he was meticulously concerned that they should not occur in the relational model.

The basic operators are all incorporated into the standard, international, relational database language, SQL, which will be described in Chapter 12. Note that SQL supports other DML operators beyond those just described and that it also supports DDL operators.

It is important that the results of use of the above listed operators on tables must themselves be tables. This is because these operators can be used sequentially in various combinations to obtain desired results. Thus each operation on completion must leave data as a table (or tables) for the next operator to use. This property which all the above operators must have is referred to as *closure*.

In this chapter the various operators are defined and examples of their use are given. This is followed by a brief discussion on the topic of *relational completeness*. Finally, another basic object (data structure) on the relational model, the *user view* will be described. This was omitted from Chapter 5 because an understanding at least of the basic operators described in this chapter is required as a prerequisite to an understanding of user views.

96   *The relational model operators*

6.2   Cartesian Product

In mathematics, the Cartesian product of two sets is the set of all ordered pairs of elements such that the first element in each pair belongs to the first set and the second element in each pair belongs to the second set. For example, given two sets:

S1 = {1,2,3}
and
S2 = {4,5,6}

then the Cartesian product S1 × S2 is the set:

{(1,4), (1,5), (1,6), (2,4), (2,5), (2,6), (3,4), (3,5), (3,6)}

An alternative definition of a mathematical relation, R, to that given in Chapter 5, is:

R is a subset of the Cartesian product S1 × S2 × ... × Sn

It follows from the fact that a Cartesian product always results in a relation, that it can be used to obtain the products of any two relations with no compromise to closure.

However, the relation resulting from a Cartesian product must be meaningful in the context of the relational model, that is, the result should not just be valid relations but also valid *tables*. Consider the two tables with sample populations as below:

```
Table FEMALE        Table MALE
name   job          name   job

-----------------------   -----------------------
Jill    clerk        Jim     clerk
June   sales        Bill    sales
```

Assume that the tables refer to male and female staff respectively. Now, in order to obtain all possible inter-staff marriages the Cartesian product of the body (relation) part of these tables can be taken, giving:

((Jill, clerk), (Jim, clerk)),
((Jill, clerk), (Bill, sales)),
((June, sales), (Jim, clerk)),
((June, sales), (Bill, sales))

At this point the tuples resulting from the Cartesian product are still presented as ordered pairs and the columns of the array consist of these ordered pairs and could only be named for female__staff and male__staff respectively. In order to get round this restriction, the relational model form of the Cartesian product extends it to a merging of the resultant ordered pairs of tuples. In the above example this simply means removing the internal brackets, so that the first tuple illustrated becomes:

(Jill, clerk, Jim, clerk)

In order to represent the result as a table, a union of the two original header sets containing the attribute names is also required and the result is:

Table MALE__FEMALE

female__name	female__job	male__name	male__job
Jill	clerk	Jim	clerk
Jill	clerk	Bill	sales
June	sales	Jim	clerk
June	sales	Bill	sales

In order to preserve unique names for attributes, the original attribute names have had to be concatenated with the original table names. The new table has also been given an identity. It can be seen that a Cartesian product in the relational model is more complex than the basic mathematical operation, involving as it does: a merging of tuples and a union operation in addition to the basic product operation; ensuring that the attribute names remain unique; the assignment of a new name to the resulting table. It would be more correct to refer to this relational model operator as an *extended Cartesian product,* but, for brevity, it will continue to be referred to as a 'Cartesian product'.

6.3   Restriction

In mathematics a set can have any number of subsets. A set is said to be a subset of another if all its members are also members of the other set. Thus, in the following example:

$$S1 = \{1,2,3,4,5\}$$
$$S2 = \{2,3,4\},$$

S2 is a subset of S1. Since the body part of a table is a set, it is possible for it to have subsets, that is, a selection from its tuples can be used to form another relation and therefore another table with the same header set but a new name. However, this would be a meaningless operation if no new information were to be gained from the new relation. One the other hand, a subset of, say, an EMPLOYEE relation, which contained all tuples where the employee represented earned more than some given value of salary, would be useful. What is required is that some explicit *restriction* be placed on the sub-setting operation.

Restriction as originally defined [22] was defined on relations only and is achieved using the comparison operators equal to ($=$), not equal to ($<>$), greater than ($>$), less than ($<$), greater than or equal to ($>=$) and less than or equal to ($<=$). An informal definition of restriction in terms of tables is:

Suppose a table T with columns whose lists of values are A and B. Let 'compare with' denote any of the comparitive operators $=, <>, >, <, > = $ or $<=$. The 'compare with' restriction of T on the value lists A and B, is defined by...

The restriction on table T is that only those tuples where the value in column A (or a literal) 'compares with' the value in column B (or a literal) applies should be selected to make a subset of the tuples of T, providing that the values are comparable and that the header part of T persists after the restriction.

98   *The relational model operators*

Note that typical RDBMSs extend restriction to include many other tests on the attribute values in tuples to enable a sub-selection to take place. Also note that the definition allows for one or both of the comparison operands to be a literal value. Indeed, in a fully defined relational procedural or declarative language, either of the comparison operands could be any valid expression in the language.

Going back to the MALE_FEMALE table of 6.2, the restriction 'female_job = male_job', if applied to it would yield:

female_name	female_job	male_name	male_job
Jill	clerk	Jim	clerk
June	sales	Bill	sales

The restriction operation is, of course, a selection and is frequently referred to as such in the literature. However, the SQL 'SELECT' operator which will be described later will be found to be more powerful than restriction as just defined.

6.4 Projection

The projection operation on a table simply forms another table by copying specified columns (both header and body parts) from the original table, eliminating any duplicated rows which result. For example, consider the table EMPLOYEE, populated as shown:

Table EMPLOYEE

personnel_number	name	age	salary
123	Smith	23	£7500
124	Jones	43	£10000
125	Brown	23	£10000

The projections of the 'age', the 'age and salary' and the 'personnel_number and name' columns would return the three tables, say, A, B and C, respectively:

Table A	Table B		Table C	
age	age	salary	personnel_number	name
23	23	£7500	123	Smith
43	43	£10000	124	Jones
	23	£10000	125	Brown

6.5 Division

Suppose two tables:

R(A1, A2,...,An, B1, B2,....Bm)

S(B1, B2,....,Bm)

The attribute names B1, B2,...,Bm are common to both tables and it is assumed that the domains of the columns associated with these names in the respective tables are domain compatible with each other. Let the concatenated value for the components corresponding to A1, A2,...An in a tuple, of R be designated RA. Similarly, RB for B1, B2,...Bm in a tuple of R and SB for B1, B2,...Bm in a tuple of S. The division of R by S results in a table whose header part is A1, A2,...An and where each tuple is a value for RA such that the values of RB occurring with this value for RA in tuples of R correspond to all values of SB in S.

For example, consider the division of the table EMPLOYEE by the table LANGUAGE as illustrated in Figure 6.1. This results in the selection of all employees who know both COBOL and PL/1. In this case only Smith is returned.

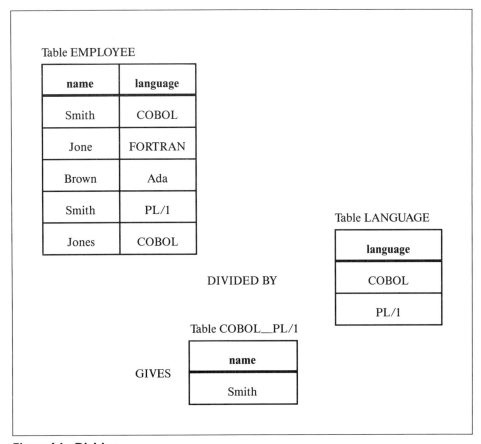

Figure 6.1 Division

100 *The relational model operators*

6.6 Join

The most general form of join operation is called a *theta* join, where *theta* has the same meaning as 'compares with' as it was used in the context of the restriction operation. That is, it stands for any of the comparative operators *equals, not equals, greater than* and so forth. A *theta* join is performed on two tables which have one or more columns in common which are domain compatible. It forms a new table which contains all the columns from both the joined tables whose tuples are those defined by the restriction applied. For example, consider the tables:

Table EMPLOYEE__PRODUCT

name	product
Smith	axe
Jones	axe
Smith	spade
Jones	hoe

Table PRODUCT__CUSTOMER

product	customer
axe	Brown
axe	Green
spade	Green

The tables list employees who make products and customers who buy those products and can be joined over the columns 'product' in both tables since the values in both columns are domain compatible. The result of a theta join, where the restriction is that the product attribute values in EMPLOYEE__ PRODUCT should be equal to the product attribute values in PRODUCT__CUSTOMER would be:

Table EMPLOYEE__PRODUCT__CUSTOMER

employee__name	product__name	customer__name	c__product__name
Smith	axe	Brown	axe
Smith	axe	Green	axe
Smith	spade	Green	spade
Jones	axe	Brown	axe
Jones	axe	Green	axe

Note that one of the 'product' columns has had to be renamed in the resultant table to preserve the uniqueness of the names in its header part. The *theta* join can be defined informally as follows:

Where R and S are tables and have union compatible columns in common, a join of R and S over these columns will result in a table with a header derived by concatenating the headers of R and S and whose tuples are the concatenation of all those tuples in R and S where the values in the common columns conform to the theta operator.

In the above example the *theta* operator was 'equals' and this, the most common form of *theta* join, is referred to as an *equi-join*. Note that an equi-join must always result in a table which has pairs of columns, like 'product' and 'c__product' in the above example, which contain identical lists of attribute values.

By far the most common form of join is a variation of the equi-join where this duplication of column values is eliminated by taking a projection of the table which

Division 101

includes only one of the duplicated columns. This is referred to as a *natural join*. The natural join of the tables in the last example would give the table:

employee__name	product__name	customer__name
Smith	axe	Brown
Smith	axe	Green
Smith	spade	Green
Jones	axe	Brown
Jones	axe	Green

It may help in understanding the different types of join if the operation is looked at from a different point of view. The join is actually a composite operator. The *theta* join is a Cartesian product operation on the two tables followed by a restriction operation on the resultant table. The tuples of the Cartesian product of the two tables in the earlier example would be:

Smith	axe	axe	Brown
Smith	axe	axe	Green
Smith	axe	spade	Green
Jones	axe	axe	Brown
Jones	axe	spade	Green
etc	etc	etc	etc
Smith	spade	spade	Green

The restriction operation on this product then selects only those tuples from this relation which conform to the restriction. In the example, the restriction was that the 'product' attributes should have equal values in each tuple and the result of this was the selection of tuples shown earlier. Since *theta* equated to 'equals', this was an equi-join. By carrying out a further, projection operation which eliminates one of the duplicated 'product' columns resulting from the equi-join, the natural join is obtained.

The examples given so far have all been of so called *inner joins*. The fact that Jones makes hoes is not recorded in any of the resultant tables from the joins, because the joining values must exist in both tables. If it suffices that the value exist in only one table, then a so called *outer join* is produced. An outer join of the EMPLOYEE__PRODUCT and PRODUCT__CUSTOMER tables exemplified above would return:

employee__name	product__name	customer__name
Smith	axe	Brown
Smith	axe	Green
Smith	spade	Green
Jones	axe	Green
Jones	axe	Brown
Jones	hoe	—

102　*The relational model operators*

6.7　Union

In mathematical set theory, the union of two sets is the set of all elements belonging to both sets. The set which results from the union must not, of course, contain duplicate elements. Thus the union of sets:

$$S1 = \{1,2,3,4,5\}$$

and

$$S2 = \{4,5,6,7,8\}$$

would be the set $\{1,2,3,4,5,6,7,8\}$.

A union operation on two relational tables follows the same basic principle but is more complex in practice.

Firstly, a (relational) table consists, as we have seen, of *two* sets, the set of attribute names in its header part and the set of tuples in its body part. Thus a union operation on a relational table is in fact two separate union operations. A union operation on the header sets of two tables results in a set containing all attribute names from both tables after removal of duplicates. A union operation on the body parts of the tables results in a set containing all tuples from both tables with duplicates removed.

Secondly, the result of this (double) union operation must itself be a table to satisfy the closure requirement, that is the header part of the result must be a set and the body part a relation. This means that the result could not be a table unless the relations had identical attributes. For example if a union were performed on the two tables:

CUSTOMER(@customer__name + status)

PROJECT(@project__name + project__status)

then a set would be produced cotaining all the tuples of both relations associated with the table and a further set would be produced part containing the attribute names from both tables. But the set of tuples would not itself be a relation, simply a set containing a mixture of two different types of tuple. Thus the result would not be a table (as described in Chapter 5). To be *union-compatible*, the relations must share the same set of attributes, the values of which would then be domain compatible. Suppose that two tables, R and S have the following tuples at some instant in time, and that their header parts are as shown:

Table R			Table S	
cust__name	cust__status		**cust__name**	cust__status
Smith	good		Jones	bad
Brown	excellent		Smith	good

These can certainly be combined in to one table containing a valid relation by the relational union operator as follows:

```
cust__name         cust__status
------------------ ------------------
Smith              good
Brown              excellent
Jones              bad
```

Normally, two such tables would not exist in a database. It would be pointless to define two tables, albeit with different names, which represent the same entity type, in this case a customer. Thus, the union operator is never used on its own but always with other operators which produce intermediate tables on closure.

The union operator is most frequently used in conjunction with projection operations, where the projections ensure that the resultant tables are union compatible. It combines the resulting tables from the two projection operations. Consider the tables:

Table EMPLOYEE__LANGUAGE		Table PRODUCT__LANGUAGE	
employee	**language**	**product**	**language**
Smith	COBOL	AA	PL/1
Jones	PL/1	AB	COBOL
Smith	FORTRAN	AB	PL/1
Brown	PL/1	AC	Ada

The first lists employees against their language skills. The second lists languages used in the construction of products. Suppose that it is necessary to survey all languages of interest to the organisation. A query can be constructed along the lines of:

> Select all languages known by employees
> UNION
> Select all languages used in products

and this would return the table...

```
           Language
           --------------------
           COBOL
           PL/1
           FORTRAN
           Ada
```

The effect of the union operator is to provide an 'either, or, or both' selection when used as above. The above query could have been phrased, 'Give me all languages which are *either* known by *employees,* or used in products, or *both.*'

104 *The relational model operators*

6.8 Intersection

In mathematics an intersection of two sets produces a set which contains all the elements that are common to both sets. Thus the intersection of the two sets:

$$S1 = \{1,2,3,4,5\}$$

and

$$S2 = \{4,5,6,7,8\}$$

would be {4,5}.

Once again, since tables contain two sets, it is possible to perform the intersection operation on them and, once again, the relations must be union compatible. The intersect operation on the R and S tables defined in 6.7 would return:

cust_name	cust_status
Smith	good

As for the union operator, the intersection operator is only used in conjunction with other operators which produce intermediate tables on closure.

The intersection operator is used in a similar fashion to the union operator, but provides an 'and' function. For example, using the same tables as above, it might be necessary to list all languages which are used in products *and* are known by employees. This query might be phrased along the lines of:

> Select all languages known by employees
> INTERSECT
> Select all languages used in products

and this would return the table:

Language
COBOL
PL/1

6.9 Difference

In mathematics, the difference between two sets S1 and S2 produces a set which contains all the members of one set which are not in the other. The order in which the difference is taken is, obviously, significant. Thus the difference between the two sets:

$$S1 = \{1,2,3,4,5\}$$

minus

$$S2 = \{4,5,6,7,8\}$$

would be {1,2,3}, and between:

$$S2 = \{4,5,6,7,8\}$$

minus

$$S1 = \{1,2,3,4,5\}$$

would be $\{6,7,8\}$.

As for the other set operations discussed so far, the difference operation can only be performed on tables which are union compatible. The difference operation on the R and S tables defined in 6.7 would return:

cust__name	cust__status
Brown	excellent

for R minus S, and:

cust__name	cust__status
Jones	bad

for S minus R.

Once again, the difference operation is used only in conjunction with other relational model operators.

It is used in a similar fashion to the union and intersection operators, but provides a qualifying 'not' function. Consider a query along the lines of:

Select all languages known by employees
DIFFERENCE
Select all languages used in products

that is, 'Give me all languages known by employees, but *not* used in products'. This would return:

Language
FORTRAN

6.10 Relational Completeness

In this section some further important aspects of relational operations are discussed informally and in outline only. A detailed discussion of them would involve the introduction of a specialised area of mathematics (the predicate calculus) and would, in any case, make no contribution to the overall practical intent of this book. Readers who wish to pursue the topics discussed into more detail can consult reference [24], or for a good tutorial treatment, reference [25].

The relational model operators were discussed above for the most part in isolation from each other. In [24], Codd defined a *relational algebra* which incorporated all of them and provided a syntax within which they could all be used. The was forwarded as a basis for a *data sub-language*. The intention was that this algebra should become a yardstick against which such a sub-language could be measured in terms of the completeness of

106 *The relational model operators*

its selection (database access) capability. The language could be a DML embedded in a conventional 3GL or a stand alone, interactive, query language. Codd recognised from the outset that his algebra provided only this selection capability and that this would need augmenting in a practical language with, for example, counting and summing capabilities.

Having defined a relational algebra using the eight basic operators, Codd then went on to define a *relational calculus*. The difference between a relational algebra and a relational calculus can be thought of as roughly analogous to the difference between a procedural and a non-procedural (declarative) programmng language. The solution to a database access problem using a relational algebra is obtained in a step by step fashion similar to the sequential statements of a program written in a 3GL. In effect, the programmer defines the solution to the access problem to the computing system. The solution to the database access problem using a relational calculus is obtained simply by stating what is required and letting the system find the answer. The algebra can be used to specify the solution to a database access problem. The calculus specifies the problem and leaves the solution to the system.

Codd's relational calculus, an applied predicate calculus, which he later developed into the programming language 'Alpha', was also defined in [24]. A data sub-language was said in this paper to be *relationally complete* if it provided the same database access power as the relational calculus. Codd also provided a reduction algorithm by means of which he was able to demonstrate that any expression in his calculus could be reduced to an expression in his algebra. Thus, his relational algebra was also relationally complete. This does not mean that a DML or query language must have the eight relational operations explicitly defined as part of its grammar, but it does mean that the function provided by these operators must be provided in some form in the grammar of the language.

6.11 User Views

User views are basic objects of the relational model rather than operators, but are best understood in the context of the latter. The relational tables described in Chapter 5 are more properly referred to as *base tables*. This is because it is possible to have a different type of table called a *view* (also known as a *user view,* or a *logical user view*). A table which is a view does not actually exist in the database as such, but is treated as if it does, whereas a base table actually exists in the database. Views are defined on one or more base tables using one or more of the relational operators just described.

Consider the resultant tables from the various examples given earlier in this chapter from use of the relational operators. Although not explicitly stated, it was implicit in the examples that these results were transient. In general, the results of some query of a database must be transient because they reflect some real world state of affairs which will change over time. All of the examples, therefore, gave 'snapshot' *views* of some information in the database at some instant in time. But it is frequently necessary to repeat such snapshots in a routine manner. Further, there may be valid reasons for restricting the views that specific classes of user can have of data in the database. It would be convenient if a user could obtain the views of the database frequently required, or be constrained to specific views without, on each occasion, having to re-formulate the query which gave rise to them. Thus, a user view is just a predefined and permanently stored operation or combination of operations on the database which results in a temporary table. This table is given a name and can be accessed like any base table, but it does not really exist in the database. It is a *virtual* table. Operations on this table are actually operations on the temporary table created as a result of the stored, predefined operation(s) on one or more base tables. Note that, in general, update, delete and insert operations are not allowed by RDBMSs on views which have been defined on more than one base table.

To give a simple example, consider an employee table containing salary and other sensitive personnel details. Access to this table is certain to be restricted to named staff in the personnel and pay-roll department and this access will be controlled by the normal access control operators provided by RDBMSs, which will be described in Part 4. But it might be company policy that even trusted personnel staff should not have access to personnel details about very senior management in the organisation. In this case a view could be created on the employee table using a restriction operation which ensured that the view did not contain data about personnel at a certain level of seniority above. This view would be the 'table' made available for access by personnel. It is unlikely that pay-roll staff would be allowed access to sensitive personnel detail other than that essential to the production of pay-slips and salary cheques. In this case a view would be formed from a projection of the base employee table and access by pay-roll staff for programs would be constrained to that view. Programs or interactive queries would use the name of the view rather than the name of the base, customer table when querying the database. The programmers using these views would not have to concern themselves with detail irrelevant to them in the base table.

7
Relational Model Integrity Rules

7.1 Nulls

In almost all of the examples given so far, an attribute value has been shown as occurring at every intersection of a row and column. There were two assumptions in this. The first assumption was that the information required to provide all attribute values for all entity occurrences in the table was available. The second was that all attributes were relevant for all occurrences of the entity types. The contents of relational tables, however, reflect some real world state of affairs, and the real world is not always as orderly and tidy as we might like it to be.

In the first place, the data in a relational database is time variant and the picture of the real world it gives at any given instant in time is a snapshot of an organisation's informational knowledge at that instant of time. It is quite normal for an organisation's knowledge of the facts about some entity type occurrence to be fragmentary at some point in time, and hence for the values of one or more attributes for that entity to be missing from the database. For example consider the table:

Table EMPLOYEE

name	age	job
Smith	-	clerk
Jones	23	-
Brown	43	sales

There is no entry for Smith's age in the table, obviously not because he does not have one, but simply because it was unknown to the organisation at the point of time the 'snapshot' was taken. Jones might have just joined the organisation and has not yet been assigned a job, therefore there is no value for the attribute 'job' which can be assigned to his row in the table. In time, it is to be expected that Smith's age will be determined and Jones will be assigned a job. A snapshot of the database at that time would reveal values in the currently blank places in the table.

Now consider a second example:

Table EMPLOYEE

name	age	job	date_pension_fund
Smith	-	clerk	-
Jones	23	-	April 1989
Brown	43	sales	-

110 *Relational model integrity rules*

In this table the attribute 'date__pension__fund' has been added which indicates the date when an employee joined the company pension fund. There are blank places for this as well as the original blanks under 'age' and 'job', but there could be differing reasons for the blanks in the 'date__pension__fund' column. The blank against Smith might indicate simply that, as for his age, the information about him is as yet incomplete. The reason for the blank against Brown, on the other hand, might be that he is a part-time employee and, as such, ineligible to join the fund. In the first case, the information was simply unknown, in the second case the information was irrelevant to that particular employee. Where blanks occur in a relational table simply because the relevant facts are unknown, they are referred to as *nulls*. Thus the above table might be more properly represented as:

Table EMPLOYEE

name	age	job	date__pension__fund
Smith	null	clerk	null
Jones	23	null	April 1989
Brown	43	sales	not applicable

The problem with this is that the date values in the 'date__pension__fund' column and the legend 'not applicable' in the same column are not syntactically or semantically compatible. This leads to practical difficulties should, for example, the RDBMS support date handling functions. The problem can be resolved in this particular instance simply by having a 'nonsense' date to indicate non-applicability as in:

Table EMPLOYEE

name	age	job	date__pension__fund
Smith	null	clerk	null
Jones	23	null	April 1989
Brown	43	sales	December 3000

But not every case is so simple and it is very easy to confuse 'missing' with non-applicable information. A considerable body of theory and opinion has built up around the handling of nulls in the relational model. Discussion of these goes beyond the scope of this book. Reference [26] gives Codd's own views for readers who wish to pursue the topic further. The important thing to note about nulls is that they are *not* values. It is not possible, for example, to say that one null equals another or is greater than another and so on. The handling of nulls is a matter of some controversy in the industry and they are currently subject to different treatment in the SQL dialects supported by RDBMSs. The support given for nulls in the RDBMS used is what matters to practising analysts and programmers.

7.2 Entity Integrity

Before introducing the entity rule, it will be useful to revise what was learned earlier (in Chapter 5) about key attribute values.

Since the tuples of a relational table are members of a mathematical set each tuple must be unique. To establish this uniqueness, a specified column, or the concatenation of a number of specified columns, must contain unique values for each tuple in the body of the table. These columns were referred to as *primary keys*. When more than one column was needed to form a key, it was referred to as a *concatenated key*. Where several different keys were possible in a table they were referred to as *candidate keys*.

There can be no ambiguity about the unique identification of any tuple in a relational table which represents an entity type and this leads to the definition of the *entity integrity rule:*

No component of the primary key of a base table is allowed to accept nulls.

The rule is just formalised common sense. If, somehow, an entity occurrence was introduced into a database without its total key attribute value, there would be no way of accessing it. What the rule means in practice is that columns which contribute values to the primary key in a table representing an entity type must all, in some fashion, be declared 'not null'. In Part 4 it will be shown how typical RDBMSs provide this facility.

7.3   Referential Integrity

In Chapter 5 foreign keys were introduced as being used to represent relationships between entities by establishing cross references amongst occurrences of them. They will now be discussed in a little more detail and some new terminology will be introduced.

Foreign keys are used to link together corresponding tuples of the primary keys of entity occurrences which have some form of relationship with each other. The foreign key is a reference to the tuple of the table from which it was taken, this tuple being called the *referenced* or *target tuple*. By the same token, the table containing the referenced tuple will be referred to as the *target table*. Thus, the matter of integrity of foreign keys is referred to as *referential integrity*. Referential integrity is about the integrity of foreign keys. The referential integrity rule is:

Foreign key values should always be matched by corresponding primary key values.

Again, the rule is just formalised common sense. Foreign keys are used to represent occurrences of relationships. Occurrences of relationships must be uniquely identifiable just as occurrences of entity types must be, otherwise they also would get 'lost' in the database. Since both foreign and target key values are needed to identify uniquely a relationship occurrence, it follows that the target key for the foreign key cannot be a null.

8
Further Normal Forms

8.1 Introduction

In Chapter 5 the first normal form of the relational model was discussed. In this chapter the further normal forms, which tables in a relational database must conform to, are introduced. The point of putting tables into these forms is to eliminate certain update insertion and delete anomalies from the design of a relational database. The normal forms are first (1NF), as already discussed, second (2NF), third (3NF), Boyce-Codd (BCNF), fourth (4NF) and fifth (5NF) and are applied progressively, in the sense that, for a table to be in second normal form it must initially be in first normal form, if in third then it must initially be in second, and so forth. 'Boyce-Codd' normal form departs from the numbering convention for the others only because it is a later refinement of 3NF.

1NF is quite different from all the others in that its only purpose is to simplify the relational model, as explained in Chapter 5. It is a fundamental property of tables in the relational model. The other normal forms, on the other hand, are constraints on the design of a database schema which is based on use of the relational model, rather than fundamental properties of the model as such.

An understanding of the conventional explanations of 2NF, 3NF and BCNF must be predicted by an understanding of *functional dependency* and of the others by an understanding of *multi-valued dependency* and these related concepts are explained prior to discussion of the appertaining normal forms.

8.2 Functional Dependency

Functional dependency is defined as follows:

An attribute in a relational model table is said to be functionally dependent on another attribute in the table if it can take on only one value for a given value of the attribute upon which it is functionally dependent.

This can be clarified by an example. Consider the tables illustrated in Figure 8.1. The first table, 'customer', is in 1NF, that is, it assumes customers have only one address and, therefore, that there are no repeating columns. The primary key attribute is 'customer__ name' and each value of this attribute must, of course, be unique within the table. For each occurrence of the primary key, therefore, there can be only one occurrence of a value for the other attributes of the table ('credit-status', 'city' and 'street'). It follows from

113

114 *Further normal forms*

the above definition that all attributes in a table are functionally dependent on its primary key, and, by extension, to any candidate key of a table.

However, the definition does not exclude functional dependencies between attributes where neither is a candidate key. Any pair of attributes in a table can be considered when considering functional dependencies. One might, for example, be tempted to think that the non-key attribute 'street' was in some way dependent on 'city', and, indeed, in the purely English sense of the word it is. But it is not functionally dependent on 'city' by the above definition, because it can take on different values for the same value of city within the table. For example, it can take on the values 'St. James St.' and 'White Ave.' for the same value, 'Bristol' of the attribute 'city'.

Table CUSTOMER

customer__name	credit__status	city	street
Jones	good	Bristol	St. James St.
Smith	bad	Bath	Park Road
Brown	excellent	Bristol	White Ave.
Green	excellent	Bath	Wilton Lane

Table EMPLOYEE

employee__name	performance	dept__name	dept__location
Jones	good	shipping	LOC-A
Smith	bad	accounts	LOC-B
Brown	excellent	shipping	LOC-A
Green	excellent	shipping	LOC-A

Figure 8.1   Functional dependency

But now consider the second table in the Figure, 'employee'. As before, the table is in 1NF, but in this case there is another functional dependency besides those of the various attributes on the primary key, 'employee__name'. If it is assumed that each department is only at one location, then a department's location ('dept__location') is functionally dependent on the department's name ('dept__name'). The functional dependence of 'dept__name' on 'employee__name' is direct. However, the functional dependence of 'dept__location' on 'employee__name' is indirect as it is established through its functional dependence on 'dept__name'. The attribute dept location is said to be *'transitively functionally dependent*' on the primary key attribute 'employee__name'.

The notation used to indicate functional dependencies is illustrated by the following examples, based on the above tables:

Second normal form 115

employee_name ---> dept_name
employee_name ---> dept_location
dept_name ---> dept_location
customer_name ---> credit_status
city --/--> street

The first of these should be read as 'employee_name determines the functional dependency of dept_name' or, more simply, 'employee_name is the *determinant* of dept_name'. The others should be read in the same way except for the last, where the slash indicates a negative, and the notation should be read as, 'city does *not* determine the functional dependency of street', or, 'city is *not* the determinant of street'.

8.3 Second Normal Form (2NF)

The rule for 2NF is:

To be in second normal form, a table must be in first normal form and no attributes of the table should be functionally dependent on only one part of a concatenated primary key.

Consider the table:

ORDER_ITEM(@order_number + @item_name + quantity + item_price)

This table lists the items contained within various orders, the quantity of each associated with the order and their unit prices. The key is formed from a concatenation of the order number and the item name since both order numbers and item names can repeat within the table. This table is in 1NF, but not in 2NF, because 'item_price' is not functionally dependent on the 'order_number' component of the primary key, but only on the 'item_name' component. 'Quantity', on the other hand, is functionally dependent on both components of the primary key. To put this information into 2NF, the single table must be decomposed into two tables as follows:

ORDER_ITEM(@order_number + @item_name + quantity)

ITEM(@item_name + item_price)

where the offending attribute and its determinant are used to form the new table.

The correctness of the 2NF decomposition of the 'order_item' table can be demonstrated in terms of how this decomposition removes certain design anomalies. Figure 8.2 shows how the original, erronous 'order_item' table might be populated and how these anomalies might occur.

It can be seen that the prices of axes and hoes are repeated in the table. Thus if the price of either or both is *updated* all corresponding entries in the table must be found and changed. Further, suppose that a new line item is to be introduced, say a hacksaw. No details about this new line item can be *inserted* into the database until an order is placed for a hack saw. (Because order_number is part of the prime key, every row must have a prime key value and no part of the concatenated prime key can have a null value in conformance with the entity integrity rule). Now suppose that order number 124 for

116 Further normal forms

twenty spades is cancelled and *deleted* from the database, all information, including their price, about spades is lost from the database. Figure 8.3 shows that all these problems are eliminated when the table is decomposed in 2NF.

Table ORDER__ITEM

order__number	item__name	quantity	item__price
123	axe	5	£15
123	hoe	10	£10
124	spade	20	£13
125	axe	50	£15
125	hoe	5	£10

Figure 8.2 Table not in 2NF

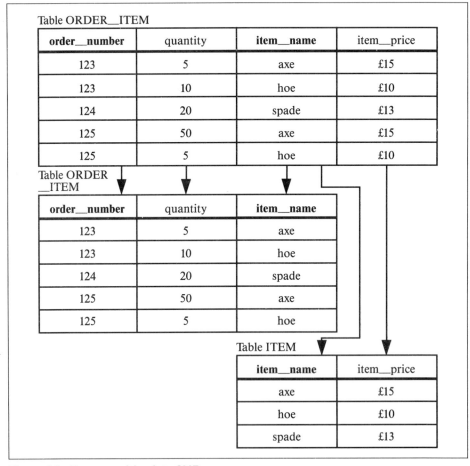

Figure 8.3 Decomposition into 2NF

Third normal form 117

The line item price is recorded once only and need only be updated at one place in the database. A new line item can be introduced simply by inserting a new row into the 'item' table and all information about orders can be deleted without affecting the information in the 'item' table.

One further simple example should help to clear up the loose end left in Chapter 5. There in order to deal with the repeating address column in the three dimensional table:

CUSTOMER(@name + credit__status + {address}),

the table was 'flattened' into 1NF giving the unsatisfactory result shown in Figure 5.6. This table can now be examined for conformity to 2NF and it can be seen immediately that the attribute 'credit__status' is functionally dependent only on the 'name' attribute part of the concatenated primary key and that the table should be decomposed into:

CUSTOMER(@name + credit__status)

CUST__ADDRESS(@name + @address),

which eliminates all the anomalies. This is an example of the progressive application of normal forms. The tables obtained from the above 2NF decomposition example, 'order item' and 'item', are, of course, *projections* from the original table.

The process just described is said to be a *non loss decomposition*. This simply means that no information has been lost in the decomposition process from one table into two. In Figure 8.3 it is clear enough that all the individual information items in the original table have been transferred in its projection onto the other two. It might at first appear that the association between order numbers and item prices in the original table has been lost, but this is not so.

The 'item__name' key attribute of the 'item' table is present as a foreign key in the 'order__item' table and this can be used to restore the associations by use of a natural join operation over the 'item name' columns.

8.4 Third Normal Form (3NF)

The rule for 3NF is:

To be in 3NF, a table must be in 2NF and no attribute of the table should be transitively functionally dependent on the primary key.

Consider the table whose header part is:

BORROWING(@book__id + @person__id + duration + librarian__id + librarian__grade)

This table lists book borrowings from various local libraries with the duration of the borrowing, the library staff member who signed out the book and the grade of that librarian. Borrowings are identified by concatenating the identification of the book and the identification of the borrower. The table is in 2NF, but not in 3NF, because 'librarian__ grade' is only transitively functionally dependent on the primary key '@book + @person'.

118 *Further normal forms*

It is functionally dependent on the identity of the librarian. To put this information into 3NF the single table must be decomposed into two tables as follows:

BORROWING(@book_id + @person_id + duration + librarian_id)

LIBRARIAN(@librarian_id + librarian_grade)

We will see in Chapter 9 that, as for 2NF decomposition, this is just good, semantic, common sense. It should be clear that the un-normalised form of the table leads to update, insertion and delete anomalies. No information about a librarian can be inserted into the database until a book is borrowed from him or her. All information about a librarian is lost when all borrowings from him/her are returned. Change to the grade of librarian will necessitate all corresponding entries in the table being found and updated. The join operation can be used to re-compose tables decomposed into 3NF as was the case for 2NF decompositions, so, again, non loss decomposition is assured.

8.5 Boyce-Codd Normal Form (BCNF)

BCNF is simply a stronger definition of 3NF. The latter does not cover the rare case where a table has multiple candidate keys, these keys are concatenated keys and two or more of the candidate keys share a common attribute. The rule for BCNF is:

To be in BCNF, a table must only have candidate keys as determinants,

where 'determinant' is used in the sense that it was used earlier in 8.2. (That is, 'employee_name *determines* the functional dependency of dept_name' or 'employee_name is the *determinant* of dept_name') If a table is in BCNF, it is also in 3NF.

An example of a table which is in 3NF but violates BCNF will be given in a moment, although such examples tend to be very contrived. However, BCNF is primarily useful because it is simpler to understand and apply than 3NF. The table BORROWING which violated 3NF, for example, can be re-examined using the BCNF rule:

BORROWING(@book_id + @person_id + duration + librarian_id + librarian_grade)

In this table the attribute 'librarian_id' is clearly the determinant of 'librarian_grade' but it is not a candidate key. Decomposition is thus called for, as before, to put it into BCNF when it will also be in 3NF. To give another example:

EMPLOYEE(@personnel_number + salary + dept_number + dept_location)

The primary key attribute in this table is the employee's personnel number. Clearly, the non_key attribute, department number, is the determinant of the department's location, assuming that a department can exist at only one location, and a BCNF decomposition is called for. In 3NF terms, of course, 'dept_location' is only transitively functionally dependent on the prime key. But now consider the (somewhat contrived) table whose header part is:

PROJECT_PART(@project_name + @ part_code + employee_name + quantity)

This table lists projects, the parts and the quantities of those parts they use, and the employees who supply these parts. Two assumptions are made. Firstly, each project is supplied with a specific part by only one employee, although an employee can supply that part to more than one project. Secondly, an employee makes only one part but the same part can be made by other employees. The primary key is shown by the use of of '@' symbols as usual. However, another, overlapping, candidate key is present in the concatenation of the 'employee_name' (assumed unique for all employees) and 'project_name' (assumed unique for all projects) attributes. These would also uniquely identify each tuple of the table as can be clearly seen in the example population of the table given in Figure 8.4.

Table PROJECT_PART

project_name	part_code	quantity	employee_name
AA	abc	5	Smith
AA	bca	10	Jones
AB	abc	20	Smith
AB	bca	50	Brown

Figure 8.4   Table not in BCNF

The table is in 3NF, since there are no transitive functional dependencies on the prime key. However, it is not in BCNF because the attribute 'employee_name' is the determinant of 'part_code' (employees make only one part). As a result of this, the table can give rise to anomalies. For example, if the bottom row is updated because Jones replaces Brown as the supplier of part bca to project AB, then the information that Brown makes part bca is lost from the database. If a new employee becomes a part supplier this fact cannot be recorded in the database until he is contracted to a project. There is also an element of redundancy present in that Smith, for example, is shown twice as making part abc. Decomposing the single table into two solves the problem. In this case the decomposition results in the two tables:

PROJECT_EMPLOYEE(@project_name + @employee_name + quantity)

EMPLOYEE_PART(@employee_name + part_code)

The reader may wish to try sample populations of these tables to prove that the anomalies have been removed.

120 *Further normal forms*

(*Note:* However, as Date points out in [25], a new problem has been introduced in that it is not possible to update the tables resulting from the BCNF decomposition independently. In the above example, it would be incorrect to update the PROJECT__ EMPLOYEE table with a new tuple indicating that an employee Brown supplied project AA, since Brown makes (only) part bca and project AA is already supplied with that part by employee Jones and can only be supplied with it by one employee. This incorrect insertion cannot be detected and rejected except by examination of the table EMPLOYEE__PART.)

8.6 Multi-Valued Dependency

Functional dependency (FD) was discussed in 6.2. The reader is reminded of the definition given there:

An attribute in a relational model table is said to be functionally dependent on another attribute if it can take on only one value for a given value of the attribute upon which it is functionally dependent.

Functional dependency concerns itself with the case where one attribute is potentially a 'single valued fact' [27] about another. For example, in the earlier example of a table:

BORROWING(@book__id + @person__id + duration + librarian__id + librarian__grade)

which was used to demonstrate violation of 3NF, 'librarian grade' is a single valued fact about 'librarian__id'. Only one value for 'librarian__grade' can occur for a given occurrence of a value of 'librarian__id'.

MVD, on the other hand, concerns itself with the case where one attribute value is potentially a 'multi-valued fact' [27] about another. Consider the table:

CUSTOMER__ADDRESS

customer__name	address
Jones	Bristol
Jones	Leeds
Smith	Leeds
Smith	Glasgow
Brown	London

In this example, 'address' is a multi-valued fact 'customer__name' and the converse is also true. For example, the attribute 'address' takes on the two values 'Bristol' and 'Leeds' for the single 'customer__name' value 'Jones'. The attribute 'customer__name' takes on the values 'Jones' and 'Smith' for the single 'address' value 'Leeds'.

MVD can be defined informally as follows:

MVDs occur when two or more independent multi valued facts about the same attribute occur within the same table.

(*Note:* The concepts of MVD's and of 4NF were introduced by Fagin in [28].)

There are two things to note about this definition. Firstly, in order for a table to contain an MVD, it must have three or more attributes. Secondly, it is possible to have a table containing two or more attributes which are *inter-dependent* multi-valued facts about another attribute. This does not give rise to an MVD. The attributes giving rise to the multi-valued facts must be *independent* of each other. Consider the table:

Table STUDENT__BOOK

student__name	librarian	text__book	date
Brown	Jill	first__year__optics	Apr
Brown	Mary	first__year__mechanics	Apr
Jones	Mary	first__year__french	Jan
Brown	Jill	first__year__optics	Jun
Jones	Mary	first__year__french	Feb
Jones	Jill	first__year__french	Jly
Jones	Fred	first__year__german	Jan

The table lists students, the text books, they have borrowed, the librarians issuing them and the date of borrowing. It contains three multi__valued facts about students; the books they have borrowed, the librarians who have issued these books to them and the dates upon which the books were borrowed. However, these multi-valued facts are not independent of each other. There is clearly an association between librarians, the text books they have issued and the dates upon which they issued the books. Therefore, there are no MVDs in the table. Note that there is no redundant information in this table. The fact that student 'Brown', for example, has borrowed the book 'First Year Optics' is recorded twice, but these are *different* borrowings, one in April and the other in June and therefore constitute different items of information.

Now consider another table example involving, this time, courses, students and text books.

Table COURSE__STUDENT__BOOK

course	student__name	text__book
Physics__1	Brown	first__year__optics
Physics__1	Brown	first__year__mechanics
Physics__1	Green	first__year__optics
Physics__1	Green	first__year__mechanics
Chemistry__1	Brown	organic__chemistry
Chemistry__1	Brown	inorganic__chemistry
French__1	Jones	french__literature
French__1	Jones	french__grammar

122 *Further normal forms*

This table lists students, the courses they attend and the text books they use for these courses. The text books are prescribed by the authorities for each course, that is, the students have no say in the matter. Clearly the attributes 'student__name' and 'text__book' give are multi-valued facts about the attribute 'course'. However, since a student has no influence over the text books to be used for a course, these multi-valued facts about courses are independent of each other. Thus the table contains an MVD. Because of this it contains a high degree of redundant information, unlike the 'student__book' example which was just given. For example the fact that Brown attends the Physics__1 course is recorded twice, as are the text books prescribed for that course.

8.7 Fourth Normal Form (4NF)

Consider another example of a table containing an MVD:

EMPLOYEE(@employee__name + @equipment + @language)

Table EMPLOYEE

employee__name	equipment	language
Smith	PC workstation	French German
Jones	workstation	French German Spanish

Table EMPLOYEE

employee__name	equipment	language
Smith	PC	French
Smith	PC	German
Smith	workstation	German
Smith	workstation	French
Jones	workstation	French
Jones	workstation	German
Jones	workstation	Spanish

Figure 8.5 Table not in 4NF

This table lists employees, the equipment they have allocated to them and the foreign languages in which they are fluent. Assuming that the table was not in 1NF, a sample population might be as per the top table in Figure 8.5. This shows clearly that 'equipment' and 'language' are independent multi-valued facts about 'employee__name' that is that it contains a multi-valued dependency. Put into 1NF it would appear as per the bottom table.

This form of the table is obviously full of anomalies. There is a high degree of redundancy which will lead to update problems. If Jones has his work station taken away, then the information about his language skills is lost and if he acquires a PC, then all the information about his language skills has to be repeated, that is, three new rows have to be inserted (because of the entity integrity rule). It might be argued that, in the example, the redundancy could be reduced since only two rows are needed to provide the information on Smith. But which rows should be left out?

The table is in BCNF, since all three attributes concatenated together constitute its key, yet it is clearly wrong and requires decomposition. Intuitively, of course, it can be seen that the problem is caused by the two independently repeating groups in the table and that decomposition should be into:

EMPLOYEE__EQUIPMENT(@employee__name + @equipment)

EMPLOYEE__LANGUAGE(@employee__name + @language)

A few moments with pencil and paper will show that this decomposition removes all the anomalies.

It would, however, be useful to have a rule to back up common sense and intuition in initiating the decomposition. Not all cases will be as simple as the above. The formal basis for the correct decomposition given above is the fact that the table contains an MVD and the rule for 4NF is:

A table is in fourth normal form if it is in BCNF and it contains no multi__valued dependencies.

The rule for decomposition is to decompose the offending table into two, with the multi-determinant attribute or attributes as part of the key of both. Looking again at the undecomposed 'employee' table, it contains a multi-valued dependency. To put it into 4NF, two separate tables are formed each of which contains the multi-determinant of the multi-valued dependency and one of the attributes which gives rise to the multi-valued facts about it. The 'course__student__book' table given in Section 8.6, which also contained an MVD would be decomposed into the two tables:

COURSE__STUDENT(@course + @student)

COURSE__BOOK(@course + @book)

to put it into 4NF.

124 *Further normal forms*

8.8 Fifth Normal Form (5NF)

5NF, as will be seen, is of little practical use to the database designer, but it is of interest from a theoretical stand point and a discussion of it is included here to complete the picture of the further normal forms.

In all of the further normal forms discussed so far, no loss decomposition was achieved by the decomposing of a single table into *two* separate tables. No loss decomposition is possible because of the availability of the join operator as part of the relational model. In considering 5NF, consideration must be given to tables where this non loss decomposition can only be achieved by decomposition into *three or more* separate tables. Such decomposition is not always possible as is shown by the following example.

Consider the table:

AGENT__COMPANY__PRODUCT(@agent + @company + @product__name)

This table lists agents, the companies they sell for and the products they sell for those companies. The agents do not necessarily sell all the products supplied by the companies they do business with. An example population of this table might be:

agent	company	product__name
Smith	ABC	spade
Smith	ABC	hoe
Smith	CDE	axe
Jones	ABC	axe

The table is necessary in order to show all the information required. Smith, for example, sells ABC's spades and hoes, but not ABC's axes. Jones is not an agent for CDE and does not sell ABC's spades or hoes. The table is in 4NF because it contains no multi-valued dependency. It does, however, contain an element of redundancy in that it records the fact that Smith is an agent for ABC twice. But there is no way of eliminating this redundancy without losing information. Suppose that the table is decomposed into its two projections, P1 and P2:

P1 agent	company		P2 agent	product__name
Smith	ABC		Smith	spade
Smith	CDE		Smith	axe
Jones	ABC		Smith	hoe
			Jones	axe

The redundancy has been eliminated, but the information about which companies make which products and which of these products they supply to which agents has been lost. The natural join of these projections over the 'agent' columns is:

Fifth normal form   125

agent	company	product_name	
Smith	ABC	spade	
Smith	ABC	axe	*
Smith	ABC	hoe	
Smith	CDE	spade	*
Smith	CDE	axe	
Smith	CDE	hoe	*
Jones	ABC	axe	

The table resulting from this join is spurious, since the asterisked rows of the table contain incorrect information. Now suppose that the original table were to be decomposed into three tables, the two projections, P1 and P2 which have already shown, and its final, possible projection, P3:

P3

company	product_name
ABC	spade
ABC	axe
ABC	hoe
CDE	axe

If a join is taken of all three projections, first of P1 and P2 with the (spurious) result shown above, and then of this result with P3 over the 'company' and 'product name' columns, the following table is obtained:

agent	company	product_name	
Smith	ABC	spade	
Smith	ABC	axe	*
Smith	ABC	hoe	
Jones	ABC	axe	
Smith	CDE	axe	

and this still contains a spurious row. The order in which the joins are performed makes no difference to the final result. It is simply not possible to decompose the 'agent_company_product' table, populated as shown, without losing information. Thus, it has to be accepted that it is not possible to eliminate all redundancies using normalisation techniques, because it cannot be assumed that all decompositions will be non-loss. If a table is in 4NF, as in the above example, and *cannot* be further non-loss decomposed, it is said to be in 5NF.

126 *Further normal forms*

But now consider the different case where, if an agent is an agent for a company and a product is made by that company, then he always sells that product for the company. Under these circumstances, the 'agent__company__product' table might be populated as shown below:

agent	company	product__name
Smith	ABC	spade
Jones	ABC	axe
Jones	ABC	spade
Smith	CDE	axe
Smith	ABC	axe

the assumption being that ABC supplies both spades and axes and that CDE supplies axes only. This table can be decomposed into its three projections without loss of information as demonstrated below:

P1

agent	company
Smith	ABC
Smith	CDE
Jones	ABC

P2

agent	product__name
Smith	spade
Smith	axe
Jones	axe
Jones	spade

P3

company	product__name
ABC	spade
ABC	axe
CDE	axe

and all redundancy has been removed. If the natural join of P1 and P2 is taken, the result is:

agent	company	product__name	
Smith	ABC	spade	
Smith	ABC	axe	
Smith	CDE	spade	*
Smith	CDE	axe	
Jones	ABC	axe	
Jones	ABC	spade	

with the spurious row as asterisked. Now, if this result is joined with P3 over the columns 'company' and 'product_name' the following table is obtained:

agent	company	product_name
Smith	ABC	spade
Smith	ABC	axe
Smith	CDE	axe
Jones	ABC	axe
Jones	ABC	spade

This is a correct recomposition of the original table and a no loss decomposition into the three projections of it was achieved. Again, the order in which the joins are performed does not affect the final result. The original table, therefore, violated 5NF simply because it was non loss decomposable into its three projections.

In the first case exemplified above, non-loss decomposition of the 'agent_company_product' table was not possible. In the second it was. If a table *is* non-loss decomposable as in the second case, it is said to be in violation of 5NF. The difference, of course, lay in certain semantic properties of the information being represented. These properties were not understandable simply by looking at the table, but had to be supplemented by further information about the relationship between products, agents and companies.

Detecting that a table violates 5NF is very difficult in practice and for this reason this normal form has little if any practical application. Nevertheless a considerable body of theory has been built up around 5NF and its ramifications and this is briefly discussed in the following paragraphs.

Suppose that the statement, 'The agent_company_product' table is equal to the join of its three projections is to hold true, this is another way of saying that it can be non-loss decomposed into its three projections and is equivalent to saying:

IF   the tuple 'agent X, company Y' appears in P1
AND   the tuple 'agent X, product Z' appears in P2
AND   the tuple 'company Y, product Z' appears in P3

THEN the row 'agent X, company Y, product Z' must have appeared in 'agent_company_product'.

If the reader cares to re-examine the projections P1, P2, and P3 from the two versions of the table which were illustrated earlier, then, it will be seen that the earlier version which was in 5NF does not conform to the above rule, whereas the later version, which violated 5NF does. The rule is referred to as a *join dependency*, because it holds good only if a table can be reconstituted without loss of information from the join of certain specified projections of it.

The notation used for a join dependency on Table T is:

$*(X, Y, ..., Z)$

where X, Y, ... Z are projections of T.

128   *Further normal forms*

Table T is said to satisfy the above join dependency if it is equal to the join of the projections X, Y, ... Z.

Thus, the second example given of the table 'agent__company__product' can be said to satisfy the join dependency:

*(P1, P2, P3)

In the discussion of the other further normal forms use was made of the concepts of functional and multi-valued dependencies. In dealing with 5NF the concept of *join dependency* has been introduced (in a very informal way). A join dependency is the most general form of depedency possible, where the term 'dependency' has the specialised meaning that has been used in reference to relational tables. What this means is that a multi-valued dependency is just a special case of a join dependency, just as a functional dependency is just a special case of a multi-valued dependency (where the set of multiple values contain only one member).

5NF is defined by the statement:

A table T is in fifth normal form if every join dependency in T is a consequence only of the candidate keys of T.

The second version of the table 'agent__company__product' illustrated earlier violated 5NF, because the join dependency *(agent, company, product__name) was not a consequence only of the primary key for the table, but also a consequence of the tuple formation rule which was given earlier.

In the first, example of 'agent__company__product' there was no application of this rule, hence no join dependency other than that on the primary key. Thus, the table was in 5NF. It can be shown that if a table is in 5NF, then, because join dependencies are the 'ultimate' form of dependency, it must also be in 4NF and thus conform to all the further normal forms. The problem with this is that detecting join dependencies is, in practice, very difficult. For this reason, 5NF is largely of academic interest.

Part 3
Information Models

The most widely accepted non-intuitive method for achieving correct relational database designs is that implied by the application of the so called further normal froms of the relational model, which were described in Chapter 8. However, the inference the reader may have drawn from Chaper 8 is that normalisation can only be used to correct a bad design, not to produce a good one. Further, the normalisation process cannot be guaranteed to remove all anomalies from a relational database design, only those which can be removed by the successive decomposition of tables.

Another method which is gaining acceptance as a basis for relational database design is the construction of an information model from which the design, that is the relational database schema, can be derived. However, the only relevant guidance given in modern methods of analysis, such as those outlined in Chapter 4, for correctness of an information model construction is that the model should be in third normal form. That is, reliance is again placed on application of the further normal forms for correctness of the design. Once again, the normalisation process cannot be guaranteed to remove all anomalies from a relational database design, only those which can be removed by the successive decomposition of tables.

What is required is a structured and disciplined method of going about the construction of information models such that the relational database schema derived from it is free from all the update insertion and deletion anomalies of the kind described in Part 3 in the first place and is, therefore, also fully in normal form in the relational model sense.

In Chapter 9, the information modelling concepts introduced in Part 1 are re-examined to determine what semantic data model objects, rules and operators are required for an information model's construction to ensure that it does not introduce distortion and ambiguity into the semantics of the information modelled. It is then demonstrated that such distortion and ambiguity free information models must also be fully in normal form in the relational model sense.

In Chapter 10, a semantic data model, referred to as the E-O (Entity-Object) model, with objects, rules and operators obtained from the analysis in Chapter 9 is defined.

In Chapter 11, practical techniques for the construction of an information model using the objects, rules and operators of the E-O model are described. All three chapters are based on practical experience gained when analysing the complex information requirements of large defence supplier and military establishments for subsequent incorporation into relational database systems.

9

Information Modelling and the Relational Model

9.1   Introduction

In Chapter 2 the basic objects of a semantic data model were introduced and in Chapter 4, a graphical and textual notation for representing these objects was described. This model, which is used as the basis for construction of information models in modern methods of systems analysis, is usually referrred to as the entity-relationship (E-R) model. Its origins lie in the work of Chen who introduced it in [29]. In Chapter 4 it was shown that information modelling, using the objects of the E-R model has become incorporated into modern methods of analysis and design and is supported by the widely available CASE tools which support these methods. Consequently, information models have increasingly become the starting point for the design of databases for systems, including, of course, relational database systems.

Chen's original E-R model was rooted in the mathematical theory of relations in a similar fashion to the relational model. However, little of this original mathematical concept has survived into what is currently referred to as the E-R model. What has survived, with considerable elaboration and change by Flavin[30], Schlaer and Mellor[17] and others over the years, is the graphical notation he used to describe its objects, the *entity relationship diagram* (ERD), together with some of the original semantic ideas.

The E-R model, as it is widely used currently in modern methods of analysis and design has become, for the most part, simply a convenient *notation* for describing the data requirements of a system. Depending on the experience, training, skill and intuition of the analyst involved, it is possible to produce a very good basis for a database design using it and it is also possible to produce a thoroughly bad one. Information modelling, in other words, despite the efforts of Flavin and others, is still very much of a black art. In the various modern analysis and design methods which support the E-R model, its objects are described, but little or no guidance is given on how to obtain correct results using them, no integrity rules are specified and no operators are described.

The only non-intuitive method which has gained acceptance as contributing to the achievement of good relational database designs is that inferred by the application of the so called further normal forms of the relational model. Most modern methods of analysis now recognise this and generally insist that information models should be in 3NF. (Few or none mention BCNF, 4NF or 5NF). However, criticism is often levelled at normalisation as an analysis/design method because of the seemingly unnatural approach it entails. The inference the reader may have drawn from Chapter 8 is that normalisation can only be used to correct a bad design, not to produce a good one. With experience, the normalisation rules can be applied intuitively as the design progresses,

131

132 *Information modelling and the relational model*

but as a design method normalisation is still fundamentally unsatisfactory. Further, as we saw in Chapter 8 when discussing 5NF, the normalisation process cannot be guaranteed to remove all anomalies from a relational database design, only those that can be eliminated by taking successive projections from (already defined) tables.

Proposals, at various times and of various types, have been made to adopt a 'synthesis' approach to the development of relational database schemata. These are based on deriving the tables from their attributes in a manner which ensures that they are in normal form. In such approaches, the analyst starts with all the attributes of interest to an enterprise and all the functional and multivalued dependencies between those attributes. He then synthesises tables by applying the normalisation rules. In effect one starts with one large table and then decomposes it until decomposition can no longer be achieved. These proposals, although theoretically sound, have not found acceptance because they run counter to the way that most analysts and designers have to work.

Systems analysis in practice involves a process of abstraction whereby the analyst abstracts the important detail of the problem first until the 'big picture' emerges, only then incorporating the minor detail in a progressive manner. The synthesis approach amounts to the reverse of this. Another, pragmatic consideration to be taken into account when considering the approach to the data analysis task is that all analysts have to produce visible interim results in as short a time scale as possible to satisfy their management and their users. The approach using abstraction, as just described, results in a series of models each successively containing more detail, and this fits in well with this need to produce early visible results. The synthesis approach does not.

What is required, therefore, is a method of going about the data analysis task which will:

- Allow visible and useful intermediate results to be produced.
- Ensure that the information model produced will be fully normalised in the first place and map directly on to an RDB schema.
- Ensure that *all* design anomalies are removed, not just those which are removable by the application of the further normal forms.

Experienced data analysts expect that an information model produced using a semantic data model will be fully normalised. This amounts to saying that if the semantics of data in the real world of an enterprise are well understood and represented *fully and without distortion* in an information model constructed using a semantic data model, then the relational database derived from that model will be in normal form.

In this chapter, this expectation is given formal shape. The E-R model concepts described so far in this book are explored further and elaborated into a definition of a semantic data model with semantically defined objects, integrity rules and operators. The purpose of this common sense model is to serve as the basis for the construction of fully normalised information models. These information models in turn can serve as the basis for the derivation of relational database schemata which themselves are fully normalised. This model is referred to as the Entity Object (E-O) model. The reason for this choice of title will become clear as the chapter progresses. It is informally demonstrated at the conclusion of the chapter that an information model constructed using the objects and integrity rules of the E-O semantic data model must be fully normalised in the relational model sense. Indeed, it will be demonstrated that use of the E-O model as an analysis and design method is more powerful than normalisation in that the latter, even when applied correctly, does not guarantee that all update, deletion and insertion anomalies can be removed, but the former, when applied correctly, does. Chapter 10 gives a summary definition of the E-O model objects, operators and integrity rules developed in this chapter.

9.2 E-O Model Concepts

9.2.1 Introductory Definitions

In the following paragraphs, many of the terms which have been used in this book, in particular the terms entity, object, relationship and attribute are re-examined and re-defined against their plain language dictionary definitions in order to arrive at some common sense definitions for the objects of the E-O semantic data model. A number of new terms are also introduced and defined. The definitions given in this Section are introductory in the sense that they provide a starting point for the rationale section which follows and which develops the ideas they represent further, refining them in the process.

Things, entities and objects

We can make a start by defining the noun with the widest possible meaning in any language, a *thing*. The dictionary definition of a *thing* is:

'Whatever is or may be thought about or perceived.'

Having defined 'thing' we can now look at the dictionary definition of an *entity*, which is:

Thing with distinct existence; thing's existence in itself as opposed to its qualities or relations

Note the use of the word 'distinct' in this definition. Another way of saying that an entity is distinct is to say that it is uniquely identifiable. Also note that the notion of an entity is simply about a thing's existence, not about its 'qualities or relations.'

Now, in a semantic data model we are concerned with the *types* of entity of interest to an enterprise rather than specific occurrences of them. An *entity type* is a generalisation into a named class of things of a number of distinct things which are observed to have similar characteristics. For example, we generalise individually observed human beings into the entity type 'person' and we generalise various types of motor propelled vehicles into the entity type 'automobile'. By elaborating on the above dictionary definition of an entity, we can define an *entity type* as:

A named class of things each of which has distinct existence; the existence of things within the class as opposed to their qualities or relations.

An entity type can be described by giving it a unique name, for example as before, 'person' and 'automobile'. Since the definition includes the notion of distinctness, that is, it conveys the idea of the ability to identify uniquely occurrences of an entity type, a complete description of an entity type must also include an indication of how this identification is to be achieved. Note that although the definition of an entity type is

134　*Information modelling and the relational model*

separate from the notion of its 'qualities or relations', it does infer that it must be possible for an entity type to have them.

The dictionary definition of an *object* is:

(Person or) thing to which action (or feeling) is directed.

This definition does not exclude the thing's qualities as was the case for an entity type. An *object type* can, therefore, be defined as:

A fully qualified entity type to occurrences of which action is directed.

This distinction between entity types and object types may seem pedantic at the moment, but will be seen shortly to be very useful.

Relations, relationships, (proportion and insistency)

The dictionary definition of a *relation* is:

Kind of connection or correspondence or contrast or feeling that prevails between (persons or) things.

and of a *relationship:*

State of being related.

All relationships between pairs of entity types have a *proportion* and an *insistency*. The proportion of a relationship can be one of the ratios 'one to many' (1:m), 'many to one' (m:1), 'one to one' (1:1) or 'many to many' (m:n).

If we say that a relationship's proportion is 1:m, then we mean that for each occurrence of an entity type on the 'one' side of a relationship, there can be many corresponding occurrences of the entity type on the 'many' side of the relationship, but that for each occurrence of an entity type on the 'many' side of the relationship, there can only be one occurrence of the entity type on the 'one' side. For example in the 1:m relationship 'Customer places order', one customer can place many orders, but an order can belong to only one customer. The m:1 case is simply the reverse of the 1:m case since all relationships are bi-directional. We could have stated the above relationship in its m:1 form as 'Order is placed by customer'. The rule is still the same in that for each occurrence of an entity type on the 'one' side of a relationship, there can be many corresponding occurrences of the entity type on the 'many' side of the relationship, but for each occurrence of an entity type on the 'many' side of the relationship, there can only be one occurrence of the entity type on the 'one' side.

If the proportion of a relationship is 1:1, then for every occurrence of an entity type on either side of a relationship, there can be just one corresponding occurrence of an entity type on the other. For example the relationship 'Husband is married to wife' is 1:1 in most societies. If the proportion of a relationship is m:n, then for any occurrence of an entity type on the 'm' side of the relationship, there can be many corresponding occurrences of the entity type on the 'n' side of the relationship, and for any occurrence of an entity type on the 'n' side of the relationship, there can be many occurrences of the entity type on the 'm' side of the relationship. For example in the m:n relationship 'Order consists of line items', a particular order can consist of many line items and a particular line item can appear in many orders.

E-O model concepts 135

The insistency of a relationship specifies whether or not for an entity on either side of a relationship there must always be a corresponding entity on the other side of the relationship. For example, in the 1:m 'Customer places order' relationship, the insistency would be that each order entity participate in an occurrence of the relationship, since every order entity must have had a customer entity who placed it. However, it is not obligatory for all customer entities to participate in an occurrence of the relationship since customers may exist who do not have orders placed at some point in time. In the m:n 'Order consists of line item' relationship, participation of all order entities in occurrences of the relationship is obligatory, since an order cannot exist unless it specifies line items, but participation of line items is not obligatory, since it is possible for certain line items not to be on order at any point in time.

Attributes, entity types and object types

The dictionary definition of an *attribute* is:

Quality ascribed to (person or) thing.

Attributes in the context of a semantic data model can usefully be divided into two broad sub-classes, *identifiers* and *qualifiers*.

An identifier is an attribute or concatenation of attributes of an entity type whose values are used to identify uniquely occurrences of the entity type.

For example, an attribute 'personnel__number' might be designed to provide for unique identification of all individual employees within an organisation. The identifier for merchant ships would require the two attributes 'ship__name' and 'port__of__registry' to be concatenated together to form an identifier, since the merchant ship's name is only unique within the context of the port at which it was registered. It is possible for an entity or object type to have more than one identifier. For example, a naval ship can be identified either by her hull number or by her name and port of registry.

Earlier, when discussing entity types, it was stated that a description of an entity type must include an indication of how occurrences of it could be uniquely identified. This, clearly, is the role of attributes which are identifiers. In principle, the existence of an entity type could be described by giving its identifier a unique name within an information model. In practice, however, it is more meaningful to give it a unique, descriptive name as well as an identifier, as in:

EMPLOYEE (@personnel__number)

We continue to signify attributes which are also identifiers by including an 'at' (@) symbol against their names as above. Note that the above constitutes a *complete* description of the entity type 'employee' in accordance with the definition of an entity type given earlier. The definition of an entity type is a description of the existence of a class of things by naming it and by showing how individual occurrences of the class are to be identified.

From a practical, semantic data model point of view, identifiers can be regarded as essentially constant in the values they can take on. If any organisation at any level frequently changed the manner by which it identified occurrences of the entity types of interest to it, it would be in a constant state of confusion of even chaos. Consider the

136 *Information modelling and the relational model*

effect of frequently changing car licence plate numbers, personnel identifications, ship names, part codes and so forth.

Such identifiers and their values can change in the real world, of course. When change to identifiers is necessary, the potentially drastic impact on the organisation's operations must be recognised and necessary plans to contain this impact need to be formulated and put into action. This sort of action applies for the most part to the populated database schema derived from an information model rather than to the information model as such. That is, containment of the impact of changing the values of identifiers is the concern of the database model in use, not of the semantic data model.

The definition given above does not exclude the possibility of an identifier conveying more information than just how occurrences of an entity type are to be identified. For example, if a small organisation wished to avoid the trouble of setting up a coding system for the types of articles it sold, it might identify them by concatenating together certain of their attributes. If it sold articles of the entity type 'garment__type', it might identify individual types of garment by concatenating together the attributes '@garment__type + @colour + @size + @material'. One occurrence of the entity type 'garment__type' might then be identified by 'dress + red + outsize + silk'.

We can now consider qualifiers. The definition of a qualifier is:

A qualifier is an attribute which is not also an identifier or part of an identifier.

(In the above definition, qualifier should be taken as meaning 'quantifier' where appropriate. This is, a qualifier could be a quality such as 'colour' or a quantity such as 'weight'.)

Employees, for example, will have, qualifying attributes such as name, age, sex, job title and salary which form no part of their identifier. The possibility that a qualifier can be a concatenated collection of attributes is excluded. That is, each qualifier is assumed to be semantically atomic. This is just common sense about the precise meaning of things. It would be pointless to specify a qualifier such as 'dimensions' when what was really meant was 'height', 'width' and 'depth'.

Note that whereas the definition of an identifier makes reference to an entity type, the definition of a qualifier does not. This is because the definition of an entity type which was given earlier included the notion of its identifier but exluded the notion of its qualifiers. However, this does not apply to object types which must, by the definition given earlier, have qualifiers. An object type is an entity type for which qualifiers have been specified. It will inherit the name and identifier of an entity type.

This distinction between entity and object types is not made simply for reasons of pedantry. In the introduction to this chapter it was stressed that systems analysis proceeds by a process of successive abstractions whereby the analyst abstracts the important detail of the problem first until the 'big picture' emerges, only then incorporating the minor detail in a progressive manner. This applies just as much to information modelling (data analysis) as to any other systems analysis activity. The initial step in constructing an information model can be to identify all the entity types of interest to an organisation and the relationships between them. This gives the required 'big picture'. Later, the entity types identified can be promoted to being object types which include all the necessary qualifying detail. We will also find this distinction to be useful and necessary in the arguments put forward in Section 9.2.2.

The degree of a relationship

The existence of a relationship depends on the existence of one or more entity types. (Only one entity type is required to support a loop relationship.) The identifier for a relationship is formed by concatenating the identifiers of the participating entity types. The *degree* of a relationship is defined as follows:

The degree of a relationship is equal to the number of entity type identifiers concatenated together to form its identifier.

If the special case of a loop relationship is ignored for the moment, all relationships must be between at least two participating entity types. That is, the minimum degree of a relationship must be two. In the case of a loop relationship, its identifier must again be a concatenation of at least two identifiers, albeit the two identifiers are taken from a single entity type's identifier. For example, consider the relationship 'Sibling has same parents as sibling'. Occurrences of the entity type 'sibling' with identifier 'sibling_name' might be:

```
@sibling_name
_____

John
Mary
Sue
Jim
Fred
Ian
```

Suppose that Ian, John and Mary are siblings and that Jim, Fred and Sue are also siblings. These occurrences of the relationship can be represented as:

```
@sibling_name1          @sibling_name2
_____

John                    Mary
John                    Ian
Ian                     Mary
Sue                     Jim
Sue                     Fred
Fred                    Jim
```

where (@sibling_name1 + @sibling_name2) is the identifier for the relationship. Thus, it is clearly impossible for any relationship, even a loop relationship, to have a degree of less than 2 by the above definition. The minimum possible degree for a relationship is binary.

The above definition given for the degree of a relationship is stricter than that commonly given in the literature. Some writers define the degree of a relationship as being equal to the number of participating entity types. By this definition, a loop relationship would have a degree of one, which is ambiguous, misleading and mathematically incorrect.

138   *Information modelling and the relational model*

Supertypes and subtypes

In Chapter 2 the notion of supertypes and subtypes was introduced. Entity types could be further generalised from subtypes into supertypes. For example, one could generalise from the entity types 'bridge', 'pontoon' and 'ford' to the supertype 'river_crossing'. 'Bridge', 'pontoon' and 'ford' would then become subtypes of the supertypes 'river_crossing'. For this type of generalisation to be useful, the subtypes must have some, but not all classes of qualifiers in common before being generalised into a supertype. The supertype can then hold these common qualifiers and the subtypes can each have qualifiers which are particular to them alone. For example, the supertype 'river_crossing' might have qualifiers like 'length' and 'width' which are common to all the subtypes, but not 'height', since this only qualifies a bridge. By the same token, 'ford' could have the qualifier 'depth' which is irrelevant to bridges and pontoons. Since only one entity type is involved, supertypes and subtypes must have at least one identifier in common.

Note that the concept of supertype and subtype does not correspond to the concept of a relationship as this was defined and discussed earlier. There is no relationship between a supertype and any of its subtypes or vice versa, simply a functional differentiation of one entity type into its subtypes, or a generalisation of subtypes into a supertype. For example, a specific river crossing cannot have a relationship with itself as a ford, since only one entity is involved.

9.2.2 Rationale

In the following paragraphs the semantic data model objects just defined are analysed in order to arrive at just two fundamental *integrity rules* which must be obeyed in the construction of information models so as to ensure that they are complete and free from semantic distortions and ambiguities. The term integrity rule is used in the sense that it was used earlier during discussion of the relational model. That is, a semantic data model integrity rule is one which applies to all information models constructed using the semantic data model, not just to specific cases.

First normal form and the E-O model

Since a prime objective of the E-O model is to assist in the development of relational database schemata and such schemata must be in 1NF, repeating attributes cannot be allowed in the E-O model. Please note both that this is assumed in the following reasoning, and that it is *not* being advocated here that *all* information models be in 1NF, only those which are to serve as the basis for relational database designs. More will be said on this topic in the postscript on E-O model applicability which is given at the end of this chapter. A construction heuristic (rule of thumb) is given later to assist the analyst in the correct removal of repeating attributes from an information model.

The primitive objects of the E-O semantic data model

In the earlier part of this section we defined five basic classes of semantic data model object, namely:

E-O model concepts   139

- Entity types
- Object Types
- Relationships — 1:m (or m:1), 1:1 and m:n
- Attributes — Identifiers and Qualifiers
- Super/Sub-Types

In the next few paragraphs it will be demonstrated that we can define three *primitive* semantic data model objects for a model, like the E-O model, which does not permit repeating attributes. These are:

- Independent Entity Types
- Dependent Entity types
- Linkages

All of the five classes defined listed earlier can be defined in terms of these primitives and, in principle, any information model which could be constructed using the above five classes of objects could also be constructed using only these three primitive classes (although this is not being advocated in practice).

Relationships, depending on their proportion, correspond either to attributes which are qualifiers, or to entity types. Consider the entity types 'customer' and 'order' which we might represent in an information model as:

ORDER(@order_number)
CUSTOMER(@customer_identity_code)

There is a 1:m relationship between customers and orders (or an m:1 relationship between orders and customers, which means the same thing). This is represented by concatenating together the identifiers of the participating entity types in the relationship, thus:

(@order_number + ?@?customer_identity_code)

If we look at some possible occurrences of this relationship, the significance of the question marks around the '@' sign will become clear.

@order_number	?@?customer_identity_code
123	A A
124	A A
125	B B
126	B B
127	C C

The 'order_number' values are unique for each occurrence of the relationship, but the 'customer_identity_code' values are not. This phenomenon stems from the fundamental nature of a relationship whose proportion is 1:m. Each occurrence of an item on the 'many' side relates to one and only one occurrence of an item on the '1' side of the relationship and consequently can only participate once amongst all occurrences of the relationship. The only identifier involved in the above example is that for the 'order' entity type.

140 *Information modelling and the relational model*

We must, in fact, represent the relationship correctly as:

ORDER(@order__number + customer__identity__code)

This shows that the 1:m relationship is semantically equivalent to a qualifier attribute for the entity type 'order'. Thus, a 1:m (or m:1) relationship is not an entity type, since it does not have an identifier of its own. It follows that it cannot participate in other relationships of any proportion. Any such relationships that we might try to identify could only be relationships with the entity type on the 'many' side of the relationship.

Now, should we choose to delete the entity type 'customer' from our model, because we are not interested in customers other than in the identities of those who have placed orders, this does not mean that the 1:m relationship between customers and orders no longer exists. It simply means that the same relationship is now being shown in the model in a 'shorthand' manner. To make this point clear, suppose that we were also interested in the dates when orders were placed, giving:

ORDER(@order__number + customer__identity__code + date__of__order)

We do not have an entity type 'date' defined in our model, but, nevertheless, we are representing a 1:m relationship between some real world entity type 'date', whose identifier is 'date__of__order', and the real world entity type 'order'. What we defined earlier as a qualifier attribute is really a shorthand way of representing an m:1 relationship between the thing being qualified and some other entity type. If follows that an object type, as defined earlier, is an entity type which is in an m:1 relationship with itself (loop relationship) and/or one or more other entity types.

Now consider the m:n relationship 'Product contains parts', where a product can be composed of many types of parts and the same part can be used in many types of products. The identifier for this relationship would then be the concatenation of the identifiers of the participating entity types, for example:

(@product__type + @part__type)

We can see how this works by looking at some possible occurrences of the relationship:

@product__type	@part__type
ABC	A
ABC	B
BCD	B
BCD	C
BCD	A

In this case, values for both of the concatenated identifiers are required to identify uniquely each occurrence of the relationship, and this is true for all m:n relationships. (The reader may wish to convince himself of this by trying a few more worked examples of m:n relationships.) The relationship must exist as an entity type in its own right *because it has its own unique identifier.* It is not a 'product' entity type or a 'part' entity type. It is an entity type formed by the relationship between these two entity types. We can, therefore, legitimately use a noun or noun phrase to name an m:n relationship and will name the above example 'product__part'. Intuitively, since m:n relationships are entity types in their own right, it should follow that they can participate in further relationships

E-O model concepts 141

of any proportion. The truth of this statement can be demonstrated by example.

Considering 1:m and m:1 relationships first, suppose that we need to know the quantities of particular parts associated with particular products. This is not a property of either of the 'product' or 'part' entity types, rather, it qualifies the entity type, 'product_part', whose data dictionary entry might then be as follows:

PRODUCT_PART(@product_type + @part_type + part_quantity)

where 'part-quantity' is just a shorthand way of representing an m:1 relationship between 'product_part' and the entity type 'part_quantity'. If specific sets of tools are needed to fit specific parts to specific products and no two individual tools are the same then a 1:m relationship would exist between 'product_part' and 'tool'. Suppose that we need to identify those employees trained to fit specific parts to specific products. Suppose also that we determine that any employee might be trained to fit any product_part combination. The relationship would then be a further m:n relationship between the entity type 'employee', with identifier, say, 'employee_id' and the entity type 'product_part'. This could meaningfully be named 'fitter'. 'Fitter' would be represented as:

FITTER(@product_type + @part_type + @employee_id)

(Note carefully that 'fitter' is *not* a ternary relationship (of degree three) as the triple concatenated identifier might dispose one to think. It is a *binary* relationship between the 'product_part' and 'employee' entity types. There are only *two* identifiers concatenated together to form its identifier, '@product_code + @part_number' from the 'product_part' entity type and 'employee_id' from 'employee'. The fact that one of these identifiers is itself a concatenated identifier is irrelevant to the degree of the 'fitter' relationship.)

Thus, we have established that an m:n relationship is an entity type, capable of having an identifier and capable of participating in further relationships of any proportion with other entity types. This includes m:1 relationships which might be represented in shorthand fashion as qualifier attributes.

Suppose that we try to form an identifier for the 1:1 relationship (in most cultures) 'Husband is married to wife'. Again, this must be formed in some way from the identifiers of the participating entity types 'husband' and 'wife', say:

(@husband_name + @wife_name)

If we assume that each husband and wife has a unique name, then some sample occurrences of this relationship might be:

@husband_name	@wife_name
John	Jill
Jim	June
Fred	Mary

In this case what stands out is that *either* of the concatenated attributes provides a unique identifier for the relationship. If we represent this 1:1 relationship in this manner, then it is an entity type, which we might call 'marriage'. It is easy to see that a 1:1 relationship identified this way can take part in further relationships of any proportion. The 'marriage'

142 *Information modelling and the relational model*

entity type could participate in an m:1 relationship with the entity type 'church'. (It does not matter to the truth of this whether this relationship is given explicit representation or is shown in a shorthand manner as a qualifier.) One marriage could produce several children (1:m relationship). One marriage could involve many guests and one guest could attend many marriages (m:n relationship). However, we could also represent the relationship as:

WIFE(@wife__name + husband__name)
or

HUSBAND(@husband__name + wife__name)

in a similar manner to that in which we represented 1:m relationship. In the first example 'husband' simply becomes an attribute of the entity type 'wife' and in the second, 'wife' of 'husband'. But if we choose to represent a 1:1 relationship in either of these two manners, then just as was the case for 1:m relationships earlier, it cannot meaningfully be regarded as an entity type and, therefore, cannot participate in further relationships of any proportion.

We can make the practical observation, therefore, that if a 1:1 relationship participates in further relationships of any proportion *which are of interest,* then it must be treated as an entity type and be separately represented in an information model. If it does not, then it need not be treated as an entity type and can be represented simply by including it as a qualifier attribute on either side of the relationship according to the choice of the analyst.

From the above reasoning it can be seen that all 1:m, all m:1 and certain 1:1 relationships are not entity types. They correspond semantically to qualifier attributes of an entity type on one or other side of the relationship. From now on we will use the term *linkage* to describe such relationships.

We have also seen that m:n relationships and certain 1:1 relationships are entity types. These entity types differ from the general run of entity types in only one significant respect. A relationship which is also an entity type cannot exist by itself. There must exist at least one other entity type to participate in the relationship. (One? Remember loop relationships.) In this sense, these relationships are *dependent entity types*. By the same token, an entity type which is not also a relationship is an *independent entity type*. We will distinguish between these two forms of entity type in what follows, wherever necessary, in order to avoid ambiguity. Note that since a dependent entity type is also a relationship, it must have a degree. It must also have a proportion which can only be m:n or 1:1.

We have now determined the three primitive object classes of the E-O semantic data model, namely:

- Independent Entity Types
- Dependent Entity Types
- Linkages

In addition to these primitives, the term 'qualifier' will continue to be used, although it should now be clear that this means a linkage which does not require explicit definition in an information model. The term 'object type' will also continue to be used though it should be clear that this is an entity type (dependent or independent) which participates on the 'many' side in 1:m linkages, or on either side in the 1:1 linkage case. We will also continue to use the terms supertype and subtype although these are not semantic model objects as such but functions (generalisation and differentiation respectively) which are performed on entity types. However, the term 'relationship' will no longer be used except where it helps to clarify the text, since, as we have seen, this is a very overloaded word which has been used to describe semantic objects with fundamentally different properties.

We will return to further discussion based on the above primitives shortly, but at this point it will be useful to re-consider what the graphic representation of relationships in an ERD and what the textual notation for data dictionary entries should be in light of what was said above.

Revised ERD notation for relationships

In the ERD notation given in Chapter 4, relationships of any proportion were represented by a diamond and named by a singular verb or verb phrase. Entity types were represented by a box and named by a singular noun or noun phrase.

No purpose is served by maintaining these distinctions for relationships which are also dependent entity types. Since they are entity types, it is more appropriate to name them using nouns or noun phrases and to represent them using boxes. However, for the ERD to convey maximum semantic information, we need to distinguish between dependent and independent entity types. To achieve this, the relationship diamond is retained, unnamed, with a pointer to the box containing the name of the dependent entity type. The ERD of Figure 9.1 shows an example of the use of this notation based on the 'product', 'part', 'product_part' and 'fitter' entity type examples given earlier and of the 'husband', 'wife', 'marriage' entity type examples just given. The convention adopted for representing the proportion of dependent entity types on the diagram is that it is not shown for the m:n case, but is shown for the much rarer 1:1 case. Representation of insistencies (not shown) is unchanged. Note that this is much the same as the notation given in Chapter 4 for associative object types. However, it is no longer necessary for a relationship to have attributes of its own for it to be represented in this way, as was the case for the associative object types encountered in Chapter 4. It simply has to be a dependent entity type as defined earlier. A further entity type has been introduced into Figure 9.1, the dependent entity type 'employee_language'. This is based on the m:n relationship between employees and languages. (One employee may known many languages and one language may be know by many employees.) If it is assumed that there is no interest in languages on the users' part, other than in the context of the employees who know them, the language entity type as such need not be introduced explicitly into the diagram. But it is still necessary to show the existence of the dependent entity type. The result has been to produce what will be referred to as a *dangling* dependent entity type in the diagram. The unshown, 'language' participating entity type in this dependent entity type can be thought of as a 'ghost' entity type.

144 *Information modelling and the relational model*

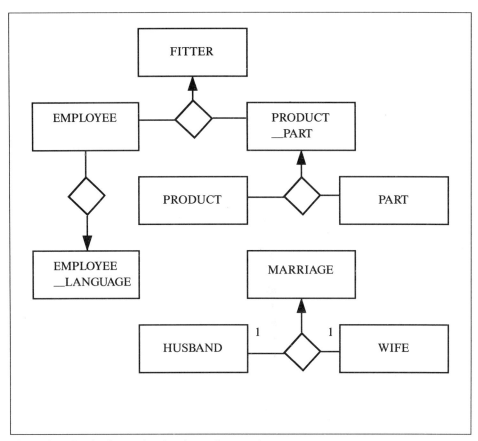

Figure 9.1 **Revised notation for dependent entity types**

Since linkages cannot participate in further linkages or dependent entity types, there seems little point in representing them with a diamond to which things can be attached. In any case, we need to distinguish them clearly from entity types. Their representation can be simplified, and it can be made clear that nothing can be attached to them, by representing them simply as arrowed lines. The lines are labelled with their names, which are given by singular verbs or verb phrases as before.

(*Note:* There is, of course, no corresponding separate entry in the data dictionary for these names, since linkages are not entity types. Only entity types, dependent or independent, can have separate data dictionary entries.)

The direction of the arrow points to the entity type which is the 'receiver' of the identifier from the other entity type and will, therefore, always point to the 'many' side of a linkage of 1:m or m:1 proportion. Where the linage is of 1:1 proportion, the direction of the arrow is at the discretion of the analyst, but must still point to the 'receiving' entity type. Nothing must be connected to a linkage's arrowed line. Using this revised notation, the 1:m 'Customer places order' and the 1:1 'Employee is allocated a company car' linkages would be represented in an ERD as shown in Figure 9.2.

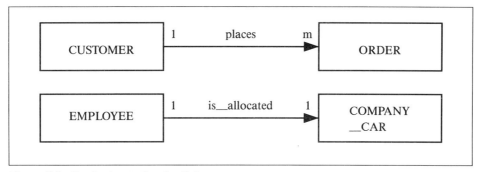

Figure 9.2 Revised notation for linkages

Insistency (not shown) can be specified as before. Where a linkage is given explicit representation in an ERD as in the Figure 9.2 examples, that is, where it is not indicated in a shorthand manner by the use of a qualifier attribute, it shows that it is of explicit interest to the user. This must be indicated in the data dictionary in some manner as well as being shown in the ERD as an arrowed line, and this is done by preceding the attribute concerned with a double 'at' sign (@@). The 'places' linkage as shown in Figure 9.2 could be indicated in the data dictionary entry for 'order' as follows:

ORDER(@order__number + @@customer__identity__code)

Qualifiers which are distinguished in this way will be referred to as *linkage identifiers*.

Removing repeating groups

The construction heuristic for removing repeating attributes or attribute groups correctly is:

'When a repeating attribute or attribute group is encountered, the proportion of the underlying relationship must be determined first in the direction of the host object type to the repeating attribute(s).

If the relationship is 1:m, then the repeating attribute or attribute group must be removed and, in the first instance, a new object type formed which contains the repeating attribute(s) as an identifier, and the identifier of the host entity type as one or more linkage identifiers. This object type should then be examined to see whether any part of its identifier is redundant and, if so, the redundant attributes should be demoted to being qualifiers. The ERD and data dictionary should be modified to show the linkage.

If the relationship is m:n, then the repeating attribute or attribute group must be removed and, in the first instance, a new dependent entity type formed which contains the repeating attribute(s) and the identifier of the host object type as a concatenated identifier. This entity type should then be examined to see whether any part of its concatenated identifier is redundant and, if so, the redundant attributes should be demoted to being qualifiers. The ERD and data dictionary should be modified to show the new, dangling dependent entity type.'

146 *Information modelling and the relational model*

A number of examples are now given to illustrate the used of the above heuristic. Consider the following object type:

CUSTOMER(@customer__id + credit__status__code + {address} + etc.)

The qualifier 'address' which is shown as being repeatable against a single occurrence of a customer. It must be either a 1:m linkage between 'customer' and the non-explicitly defined entity type 'address', or an m:n relationship between the two. This can be seen clearly in the following example occurrences of the object type:

1:m Linkage Case:

@customer__id	credit__status__code	{address}
Jones	good	Bristol
		Bath
		Leeds
Smith	bad	London
		Manchester
		Glasgow

(The assumption in this case is that no two customers can be at the same address.)

m:n Relationship case:

@customer__id	credit__status__code	{address}
Jones	good	Bristol
		Bath
		Leeds
Smith	bad	Bristol
		Bath
		Glasgow

(The assumption here is that they can.)

In the first case, following the heuristic, the repeating attribute must be removed by defining a 'customer__address' entity type, whose identifier is '@address' and a 1:m linkage between 'customer' and 'customer__address':

CUSTOMER__ADDRESS(@address + @@customer__id)

with an ERD entry as in Figure 9.3. In the second case, the repeating attribute must be removed by defining a dependent entity type on 'customer' and 'address', thus:

CUSTOMER__ADDRESS(@customer__id + @address)

and the ERD would show a dangling dependent entity type as depicted in Figure 9.3. In the example just given, only one attribute, 'address' was shown as having repeating values against a single occurrence of the entity type 'customer'. It is also, of course, possible to have attributes which repeat in a group as in:

CUSTOMER(@customer__id + credit__status__code + {city + street__name + street-__number} + etc.)

Now suppose that no two customers can exist at the same address as defined by 'city+street_name+street_number'. This means that the relationship between 'customer' and this repeating group is 1:m. Following the heuristic we would obtain:

CUSTOMER_ADDRESS(@city+ @street_name+ @street_number+ @@customer_id}

as our new data dictionary entry and the ERD would now show a linkage between 'customer' and the new object type 'customer_address' as shown in the top half of Figure 9.3.

On the other hand, has it been possible for more than one customer to exist at the same street number in the same city the relationship would have been m:n, the data dictionary entry for 'customer_address' would have been:

CUSTOMER_ADDRESS(@city+ @street_name+ @street_number+ @customer_id)

and the ERD would have shown a dangling dependent entity type as in the lower half of Figure 9.3.

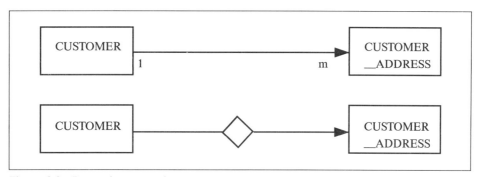

Figure 9.3 Removing repeating groups

Finally, in this discussion of repeating groups, consider the case where the 'customer' object type is initially defined as:

CUSTOMER(@customer_id+credit_status_code+{city+street_name+street_number+postal_code}+ etc.)

Assuming the underlying relationship to be m:n, in the first instance removing the repeating group would give the 'customer_address':

CUSTOMER_ADDRESS(@city+ @street_name+ @street_number+ @customer_id+ @postal_code}

But a postal code (in the UK) identifies an address to within a city and street and even to a section of a street. Therefore the identifier obtained in the first instance for 'customer_address' contains redundancy and this would be corrected by redefining the entity type 'customer_address' as the dependent object type:

148 Information modelling and the relational model

CUSTOMER_ADDRESS(@postal_code+@street_number+@customer_id+street_name+city).

The two integrity rules of the E-O model

With the assistance of the above revised notation and using the primitive semantic data model objects just defined, two integrity rules for the E-O semantic data model can be developed. These rules are constraints which must be placed upon any information model constructed using the objects of the E-O model in order to avoid introducing ambiguity and/or distortion into the picture the information model gives of the real world information requirements of an organisation and to ensure its completeness.

The First Integrity Rule

Consider the case where we have two object types, 'employee' and 'department':

EMPLOYEE(@employee_id+birth_date+salary+@@department_number+building_number)

DEPARTMENT(@department_number+building_number)

Normally these would be represented compactly in an ERD as two boxes, one for each of the object types, with a 1:m linkage between them. However, we can also represent these two object types, using the primitive E-O model objects, entirely as entity types and linkages as in the ERD of Figure 9.4.

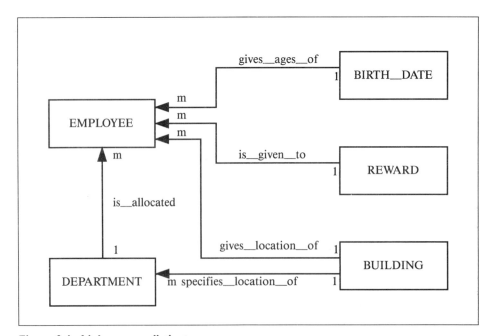

Figure 9.4 Linkages are distinct

The first integrity rule   149

The qualifiers 'salary' and 'date__of__birth' are shown as 1:m linkages from the entity types 'reward' and 'birth__date' respectively to 'employee'. The original, explicitly defined 1:m linkage between 'department' and 'employee' is also shown.

Now, the qualifier 'building__number, in the object type 'employee' is shown as the m:1 linkage 'gives__location__of' between employee and an entity type 'building', whose identifier is 'building__number'. Similarly, the qualifier 'building__number' in the object type 'department' is shown as the m:1 linkages 'specifies__location__of' between 'department' and 'building'.

The important point to note is that these two linkages are quite distinct in their meaning. The first means that an employee is located in some building. The second means that a department is located in some building. We cannot infer from the presence of these two separate linkages that an employee is always in the same building as his department. *We could only draw this inference if there were a relationship between 'employee' and the linkage 'specifies__location__of'.* Since linkages cannot partake in further relationships, this means that the same qualifier used as an attribute in two or more different object types must have a different meaning in each, that is its meaning must be *private* to each object type it qualifies. This leads to the observation that *all qualifiers must be semantically private to one object type.*

Now suppose that we have defined just one object type in an information model, 'equipment', as:

EQUIPMENT(@equipment__ser__number + @equipment__type + engineer__id + age + manufacturer__id + weight + engineer__grade + etc)

Since there is only one object type, we might be tempted to assume that all of its qualifiers must be private to it. But this is not the case. If we eliminate the 'shorthand' and expand the above object type definition into its definition as entity types and linkages, we would obtain the following:

EQUIPMENT(@equipment__ser__number + @equipment__type + @@engineer__ id + @@age + @@manufacturer__id + @@weight + ?@@engineer__grade? + @@etc)

ENGINEER(@engineer__id + @@engineer__grade)

TIME__OF__EXISTENCE(@age)

MANUFACTURER(@manufacturer__id)

WEIGHT(@weight)

ENGINEER__GRADE(@engineer__grade)

Obviously this is wrong. From the analysis it is clear that we have made 'engineer__grade' into a *public* qualifier. It is used in two linkages with the same meaning. The problem was caused by the fact that we did not have the correct entity type in the information model, namely 'engineer', to associate 'engineer__grade' with. But 'engineer' in the above example is also an *object type*, since it has the qualifier 'engineer__grade'. This leads to the observation that *all object types (entity types with qualifiers) of interest must be explicitly defined in the model.* The above analysis leads to the first integrity rule for the E-O model:

150   Information modelling and the relational model

All object types (entity types with qualifiers) of interest must be explicitly and separately defined in the model and all qualifiers must be semantically private to one object type.

Note that if it were necessary for the value of a qualifier of one object type to change solely because the value of a qualifier in another object type had changed, then the qualifier would not be private for one or other of the object types.

The Second Integrity Rule

Consider that we have only one object type, 'product_part', in an information model, which might be defined as:

PRODUCT_PART(@product_type+@part_type+quantity+etc)

This object type identifies various product types, the various part types from which they are made and the quantity of each of these part types which must be fitted to a given product type. Since we have only one object type in the model, we might be tempted to think that it must be an independent object type. But the identifier for this object type is a concatenation of the attributes '@product_type' and '@part_type'. It might be that for the moment we have no interest in details of products or parts as such and, therefore, have not included a 'product' or 'part' object type in the model. Nevertheless, we can represent this object type entirely in terms of independent and dependent entity types and a linkage as shown in Figure 9.5.

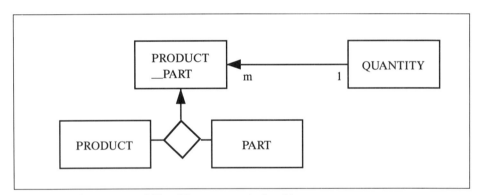

Figure 9.5 Concatenated identifier as mn-relationship

The qualifier 'quantity' is shown, as expected from our earlier discussion of qualifiers as linkages, as a 1:m linkage between 'quantity' and 'product_part'. The m:n relationship between the entity types 'product' and 'part', which were not explicitly shown in the model, gives rise to the identifier for 'product_part', since each occurrence of this m:n relationship is equivalent to an occurrence of 'product_part'. The concatenated identifier for our 'product_part' object type is equivalent to an m:n relationship and 'product_part' is, therefore, a dependent object type.

Now let us consider the case where an identifier is made up by the concatenation together of *three* attributes. Suppose, for example, that our users require that suppliers of parts for products be identified against the product types and the part types they use.

The information model would now have the same object type 'product_part' as before and an additional entity type which we will call 'supply', thus:

SUPPLY(@product_type+@part_type+@supplier_name)

In Figure 9.6 we show that this is a dependent entity type. It is founded on the m:n relationship between the 'ghost' entity type 'supplier' and the dependent object type 'product_part'. Note carefully that this is a *binary* dependent entity type, despite the fact that it has a triple concatenated identifier. The fact that 'product_part' itself has the concatenated key '@product_type+@part_type' is irrelevant to the degree of 'supply'. There are only two identifiers involved, and, by our earlier definition of the degree of a relationship, this means that the degree of 'supply' is two.

In the example, although the concatentated identifier was composed of three attributes, the degree of the corresponding dependent entity type was two. We could continue to demonstrate the build up of the number of concatenated attributes in an identifier in the above manner. For example if we needed to express some m:n relationship between 'supply' and any independent entity type, the number of attributes in the identifier for this dependent entity type would be four. The point is that we can build up a concatenated identifier with any number of attributes by defining a series of *binary* dependent entity types *and the result is always a binary dependent entity type*. Intuitively, the converse must also be true, that is, it must be possible to decompose a dependent entity type with more than two concatenated attributes in its identifier into two or more binary dependent entity types.

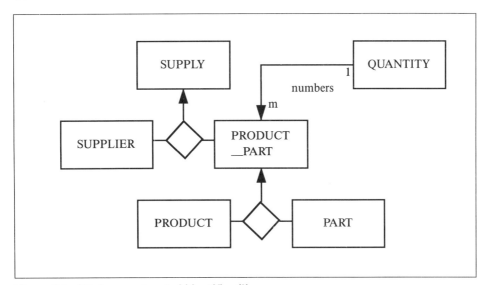

Figure 9.6 Triple concatenated identifier (I)

Now consider the case where *only* the 'supply' entity type:

SUPPLY(@product_type+@part_type+@supplier_name)

is defined in an information model. What information does this give us? Firstly, can we unambiguously decompose it into its constituent dependent entity types? The answer

152 *Information modelling and the relational model*

is 'No', simply because by itself it does not convey enough information for us to be able to do so. Figure 9.7 shows that, in the absence of any further information, the decomposition of 'supply' into its constituent dependent entity types can be interpreted as one of three possibilities. None of these three possible interpretations means the same thing.

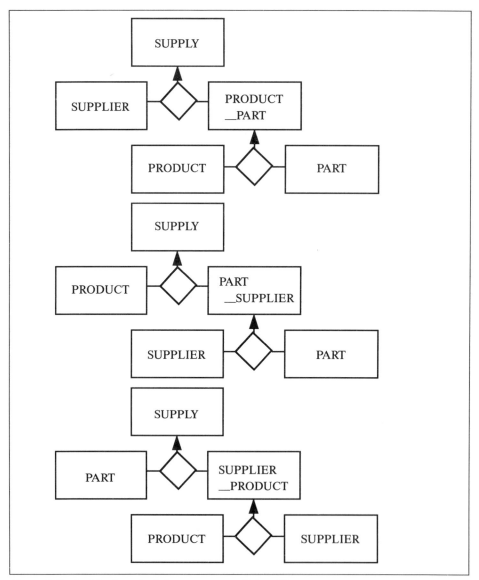

Figure 9.7 Ambiguity of triple concatenated identifier

At the top of the figure 'supply' is shown as meaning that there is a relationship between the independent entity type 'supplier' and the dependent entity type 'product_part'.

We would expect in this case that a real world relationship of this type actually existed and that it would therefore be possible to write down a list of product parts without any consideration of suppliers. The next possibility is that there is a relationship between the independent entity type 'product' and the dependent entity type 'part_supplier'. In this case we would expect to be able to write down a list of part suppliers without taking any consideration of products. The last possibility is that there is a relationship between the independent entity type 'part' and the dependent entity type 'supplier_product', and in this case we would expect to be able to write down a list of suppliers in relation to products without any consideration of parts.

Now consider what this means in business terms. If we interpret 'supply' as per the first of the above cases, it implies that the way our users conduct their business in this area is on a basis of allocating specific product part combinations for supply by specific suppliers. If we interpret 'supply' as per the second option, it implies that the users conduct their business on the basis of allocating parts for supply by suppliers regardless of which products these parts will be used in. If we take the last interpretation, it means that our users allocate suppliers who supply parts for specific products only.

The inference we must draw from the above is that a dependent entity type with a triple concatenated identifier, taken in isolation, is *an ambiguous and incomplete statement about the semantics of the information being modelled*. It is intuitive that as the number of attributes required to make up a concatenated identifier increases, then the statement it represents about the semantics of the data being modelled becomes increasingly ambiguous and incomplete. This means that, in order to represent information completely and unambiguously in an information model, all dependent entity types with more than two attributes concatenated together to form their identifier must be explicitly defined as binary, by showing the two participating entity types upon which they are founded.

Now suppose that if a certain product used a certain part and a supplier both supplied parts for that product and supplied that part, the supplier would always supply that part for the product there would be no need for the 'supply' entity type. The 'product_part', 'part_supplier' and 'supplier_product' entity types, if defined, would provide all the needed information.

The conclusion to be drawn from the above is that all dependent entity types containing only two attributes in their identifiers (that is, all dependent entity types founded on independent entity types), should be defined first, and only then further dependent entity types if these are required. This would ensure that the model was complete and unambiguous, but cannot, to be practical, be an unconditional rule.

In the practical world people − analysts, end users and the like, share a great deal of common knowledge. For example, the entity type we discussed earlier:

CUSTOMER_ADDRESS(@city + @street_name + @street_number + @customer_id)

which was pictured in the lower half of Figure 9.3 as a dangling relationship, has four attributes making up its identifier. The identifier is made up from the two identifiers '@customer_id' from the explicitly defined 'customer' object type and '@city + @street_name + @street_number' from the entity type 'address' which is not shown. Had 'address' been explicitly shown as the missing participant in the dangling 'address' dependent entity type, it would still have had a triple concatenated identifier.

154 *Information modelling and the relational model*

To model completely and unambiguously all the semantics of the information being analysed would have entailed including another dependent entity type founded on a dependent entity type with identifier '@street_name + @street_number' and the independent entity type with identifier 'city'. (We cannot assume that street names/numbers are unique to cities.) But it would have been pointless, of course, to include this information in the model since it is common knowledge – *and it has nothing to do with the way the organisation does its business*. The above considerations lead to the second and final integrity rule of the E-O model . . .

Binary dependent entity types founded on independent entity types must all be defined where this is required to show how the organisation conducts its business. Dependent entity types should not participate in the definition of further binary dependent entity types unless this is required to provide information which could not otherwise be inferred from the model.

(*Extended Note:* It may be objected that this rule would force the analyst to include entity types in an information model which later would not need to be included in a database schema. For example, if our users were interested only in the 'supply' dependent entity type, then the inclusion of one of the options for the underlying dependent entity type shown in Figure 9.7 could be said to be redundant. But it would only be redundant with respect to the database schema, *not* with respect to the information model. One must not lose sight of the purpose of the information model, which is first and foremost a vehicle for recording our understanding of the semantics of our users' information requirements. If integrity rule 2 is not obeyed, an information model might not completely record that understanding (or could indicate that the understanding has not been fully obtained) and might contain a degree of ambiguity. It does not necessarily follow that all entity types in the information model must also be included in the database schema derived from it.

A few common sense observations, still in the context of concatenated identifiers, about what *must* be included in a database schema may be useful. Consider that we have modelled 'supply' following rule 2. It might then appear as in Figure 9.8.

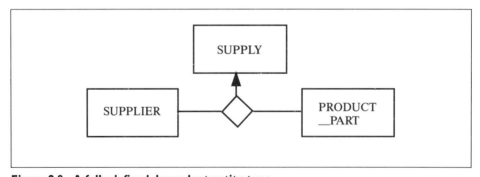

Figure 9.8 A fully defined dependent entity type

Now suppose that we decide, for whatever reason, to transfer only the 'supply' entity type into a relational database schema. This tells us which suppliers provide specific parts for specific products. However, it does *not* tell us about:

Normalisation and the E-O model 155

- All possible suppliers – only those who supply parts for products.
- All part-product combinations possible – only those for which suppliers exist.

If we require either or both of these items of information, we must include the appropriate entity types from the information model in the database schema. Suppose that we have included the 'product__part' entity type. This tells us which part types must be fitted to which product types. It does *not* tell us:

- All product types – only those which have parts fitted to them.
- All part types – only those fitted to products.

If we require this information, then we must include the participating 'product' and 'part' entity types in both the information model and the schema. Note that if only one of these entity types were of interest, then it would have to be represented as a 'dangling' dependent entity type in the information model ERD.)

E-O Model operators – promote and demote

The operators required for the E-O model are for the most part self evident from the above discussion. Clearly, we must be able to create and delete dependent and independent entity and object types, linkages and so forth. These operators are listed in Chapter 10 where a summary definition of the E-O model is given. However, two special operators are also given in that chapter, the *promote* and *demote* operators and a few preliminary words of explanation are given about them here. Earlier the possibility of promoting qualifiers to being entity types in their own right was discussed. It would be useful to have an operator specifically designed to do this and this is relatively straightforward. However, during the course of building an information model we may introduce entity types which will not be carried through into the database schema for the reasons discussed in the extended note to integrity rule 2 which was just given, or, indeed, we may introduce them simpy to clarify our thinking about some complex relationships and wish to remove them when that need has been satisfied. Now, if we *delete* an entity type form an information model we must also, inter alia, delete all the dependent entity types and linkages which were founded on it. But if we have introduced an entity type into the model simply to clarify our understanding of the underlying relationships as we did, for example, in Figure 9.4 or to satisfy rule 2 as we did for example in Figure 9.8, then we must delete only that object from the model and not the dependent entity types and linkages it takes part in. We need a separate demote operation to cater for this case.

9.3 Normalisation and the E-O Model

Introduction

The further normalisation rules which were described in Chapter 8 are useful, indeed essential, checks on the correctness of a relational database design, which reduce the probability that the resultant database system will be difficult and expensive to maintain and enhance because of the presence of updating, deletion and insertion problems. Most analysis and design methods now stipulate that information models should be in normal

156 *Information modelling and the relational model*

form. If the objective is to use the information model as the basis for derivation of a relational database schema, then the advantage of having it fully normalised is self evident. In this section it will be demonstrated that if the objects of the E-O model are used to construct an information model and its two simple integrity rules are obeyed, then the information model will be normalised in the sense that it will conform to the further normal forms of the relational model.

The two important differences between this approach to normalisation, and that of applying the normal forms are that: whilst the latter involves the *decomposition* of a bad design, the former involves the *construction* of a good design in the first place; the limitations of the latter as a method of removing design anomalies are not present in the former. In the following paragraphs each of the further normal forms as described in Chapter 8 is reviewed against the objects and integrity rules of the E-O model and conclusions are drawn.

First normal form

The rule for 1NF is simply that all attributes must be atomic, in other words that there can be no repeating groups of attributes and this rule also applies to the E-O model. It is not defined as an integrity rule for the E-O model any more than it is for the relational model. 1NF is simply a property of the relational model (to simplfy it) and the E-O model must also have the same fundamental property, since it is intended to be the basis for derivation of relational database schemata. The E-O model construction heuristic for the removal of repeating fields or repeating groups of fields ensures that correct primary keys will have been identified for the relational tables which will later be derived from the information model.

Second, Third and Boyce-Codd normal forms

Violations of second, third and Boyce-Codd normal forms correspond to violations of the first integrity rule of the E-O model:

All object types (entity types with qualifiers) of interest must be explicitly and separately defined in the model and all qualifiers must be semantically private to one object type.

If the second clause of this rule is followed then each qualifier can be functionally dependent only on the identifier of the entity type it qualifies, that is, in relational model terms, on its primary key. Functional dependency was defined in Chapter 8.

An attribute in a relational model table is said to be functionally dependent on another attribute in the table if it can take on only one value for a given value of the attribute upon which it is functionally dependent.

It has been demonstrated that all qualifier attributes, in E-O model terms, are m:1 linkages between the entity type qualified and the identifier for some other entity type. In other words, the qualifier is functionally dependent on the identifier for the qualified entity type.

For example, in the m:1 linkage 'order is placed by customer', 'order_number' is in an m:1 linkage with 'customer-id', and example occurrences of this linkage would be:

Normalisation and the E-O model   157

ORDER Table

@order__number	customer__id
123	Jones
124	Jones
125	Smith
126	Brown

The qualifier 'customer__id' can take on only one value for an occurrence of a value for 'customer__id' and hence is functionally dependent on 'customer__id'. If, on the other hand, we take an example of an *m:n relationship*, say:

ORDER__LINE__ITEM Table

@order__number	@line__item__name
123	hoe
123	spade
124	axe
125	hoe

then attribute '@line__item' is not functionally dependent on '@order number' since it can take on different values for a given value of 'order__number'. Likewise, 'order__number' is not functionally dependent on '@line__item'. To be functionally dependent on some other attribute, an attribute must be in a 1:m relationship with it.

3NF

Suppose that we try to introduce a qualifier for the 'order' table which is functionally dependent on the qualifier 'customer__id', for example 'customer__credit__status'. This is a violation of 3NF, since 'customer__credit__status' would only be transitively dependent on the prime key '@order__number'. But it is also in violation of rule 1 since, if 'customer__credit__status' is in a 1:m linkage with 'customer__id', it is a qualifier for that entity type and private to it. Rule 1 would have directed us to form an object type 'customer' to contain the qualifier 'customer__credit__status' and would have forbidden us from making it public by using it also to qualify 'order'.

2NF

Now suppose that we try to introduce the qualifier 'item__price' into the table 'order__line__item'. This is in violation of 2NF because it is functionally dependent on only the 'line__item__name' attribute of the concatenated primary key for the table. But it is also in violation of rule 1 since, if 'item__price' is in a 1:m linkage with 'line__item__name', it is a qualifier for that entity type and private to it. Rule 1 would have directed us to form an object type 'line__item' to contain the qualifier 'line__item__price' and would have forbidden us from making it public by also using it to qualify 'order__line__item'.

158 *Information modelling and the relational model*

BCNF

In Chapter 8 we learned that BCNF is simply a stronger definition of 3NF. The latter did not cover the rare case where a table has multiple candidate keys, these keys are concatenated keys and two or more of the candidate keys share a common attribute. The rule for BCNF was:

To be in BCNF, a table must only have candidate keys as determinants.

The (somewhat contrived) example given of a table which violated BCNF, yet was in 3NF, was:

PROJECT__PART(@project__name + @part__code + employee__name + quantity)

In this table the relationship between projects, the parts and quantities of those parts they use, and the employees who supply these parts was listed. Two assumptions were made. Firstly, each project is supplied with a specific part by only one employee, although an employee can supply that part to more than one project. Secondly, an employee makes only one part but the same part can be made by other employees.

Now the second of these assumptions means that there is an m:1 linkage between employees and parts, thus making 'employee' an object type, and this would have to have been explicitly and separately defined according to rule 1. Thus, in the data dictionary we would have had the entries:

PROJECT__PART(@project__name + @part__code + @@employee__name + quantity)

EMPLOYEE(@employee__name + part__code)

and these would both have appeared as tables in the schema derived from it.

The original table, taken in isolation, gave rise to certain update, insertion and deletion anomalies shown originally in Figure 8.4 which is reproduced below.

Table PROJECT__PART

project__name	part__code	quantity	employee__name
AA	abc	5	Smith
AA	bca	10	Jones
AB	abc	20	Smith
AB	bca	50	Brown

Figure 9.9   Table not in BCNF

If the bottom row is updated because Jones replaces Brown as the supplier of part bca to project AB, then the information that Brown makes part bca is lost from the database. If a new employee becomes a part supplier, this fact cannot be recorded in the database until he is contracted to a project. There is also a seeming element of redundancy present in the fact that Smith, for example, is shown twice as making part abc.

But now consider the effect of explicitly introducing the separate table 'employee' by following rule 1 in constructing the information model. There are no longer any insertion or deletion anomalies. If the information that Brown makes part bca is lost from the 'product_part' table because he has been replaced by Jones as a supplier of that part to project AB, it is not lost from the database, since it will still be recorded in the 'employee' table. Similarly, if a new employee becomes a part supplier, this can be recorded immediately in the 'employee' table, there is no need to wait until the employee is assigned to a project. Furthermore, the problem (described in Chapter 8) caused by the BCNF decomposition of the table 'product_part' into:

PROJECT_EMPLOYEE(@project_name + @employee_name + quantity)

EMPLOYEE_PART(@employee_name + part_code)

whereby it was not possible to update these tables independently, no longer exists, *because we have not decomposed the table*. We have not come up with the same 'solution' which was obtained by the BCNF decomposition shown earlier in applying rule 1, *because we did not need to*. The real problem was that too little of the semantics of the data were modelled in the 'product_part' table and this led directly to the insertion and deletion anomalies described above. With the explicit definition of the 'employee' table as a consequence of applying rule 1 in constructing the information model the real problem was addressed and there was no need for decomposition to the 'product_part' table. It might be argued that the 'product-part' table still contains an element of redundancy in that, for example, Smith is still shown twice as making part abc (in Figure 9.9). Firstly, there is no semantic redundancy in this. In E-O model terms, the qualifier 'employee_name' is a link identifier and the two occurrences of Smith in the figure represent two distinct occurrences of a linkage. In relational model terms, 'employee_name' is a foreign key. It is certainly true that if the value of the target key of a foreign key changes, then there will be severe update problems in the sense that all occurrences of the foreign key in the database will have to be found and changed. But this applies to *all* foreign keys, and will continue to apply to them all until current moves to extend the SQL language to safeguard referential integrity and then implement them in RDBM SQL dialects come to fruition. Meanwhile note that foreign keys inherit the essentially constant nature of their target primary keys.

By following integrity rule 1 of the E-O model, the analyst can ensure that the model conforms to 2NF, 3NF and BCNF.

Fourth and Fifth normal forms

Violations of fourth and fifth normal forms correspond in to violations of the second integrity rule of the E-O model:

Binary dependent entity types founded on independent entity types must all be defined where this is required to show how the organisation conducts is business. Dependent entity

160 *Information modelling and the relational model*

types should not participate in the definition of further binary dependent entity types unless this is required to provide information which could not otherwise be inferred from the model.

4NF

An example of a table violating 4NF was given in Chapter 8 as:

EMPLOYEE(@employee_name + @equipment + @language)

This table contained two *independent* multi-valued facts about employees: firstly that an employee could have many items of equipment allocated to him; secondly that an employee could know a number of languages. The table therefore contained an MVD and was in violation of 4NF.

This table corresponds in E-O model terms to a dependent entity type with more than two attributes in its concatenated identifier. Therefore rule 2 of the E-O model is applicable to it. In following rule 2 we would have constructed the following two binary dependent entity types:

EMPLOYEE_EQUIPMENT(@employee_name + @equipment)

EMPLOYEE_LANGUAGE(@employee_name + @language)

which is the same solution as that was obtained by the 4NF decomposition in Chapter 8. We could not have arrived at the incorrect 'employee' construct simply because it contains no information which could not be inferred from the above dependent entity types. It is not possible to violate 4NF using the objects of the E-O model, if integrity rule 2 is followed, because it does not allow us to invent binary relationships which do not exist.

5NF

In essence, 5NF was violated if it was possible to do a non-loss decomposition of a table into three or more tables without loss of meaning in order to remove certain insertion and deletion anomalies and this was not done. The example given of a table which, under certain specified conditions, violated 5NF was:

AGENT_COMPANY_PRODUCT(@agent + @company + @product_name)

The first condition given was that agents did not necessarily sell all the products made by the companies they did business with. In this case the table was in 5NF because non-loss decomposition of it was not possible. The second condition given was that agents sold all the products of the companies they did business with. In this case the table violated 5NF because non-loss decomposition of it into three normalised tables was possible.

It is not possible to violate 5NF using the E-O model when following integrity rule 2. We know in the above example that there are relationships between agents and companies, between agents and products and between companies and products all of which provide specific information about the way the (imaginary) company does its business. Rule 2 specifies that we define these explicitly as binary dependent entity types in our information model. This is shown by the unshaded dependent entity types in Figure 9.10. If, when an agent is an agent for a company, the company makes a product and the agent sells that product, then the agent sells that product for the company, nothing more need be modelled than these three entity types, we have all the information required. This corresponds to the correct decomposition for conformity with 5NF.

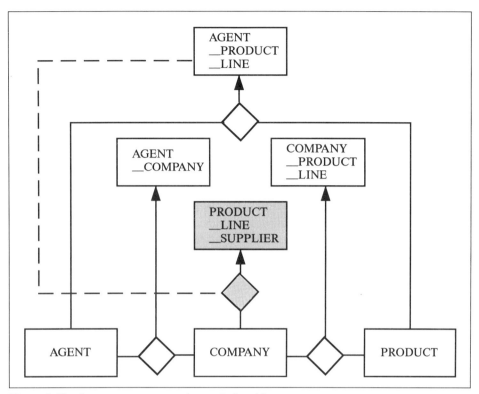

Figure 9.10 Agent company product relationships

If, on the other hand, an agent does not necessarily sell all the products stocked by the companies he is an agent for, rule 2 insists that we need to specify explicitly a further relationship, 'Company supplies product sold by agent'. This is shown as the shaded dependent entity type 'product_line_supplier' in Figure 9.10 and its data dictionary entry would be:

PRODUCT_LINE_SUPPLIER(@agent + @product_name + @company)

Now, seen in isolation from the relational model point of view as in Chapter 8, this is a table which has insertion and deletion anomalies, but is in 5NF and cannot be decomposed further to remove these anomalies. But there are no such insertion and deletion anomalies when it is seen in the context of the other dependent entity types shown in Figure 9.10.

In Chapter 8 it was observed with respect to 5NF decomposition that it had to be accepted that certain tables could not be decomposed in order to eliminate all possible design anomalies. This statement is true if one regards the design process as one of successive *decomposition* of tables as in the (further) normalisation approach, because

162 *Information modelling and the relational model*

we can specify tables with insufficient semantic content to allow for their decomposition as we saw in the example just given and in the earlier BCNF example. However, this does not apply where the process is one of *construction*. When we construct an information model following rules 1 and 2 of the E-O model, we simply do not run into the design anomalies 5NF decomposition was conceived of to remove, and the question as to whether or not they can be removed by decomposition is simply irrelevant.

9.4 Applicability of the E-O Model

Earlier, it was stated that it is not being advocated in this book that all information models be in 1NF, only those which are to serve as the basis for relational database designs. The E-O model, which is fully summarised in the next Chapter, has been specifically defined to assist in the production of information models from which correct relational database schemata can be derived. No claim is made that it is suitable as the basis for producing schemas for formatted database models like CODASYL since these both allow repeating fields to be specified and rely for the most part on the positioning of data in storage (using pointers) to establish relationships rather than the semantics of the data as such. These remarks also apply where the storage schema of the system being analysed and designed is to be implemented using traditional file management techniques, unless these techniques exclude the use of repeating fields and pointer based data structures.

Note that many information modelling methods whether promoted by CASE tool vendors or in the literature in general, now insist that the information models should be in 3NF, that is in 1NF, 2NF and 3NF. This makes the restriction on their applicability the same as that just described for the E-O model.

10
The Entity-Object (E-O) Semantic Data Model

10.1 The Objects of the E-O Model

Figure 10.1 summarises all the E-O semantic data model objects which were introduced during the course of Chapter 9. The definitions which follow, where they differ from the introductory definitions given in Section 9.2.1 of Chapter 9, have been modified to take into account the rationale of section 9.2.2. These objects are defined in the following paragraphs.

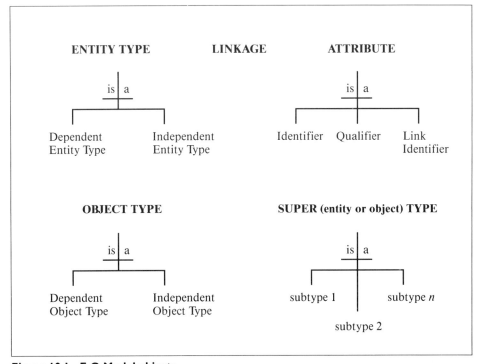

Figure 10.1 E-O Model objects

Entity type

A named class of things each of which has a distinct existence; the existences of things within the class as opposed to their qualities or relations.

164　*The entity-object (E-O) semantic data model*

An entity type must have a unique name and an identifier (see below), but does not have qualifiers (see below). Entity types are named by unique nouns or noun phrases. An entity type can be independent or dependent.

- *Independent Entity Type*

An idependent entity type is an entity type which depends on no other entity type for its existence

- *Dependent Entity Type*

A dependent entity type depends on at least one other entity type for its existence.

The identifier for a dependent entity type is obtained by concatenating together the identifiers of the entity type(s) upon which it is founded.

Object Type

An object type is an entity type with qualifiers defined for it.

An object type makes its name and identifier from the entity type for which it is defined. An object type can be independent or dependent.

- *Independent Object Type*

An independent object type is an independent entity type with qualifiers defined for it.

- *Dependent Object Type*

A dependent object type is a dependent entity type with qualifiers defined for it.

Linkage

A linkage corresponds to a relationship of proportion 1:m, m:1 or 1:1 that prevails between two entity types.

A linkage is identified by a link identifier (see below) and named by a verb or verb phrase which need not be unique.

Attribute

An attribute is a quality ascribed to a (person or) thing.

An attribute can be an identifier, a link identifier or a qualifier.

- *Identifier*

An identifier is an attribute or concatenation of attributes of an entity type whose values are used to identify uniquely occurrences of the entity type.

- *Link Identifier*

A link identifier is an attribute or concatenation of attributes of one entity type whose values are used to identify uniquely occurrences of a linkage with another entity type.

In the case of 'many to one' and 'one to many' linkages, the link identifier is formed by taking the identifier from the entity type on the 'one' side of a linkage and making it an attribute of the entity type on the 'many' side of the linkage. In the case of a 'one to one' linkage, the link identifier is formed by taking the identifier of an entity type on either side of the linkage and making it an attribute of the entity type on the other side, according to the choice of the analyst.

- ● *Qualifier*

A qualifier is any attribute which is not an identifier or a link identifier or part of either.

A qualifier is a shorthand way of indicating an m:1 linkage between the entity type qualified by it and some other entity type which is otherwise of no interest.

Supertype and Subtype

A supertype is a functional generalisation of subtypes into a supertype. A subtype is a functional differentiation of one entity type into its subtypes.

10.2 The Integrity Rules of the E-O Model

Integrity rule 1

All object types (entity types with qualifiers) of interest must be explicitly and separately defined in the model and all qualifiers must be semantically private to one object type.

Integrity Rule 2

Binary dependent entity types founded on independent entity types must all be defined where this is required to show how the organisation conducts its business. Dependent entity types should not participate in the definition of futher binary dependent entity types unless this is required to provide information which could not otherwise be inferred from the model.

10.3 The Operators of the E-O Model

(Note: The graphic representations of an E-O model objects given below are based on an adaptation from that used in the structured analysis method. Any other graphic notation which serves the same purpose can be used. The data dictionary syntax used is also adapted from the structured analysis method. Any other data dictionary syntax which serves the same purpose can be used.)

Define Independent Entity Type

An independent entity type is defined by drawing a uniquely named box on the ERD and creating a data dictionary entry against this name which contains the identifier for the entity type. The identifier may or may not be concatenated.

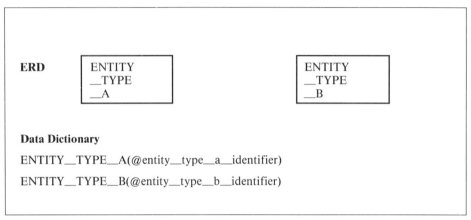

Figure 10.2 Independent entity type definition

Define Dependent Entity Type

A dependent entity type is defined by drawing a uniquely named box on the ERD and creating a data dictionary entry against this name in the data dictionary which contains the identifier for the dependent entity type. The identifier is constructed by concatenating the identifiers from the participating entity types in the dependent entity type. A diamond is used to connect together the boxes representing the participating entity types and the dependent entity type. An arrowed line points to the dependent entity type. The proportion of the dependent entity type need only be shown if the underlying relationship is 1:1.

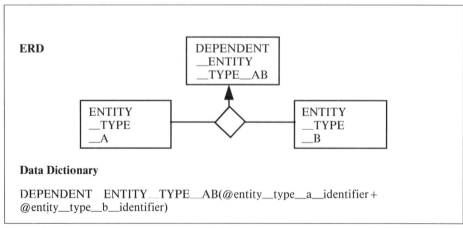

Figure 10.3 Dependent entity type definition

Define Linkage

A linkage is defined by drawing a named arrowed line on the ERD connecting the associated entity types. The proportion of the linkage must be shown. The arrowed line should point to the entity type on the 'many' side of the linkage. In the degenerate case of a 1:1 linkage, the arrow may point in either direction depending on the decision of the analyst. The identifier for the entity type pointed from must be included as a link identifier in the data dictionary entry for the entity type pointed to.

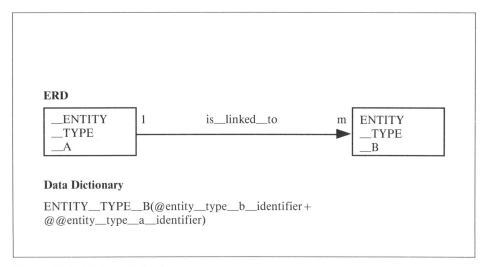

Figure 10.4 Linkage definition

Define Object Type

An (independent or dependent) object type is defined by adding all qualifiers of interest to the data dictionary entry for the entity type from which it is derived.

Define Super-entity-type, Sub-entity-type

Super and subtypes are defined by drawing uniquely named boxes on the ERD for them and creating data dictionary entries against these names which contain the identifier for the super type. The identifier may or may not be concatenated. The boxes are connected together by straight lines as a hierarchy, the supertype being identified by a bar on its connecting line.

Define Super-object-type, Sub-object-type

A super-object-type is defined by adding all those qualifiers of interest to the data dictionary entry for the super-entity-type from which it is derived which are common across all of its sub-types. A sub-object-type is defined by adding all those qualifiers of interest to the data dictionary entry for the sub-entity-type from which it is derived which are not defined for the super-object-type.

168   *The entity-object (E-O) semantic data model*

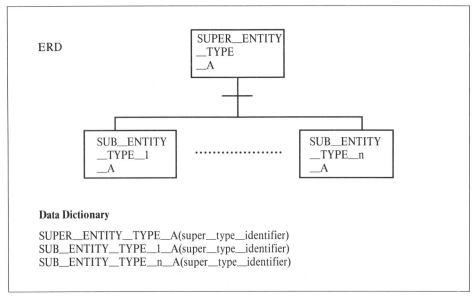

Figure 10.5 Super-entity-type, sub-entity-type definition

Delete Entity or Object Type

Deletion of an object or entity type from the ERD and data dictionary means that any dependent entity or object types in which it participates must also be deleted and that any dependent entity or object types which participate in these latter must also be deleted an so forth. All linkages associated with these deleted entity or object types must also be deleted.

Delete Linkage

If a linkage is deleted, then the link identifier in the entity or object type pointed to in the linkage must be removed and the corresponding arrowed line and label removed from the ERD.

Delete Supertype or Subtype

Deletion of super or subtypes from the ERD and data dictionary has the same impact as for any deletion of entity and object-types as already defined. Deletion of a subtype has no impact on its super-object-type. Deletion of a super-object-type means that each of its sub-object-types must inherit its qualifiers.

Demote Entity or Object Type

Demotion of an entity or object type means that the data dictionary and ERD entries corresponding to it must be deleted but has no other effect except that any link identifiers associated with it become simple qualifiers.

Promote Attribute

When a qualifier is promoted, it is preceded by a double at sign (@@) in the data dictionary, an entity type is named for it on the ERD and introduced into the data dictionary with the qualifier's name as its identifier, and a linkage is shown in the ERD between this entity type and the object type qualified. When part of an identifier (a 'ghost' entity type) is promoted, an entity type is named for it on the ERD and connected to the appropriate relationship diamond and it is introduced into the data dictionary.

Remove Repeating Qualifier or Qualifier Group

When a repeating attribute or attribute group is encountered, the proportion of the underlying relationship must be determined first in the direction of the host object type to the repeating attribute(s).

If the relationship is 1:m, then the repeating attribute or attribute group must be removed and, in the first instance, a new object type formed which contains the repeating attribute(s) as an identifier (concatenated), and the identifier of the host entity type as one or more linkage identifiers. This object type should then be examined to see whether any part of its concatenated identifier is redundant and, if so, to demote the redundant attributes to being qualifiers. The ERD and data dictionary should be modified to show the linkage.

If the relationship is m:n, then the repeating attribute or attribute group must be removed and, in the first instance, a new dependent entity type formed which contains the repeating attribute(s) and the identifier of the host object type as a concatenated identifier. This entity type should then be examined to see whether any part of its concatenated identifier is redundant and, if so, demotion of the redundant attributes to being qualifiers should take place. The ERD and data dictionary should be modified to show the new, dangling dependent entity type.

11
Constructing an Information Model

11.1 Introduction

The objects, operators and integrity rules of a sematic data model can be used in constructing a model of the information requirements of an enterprise. If the E-O semantic data model which was defined in Chapter 10 is used, then a complete, undistorted and unambiguous picture will be obtained of the semantics of the information being modelled. The resulting data dictionary entries will map on a one to one basis with the tables of a relational database schema and that schema will conform to the normalisation rules of the relational model.

(*Note:* Translating the data dictionary entries into relational database tables is a relatively simple step which will be achieved by coding CREATE TABLE statements in the international standard relational database access language SQL, or may even be achieved automatically using one of the CASE tools now available. SQL and the mechanics of moving from the information model to a relational database schema will be described in Part 4.)

In this chapter the first and most fundamental step on the way to designing a relational database schema following moderm techniques is described, that of constructing the information model from which it will be derived. This step consists itself of a number of sub-steps, namely:

- Identify Enterprise Information Goals

- Identify Information Sources

- Partition the Problem

- Produce Information Models

- Integrate the Models

- Balance with Functional Model

- Add Supplementary Information to the Models

These steps are not rigidly sequential in the sense that one must be entirely completed before the next can start. There is always a degree of overlap across them and iterations can take place through them, but they do broadly represent the way that the data analysis task must progress. In the rest of this chapter we will be examining each of these steps in some detail.

172 *Constructing an information model*

11.2 Identifying the Use of Information in Serving the Goals of the Enterprise

It is important, wherever possible, that the data analyst (or team of data analysts) work within some defined framework of enterprise objectives with respect to information when carrying out the information modelling task. The information model will be a model of the information the staff at all levels of that enterprise need to help them in making their contribution to meeting the enterprise's goals. It is impossible to be specific about what these goals might be, but it is possible to divide the information needs of an enterprise into two broad categories which need not be mutually exclusive, namely:

- Operational Data

- Management Decision Data

Into the first category fall the data which are most commonly associated with database contents, for example (in a commercial enterprise) data about customers, the orders they have placed the line items contained in these orders, inventories of line items and parts, employee details, accounts receivable and payable and so forth. These data are used to support the routine operations of the enterprise such as sales order entry, payroll, inventory management and the production of regular or ad hoc management reports. They constitute a day to day model of the real world operations of the enterprise.

Operational data as described above are, of course, used by management where it is appropriate for them to use them and it has been made convenient for them to access them. But management of various types and levels also need other data to assist them in meeting their goals. For example, a company chairman might regard his main goal in business life as ensuring the survival of his company. To support him in this he will require information, inter alia, about the possibility of hostile take over bids from other organisations. That is, he will need intelligence data (in the military sense) to be available to him about other, potentially hostile enterprises. A company director might see his role as principally that of establishing policies and would then require data which allowed him to monitor the implementation of these policies and their success or otherwise. A marketing manager will be interested in intelligence data about his company's competitor's, their products, prices, discounting policies, plans for new product launches, customer service charges and so on. Line and staff managers at all levels may need access to a database which models their part of the enterprise and allows them to make 'what if' calculations using, for example, a spreadsheet on a desk top personal computer to assist them in their decision taking.

Perhaps the most important enterprise goal with respect to information is that the need for sharing it where necessary across the various functions of the enterprise should be recognised at the very top and be promulgated as enterprise wide policy. In the absence of such a policy, any attempt to establish an integrated enterprise wide database may founder in the face of entrenched attitudes and intra-enterprise politics.

Having identified, if possible, the broad goals that information has to serve in the enterprise, the analyst is ready to move on to the next stage, that of establishing in detail the sources of information to be used in the information modelling activity.

11.3 Identifying the Information Sources

The information model is a semantic data model representing an enterprise's information requirements. *It is impossible to construct a semantic data model without understanding the semantics of the data being modelled.* This can be a surprisingly difficult idea to get across, even to professional computer staff within an organisation. What it means in practice is that it is not possible to produce an information model without a detailed understanding of the operations of the enterprise the model is being developed for and the specialised jargon which is frequently in use to describe these operations. Without this understanding it is quite impossible to identify the entity types, attributes and relationships of interest to the enterprise. The sources of information identified and used by the analyst *must* enable the acquisition of this understanding. The analyst may have acquired some such understanding already by a period of service in the enterprise, but this is unlikely to be the all embracing knowledge required to construct an enterprise wide information model. Thus the second task on the way to the construction of an information model is that of identifying the information sources from which the analyst, or team of analysts, can acquire the necessary detailed understanding of the data used and required by an enterprise.

These sources will usually include documents of various kinds, for example:

- Feasibility Studies

- Narrative descriptions of existing manual or computerised systems.

- Technical documentation of existing computer systems.

- Standard Operational Procedures

- Management Directives

- etc.

The one thing all such documents are likely to have in common is that they will raise as many questions of semantic detail in the analyst's mind as they answer. Most narrative descriptions of current systems, for example, are either too undetailed to serve as more than general guidelines to the required enhanced or replacement system's data content, or are out of date, or both. A situation which frequently occurs is that the data analyst is presented with program listings containing, for example, COBOL data declaration sections which describe existing file structures in minute detail. The problem with these is that they rarely contain anything other than a synactical specification for data items. The semantics of the data held in the files remain firmly in the heads of those who originally designed them.

Thus, in the great majority of cases, existing documentation will have to be supplemented by access to people within the enterprise who have the necessary understanding of the information needs of the business. Ideally, such staff would be allocated to the analyst team on a full time basis, but this is rarely possible in practice. More frequently the analysts will have to set up a series of dialogue sessions with key staff both in user departments and in the data processing (DP) department. A series of short sessions should be planned, since they are usually more acceptable to user and DP staff than one long session away from their main tasks. The analyst will then also have

174   *Constructing an information model*

time in the period intervening between sessions to consolidate what was learned and prepare a fresh set of questions and/or proposals for discussion and resolution at the next.

11.4   Partitioning the Problem

If data analysis is to be conducted for a small enterprise or a single department of a larger enterprise, then a single information model may be all that is required. If the database is to be introduced for a larger enterprise, or for a significant part of it, then attempting to produce a single information model in the first instance is unlikely to be practical because of the sheer size and complexity of the task. The problem must first be divided up into manageable areas and an information model produced for each area. Later these will be consolidated into a single model in order to eliminate redundancies. The choice of how to partition the problem will usually follow in a natural and intuitive way from the natural partitioning within the enterprise itself. Initial models, for example, might be produced for the accounts, sales, factory, warehouse, etc, departments of an enterprise.

11.5   Producing the Information Models

11.5.1   Background Notes

In the following, the reader is assumed to be familiar with Chapter 10, which summarises the objects integrity rules and operators of the E-O model.

It is the semantic data model objects, integrity rules and operations used which are of fundamental importance, not any specific graphical and/or structured textual notation which may be used to represent them. The notation used in this book is based on a slight elaboration of the information modelling notation prescribed by the structured analysis method and as such is supported by a number of CASE tools. Other tools supporting different notations are also available and these notations can generally be adapted to the needs of the E-O model.

Unless the CASE tool provided by an RDBMS supplier, or in close cooperation with one, it is unlikely that it will have been created with the specific purpose of assisting in the design of relational database schemata. This can mean that its facilities for running checks on ERDs and data dictionary entries will fail if the information model is optimised against the relational model requirements. For example, if an information model does not provide separate data dictionary entries for 1:m relationships it may fail a tool imposed rule that this should be so. The tool must then be 'fooled' in some manner to pass its tests, or the negative results of some of its checks ignored. A CASE tool's sole purpose is to help the analyst to do his or her job. Checks which would force the analsyt to do that job incorrectly must be bypassed or ignored.

11.5.2   Getting Started

Three useful rules of thumb to bear in mind when getting started on the construction of an information model are:

Producing the information model 175

Look for the Identifiers

The analyst should concentrate initially on homing in on those things of interest to his/her users, instances of which they require to be identified *uniquely.* The identifiers for many of these things will probably already exist in the current automated or manual systems — things like personnel numbers, coding schemes used in warehouses, coding schemes for invoices, statements, orders, deliveries and so forth. Finding these identifiers is normally equivalent to finding entity types.

Look for Relationships and Identify their Proportions

Identifying relationships and hence linkages and dependent entity types is for the most part intuitive. Some assistance may be obtained from examination of cross references between things in existing automated and manual systems, but ultimately the process can only be based on a thorough understanding of the semantics of the information requirements being examined. Identification of the proportion of relationships is, as we have seen, of critical importance, but is frequently less intuitive. It is easy to confuse 1:m with m:n relationships, even when the advice of a subject matter expert is available. A useful rule of thumb, when faced with this problem, is for the analyst to ask himself/herself whether the relationship can have qualifier attributes of its own, that is, attributes which cannot meaningfully belong to the entity types on either side of the relationship. It does not matter whether these attributes are actually of interest to the user. If the answer to this question is 'Yes', then the relationship *must* be m:n or 1:1.

Build Skeleton Models First

A *skeleton* information model is one that contains the minimum amount of information needed to identify entity types and linkages of importance to the user. This entails the construction of an ERD, whose data dictionary entries need only contain identifiers and linkage identifiers. The inclusion of qualifiers can be left to a later stage once the analyst has established the fundamental framework into which they can be fitted.

The purpose of a skeleton model is to enable the analyst to abstract a clear, accurate and unambiguous 'big picture' of the organisation's information requirements as a first step, prior to introducing the voluminous detail represented by qualifier attributes. A complete skeleton model could be produced for the whole problem area under analysis prior to filling in the qualifier detail. This would be the ideal first step if circumstances permitted, but can be impractical where the analyst, as is the normal case, is also uncovering qualifier detail as he examines the problem and needs 'somewhere to put it'. It is still, nevertheless, very beneficial to progress by analysing small sections of the problem, producing and checking carefully skeleton models for these sections and only then filling in the qualifier detail before moving on to the next 'mini' skeleton model. The analyst is then focussing on the most critical task first, identifying dependent and independent entity types and linkages, and avoiding distraction from this task by avoiding unnecessary examination of detail whilst it is being carried out.

The analysis task will be accomplished to a greater or lesser extent in joint sessions with user or DP department members who are expert in the subject matter being modelled. If a suitable information modelling tool can be made available during such

176 *Constructing an information model*

sessions, jointly agreed decisions can be easily recorded on the spot, saving valuable time during the sessions and providing both parties with an agreed output from the session for later review. It is essential for the analyst to give a short and simple explanation of the semantic data model objects and the graphic and textual notations being used to represent them to the subject matter experts, before getting too deeply into these sessions. Time spent on this early on will be amply repaid by the improvement in communication which results.

An imaginary example is given to show how one would get started on the construction of an information model using the above rules of thumb.

(*Note:* Unfortunately a realistic example of a typical information model of moderate size would well exceed the size of this book.)

Suppose that an analyst has been given the task of modelling the information requirements of managers and staff whose responsibility it is to look after the transport fleet of a very large wholesale organisation. We will assume that this organisation has a head office and multiple branches. At each branch there is a sales office and a warehouse holding stocks of goods. The organisation's goals with respect to information are: that its prime purpose is to enable managers and staff to keep capital costs to a minimum and to maximise cash flow; that it be made freely available at the head office and at branches; that branches will as far as is practicable use a common database schema so that applications designed for one branch can be used by other branches without change. A centralised database, available to all branches via a communications network, is envisaged as serving the needs of both head office and branches. The analyst, after reading available documents and conducting initial short interviews with key staff, has written down the following statement about company policy with respect to transport management.

'The company operates both a hiring and a buying policy for the fleet of vans which it uses to deliver goods from the branch warehouses to its customers. The normal policy is for each branch to buy and maintain its own vans under capital sanction from head office, but this is supplemented by the right of branch managers to rent vans to cope with peak periods, like Christmas, when deliveries are normally at an exceptionally high rate, or simply to cope with the aftermath of an exceptionally successful period of sales activity. The company normally buys its vans from the range of a single manufacturer, but can supplement these for tactical reasons with other manufacturer's models. Different models are purchased from these manufacturers according to need. Overall responsibility for management of the transport fleet lies with a head office manager and all capital purchasing decisions with respect to it are made by him. Branch managers are responsible for the care and maintenance of vans allocated to them and for rental decisions.

A decision is made to partition the problem and produce two information models initially, one for the head office and another for the branches and then integrate these into a single model from which the centralised relational database schema will be derived. No specific requirements have been written down for the information needed by the transport function, although manual systems exist at the head office and branches which have grown over the years in an ad hoc and uncoordinated manner, and these are available for the analyst's inspection. Having gleaned as much as he was able to from this material, the analyst has set up a series of interviews with head office and branch staff to ascertain their respective requirements and produce two information models in line with the initial partitioning of the problem.

Producing the information model

The first session the analyst has organised is with the head office transport manager who has overall responsibility for running the company's fleet of delivery vans. During the course of this session the analyst uncovers the following information needs of his manager:

- Particulars of specific makes and models of vans used by the company.
- Numbers of company owned vans of a given make and model at each branch.
- The numbers of rental vans of a given make or model at each branch.
- Serviceability status of all vans at branches, whether on or off the road.
- Names and telephone numbers of staff appointed by branch managers to oversee the day to day management of their local van fleet.
- Average cost of ownership per annum of each van type for company owned vans.

The analyst might initially have thought that 'van' would be an entity type of interest to this manager, but this is not the case. Since it is a large company, the head office transport manager is not interested in information about individual vans at all. He requires information about the individual numbers of vans of a given make and model at given branches of the company. The principle entity type of interest to this manager is not vans, but *van types* and this information is only meaningful to him in the context of a *relationship* between such van types and *company branches*.

Before taking this information any further, the analyst must determine the proportion of this relationship. If only one type of van is used at any branch, then the proportion (in the direction 'van_type' to 'branch') is 1:m. If a branch can use more than one van type then the proportion of the relationship between van types and branches is m:n. Assuming that the latter is the case, then the analyst at this point would have an ERD as in Figure 11.1

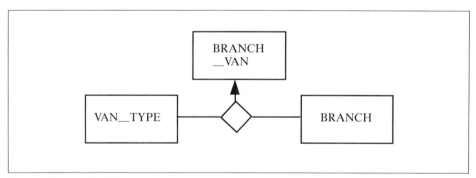

Figure 11.1 Initial ERD

The corresponding data dictionary entries might be:

VAN_TYPE(@manufacturer + @model)

BRANCH(@branch_name)

BRANCH_VAN(@manufacturer + @model + @branch_name)

178 *Constructing an information model*

Note the application of Rule 1. The analyst has established that the 'van type', 'branch' and 'branch__van' entity types will all have qualifiers of their own, will become object types and must therefore have separate definition in the model. The rule (or just his own common sense, since the rule is only formalised common sense) has not allowed him to make the mistake of thinking that 'branch__van' alone could represent all the information required and, therefore, of leaving the other two entity types out of the model. Had there been no requirement to store information about branches and van types as such, then they could have been left out of the model without breaking the rule. But a cautious analyst would be unlikely to do this at this stage. Our analyst, for example, has not yet interviewed a branch manager with responsibility for transport.

The skeleton model so far produced can now be fleshed out with qualifier detail, giving the data dictionary entries:

VAN__TYPE(@manufacturer + @model + average__miles__per__gallon + service__interval + cost__price + company__discount__price + average__depreciation__per__annum + etc)

BRANCH(@branch__name + address + telephone__number + manager__name + warehouse__manager__name + warehouse__manager__extension__number + etc)

BRANCH__VAN(@manufacturer + @model + @branch__name + total__number__own__van + total__number__rented__van + total__on__road + total__off__road + etc)

The analyst has not yet addressed the requirement that the average cost of ownership per annum of each van type for company owned vans to be provided. This involves a calculation, therefore it must be a subject of functional rather than data analysis and we will assume that that problem is passed to another analyst for this functional analysis. Later, the results of this functional analysis will have to be balanced with the information model. This topic will be covered in section 11.6.

We assumed in the above data dictionary entries that, at all branches, the warehouse manager has been made responsible for the day to day running of the local fleet. We will also assume (very unrealistically), to keep this example short, that the branch warehouse managers have mutually agreed their information requirements and appointed one of their number as spokesman on the topic.

At his interview with this manager, the analyst uncovers the following needs for transport related information on the part of the branch warehouse managers.

- Details, such as the local service garage, for specific types of van.
- Details, such as serviceability status, of all vans under their control.
- Details of the present and planned delivery journeys of all vans.
- Details of average runinng costs for each company owned van type per annum.
- Financial details of individual rentals.

The analyst has established that at branch level, unlike at head office, vans are an entity type for inclusion in the model since they have to be identified individually, although there is still an interest in van types. Van rentals are also an entity type of interest since they also require individual identification. We will also assume that the analyst has established that: each rental can be for several vans at a time to take advantage of quantity discounts; several deliveries can be made by one van during one journey; several vans can be involved in one delivery; data must be kept about both journeys and deliveries, each of which needs to be uniquely identifiable; whilst rental and company owned vans have certain details, including their identifier, in common, there are also details which are specific to company owned vans which are not shared by rented vans and vice versa. Figure 11.2 shows how an ERD for the branch might look at this stage.

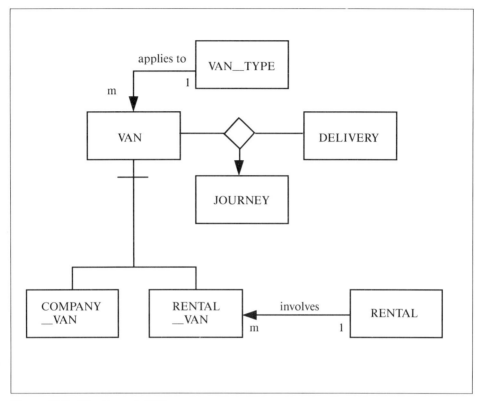

Figure 11.2 The Branch ERD

Four independent entity types have been defined, 'van_type', 'van', 'rental' and 'delivery'. Since deliveries and vans are in a *mn*-relationship with each other and this relationship constitutes a journey about which details must be kept, the dependent entity type 'journey' is defined as shown, on 'van' and 'delivery'. 'Van' has been defined as having two sub-types, 'company_van' and 'rental_van', because whilst these sub-types share the same indentifier and some of their qualifiers, there are certain qualifiers which are particular to one or the other. A 1:m linkage is shown between 'rental' and 'rental_van', indicating that many vans can be involved in one rental. Note that this in itself will result in 'rental_van' having an attribute, the linkage identifier taken from 'rental', which is not an attribute of either the super-type 'van' or the other sub-type 'company_van'. Finally, a 1:m linkage is shown between 'van-type' and 'van'. At this point the data dictionary entries would look like the following:

180 *Constructing an information model*

VAN__TYPE(@manufacturer + @model)

VAN(@licence__plate__number + @@manufacturer + @@model)

COMPANY__VAN(@licence__plate__number)

RENTAL__VAN(@licence__plate__number + @@rental__number)

RENTAL(@rental__number)

DELIVERY(@delivery__number)

JOURNEY(@delivery__number + @licence__plate__number)

On completion of fleshing out the branch skeleton model with qualifiers, the data dictionary entries might look as follows.

VAN__TYPE(@manufacturer + @model + local__service__garage + etc)

VAN(@licence__plate__number + @@manufacturer + @@model + mileage + average__miles__per__gallon + serviceability__status + etc)

COMPANY__VAN(@licence__plate__number + service-cost__to__date + fuel__cost__to__date + etc)

RENTAL__VAN(@licence__plate__number + @@rental__number)

RENTAL(@rental__number + number__of__vans + date__of__rental + duration__of__rental + cost__of__rental + etc)

DELIVERY(@delivery__number + weight + volume + value + etc)

JOURNEY(@delivery__number + @licence__plate__number + date + total__mileage + etc)

Finally, the branch and head office models need to be integrated together. Figure 11.3 shows how the ERD for this integrated model might look.

Note that in this ERD there is only one occurrence of 'van__type'. Even though the branch and head offices needed to know different facts about a van type, there was no need to include two 'van__type' object types (such as 'branch__van__type' and 'head__office__van__type') in the integrated model. It is sufficient to make sure that all the qualifiers required are present in one, as in:

VAN__TYPE(@manufacturer + @model + average__miles__per__gallon + service__interval + cost__price + company__discount__price + average__depreciation__per__annum + local__service__garage + etc)

Note also that the 'branch__van' object type defined in the original head office model has been removed. This is because all the information defined by that object type can be acquired from the information model as it now stands. The total number of vans at a branch and the subtotals reflecting rental and owned vans, together with the overall serviceability status can all be obtained from the information modelled. In the eventual database, the information called for by the head office manager which was originally modelled as 'branch__van' will be provided by regular or ad hoc computed *reports* from the database based on data which will be subject to continuous change. Unless there is

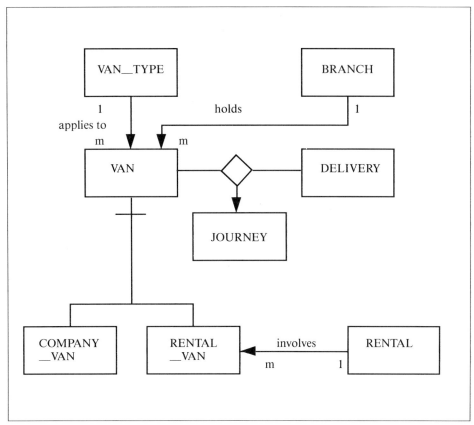

Figure 11.3 The Integrated Branch and Head Office ERD

a good reason for doing so, these reports will not be stored in the database. The actual computation required is the subject of functional rather than data analysis, albeit in this example the analysis would be very trivial. However, if we assume that it is done using structured analysis as described in Chapter 4, there would be no problem about balancing the resultant DFD and the information model. The 'functional' analyst would have the information model available at the outset and would name his stores and data flows to line up with the information model object types names and the names of their qualifier attributes.

11.6 Balancing the Information Model with the Functional Model

In our imaginary transport example, the analyst uncovered that there was a requirement to compute the average cost of ownership per annum of company vans per van type. If we suppose that the problem was tackled by another analyst, he might have come up with a DFD along the lines of Figure 11.4.

182 *Constructing an information model*

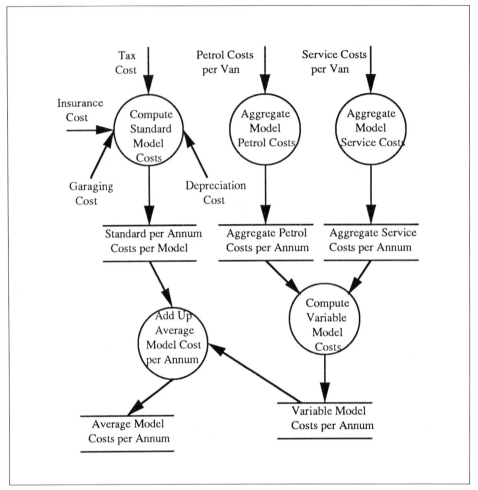

Figure 11.4 DFD

The average standard overhead cost to the company per annum per van type is computed from average tax, insurance, garaging and depreciation costs. The average variable costs per van type are computed from actual petrol and servicing costs and these are used with the standard overheads to arrive at the average ownership cost to the company for its vans per annum. In order to balance the data stores and data flows in the DFD and the information model, the analyst must ask the following questions:

- Do we have any new qualifiers for existing object types?
- Do we have any new object types?
- Are these to be stored or only reported?

Taking the first question, we can see from the data flows input to the top left hand bubble that we have three new qualifiers for the object type 'van_type', namely, (annual)

Balancing the information model with the functional model 183

'insurance__cost', garaging__cost' and 'tax__cost'. This object type already has the qualifier 'average__depreciation__per__annum'. We can also see, from the data flows into the two topmost right hand bubbles, that we have two new qualifiers for the object type 'van', namely, 'petrol__cost', meaning accumulated actual petrol cost in a year and 'service__cost', meaning accumulated actual service costs for a year. These would be added to the data dictionary entries for these object types giving:

VAN__TYPE(@manufacturer + @model + average__miles__per__gallon + service__interval + cost__price + company__discount__price + average__depreciation__per__annum + insurance__cost + garaging__cost + tax__cost + etc)

VAN(@licence__plate__number + @@manufacturer + @@model + mileage + average__miles__per__gallon + serviceability__status + petrol__cost + service__cost + etc)

Now consider the data store 'standard per annum costs per model'. This is the result of adding together average annual depreciation, insurance, tax and garaging costs for a given make and model of van and could be included as a qualifier for van type if so desired. However, if we only need to look at this figure very infrequently, it can always be produced as a *report* from the database. That is, the simple calculation required could be performed as often as required and reported to screen or printer. Alternatively, it could be done once and the result stored permanently in the database. Design trade off decisions of this nature have to be made frequently when balancing the functional and information models. The trade off, of course, is between use of storage space in the computer and the added complexity of the eventual database schema and the use of computing power necessary to do the same calculation more than once. If we assume that no user has any interest in seeing this figure at all, the store would then become part of the private working space of the program used to arrive at the ultimate value required. No object type would exist for this store in the information model. Assuming (on the other hand) that the head office transport manager required access to this figure very frequently and that he also wanted to keep history of what it had been in previous years, then an object type would have to be created to hold it, thus:

VAN__COST__PA(@manufacturer + @model + @company__year + average__van__cost__pa)

and a box named for it would be included in the ERD.

If we assume that the other stores holding intermediate calculation results are of no interest and are not, therefore, included in the model, the information model has now been balanced against the new information obtained from the results of functional analysis as presented in the DFD. The DFD must now be balanced in line with this updated information model. The manner of doing this is shown in Figure 11.5.

The information model object types 'van__type', 'van' and 'van__cost__pa' have now been introduced into the DFD. The data flows into the top three bubbles are as before, but are now shown as flowing from the appropriate information model object types, and the final output is shown as being written to the 'van__cost__pa' object type. The remaining stores shown on the DFD will not form part of the eventual relational database schema. They are simply repositories for intermediate calculation results, and in the

184 *Constructing an information model*

eventual design, the functional analyst will decide what storage structures will exist to hold these intermediate results, whether they will exist in main memory or backing storage and so forth.

In Chapter 1 the notions of public and private data were introduced in the context of database transactions. In balancing the DFD and the information model, the analyst must also apply his or her judgement as to which of these categories the various data stores and data flows in the DFD fall into.

11.7 Adding Supplementary Information to the Model

The ERD and the data dictionary of an information model provide a graphical and structured textual description of the data of interest to an enterprise. These will require supplementing with further detail in order to lay down a realistic basis for later implementation of a database. The manner in which this detail is recorded will vary depending on whether an information modelling tool is in use or not and, if so, the particular tool. At the very least, an information modelling tool is likely to allow comments and/or notes to be added to data dictionary entries and this feature can be used to record extra information. In the following paragraphs the supplementary information required is described.

Independent Object Type Specificiation

An independent object type specification supplements the information given about it in the ERD and data dictionary by:

- DESCRIPTION: A brief description of what the object type is in the context of the enterprise.

- PURPOSE: A brief description of the purpose the object type serves within the enterprise.

- CONSTRAINTS: Constraints/business rules appertaining to occurrences of the object type within the context of the enterprise.

- MAX OCCURRENCES: Estimates of the maximum number of occurrences of the object type liable to occur at points in time.

- TUPLE OCCUPANCY: Total, in bytes, of the data storage required by its attributes.

For example, the specification for the object type 'military__radar' might be:

MILITARY__RADAR:

Description:

Apparatus using higher power radio pulses, reflected or regenerated, for locating objects or determining one's own position.

Adding supplementary information to the models 185

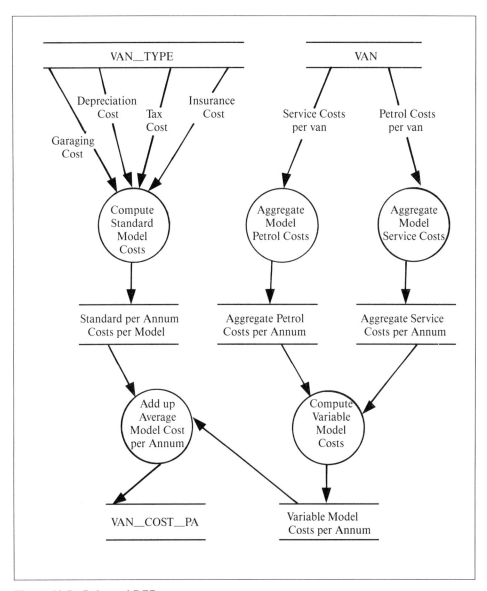

Figure 11.5 Balanced DFD

Purpose:

Used for defensive and offensive purposes.

Constraints:

Only ground based RADARs are of interest to the organisation. All performance data about RADARs is classified secret.

186 *Constructing an information model*

Max Occurrences:

Current number is around 3000 and expected to reduce about 1500 over the next five years.

Tuple Occupancy:

Total bytes are 256.

Dependent Object Type Specification

A dependent object type specification contains the same information as for independent object types and in addition:

- RELATIONSHIP: A brief description of the underlying relationship which includes a justification for the selection of its proportion and insistency.

For example the full specification for the dependent object type 'line__item__quantity' might be as follows:

LINE__ITEM__QUANTITY

Description:

The quantity of a line item which has been included in an order.

Purpose:

Used to form picking list by warehouse staff and for computing the order value by accounts.

Constraints:

Orders for bespoke items are not to be included in this.

Max Occurrences:

Based on archiving orders once they have been delivered and paid for and on current sales forecasts, it is estimated that about 250,000 occurrences are likely in the first six months of operation, and this may increase to a million over the next two years.

Tuple Occupancy:

512 bytes.

Relationship:

The relationship between orders and line items is many to many because orders containing mixed line items are permissible and any line item can be included in any order. It is possible for a line item not to be in any order, but it is not possible for an order not to include a line item.

Linkage Specification

This simply consists of a brief description of the underlying relationship which includes a justification for the selection of its proportion and insistency. For example the 1:m relationship 'places' as between customers and orders might be described as follows:

Places:

Relationship:

The relationship between customer and order is one to many since it is possible for a customer to have more than one current order on the books, but it is not possible for a specific order to be attributed to more than one customer. A customer can exist who has no current orders on the books, but an order cannot exist which cannot be attributed to a customer.

Attribute Specification

Each attribute in the data dictionary will be qualified with the following information. (It will usually be possible to include this information as comments against the data dictionary entry for the attribute.)

- *An Attribute Definition:* This spells out the full name of the attribute and, where necessary, gives a brief explanation of its meaning. For example:

naval__ship__id

Definition:

Naval ship identification. The hull number painted on a naval ship which is used to identify visually each ship in the navy in times of peace.

- *A Data Type Definition:* Description of the attribute's syntax.

The data type (type and picture in COBOL) of the attribute must be specified. Information modelling CASE tools vary widely in how they allow this to be done, that is in the data types they support and the means of describing them. However, the analyst must bear in mind that the data type definition for an attribute must eventually conform to one of the data types supported by the RDBMS in use. If the CASE tool does not match the RDBMS in this respect, then the analyst will have to supplement or replace its data type descriptions with those appropriate to the RDBMS. Typical data types supported by RDBMSs will be described in Part 4. For example:

naval__ship__id:

Data Type: integer

- *Data Integrity Specifications:* Providing any further information available which will be useful in the later development of integrity checks on data being input to the database. These typically would include ranges within which an attribute's value must fall or lists of legal values which it could take on. For example:

naval__ship__id

range: 0-9999

car__body__style:

emuneration: saloon, coupe, hatchback, limousine, cabriolet

- *Mandatory/Optional Specification.* Specifying whether or not a value for the attribute is mandatory for each occurrence of an object type. This amounts in relational database terms to specifying whether the attribute is 'nullable' or 'not nullable'. For example:

188 *Constructing an information model*

naval__ship__id: not null

Data Ownership Specification

It is important to record in some formal manner during the course of data analysis exactly who (meaning which department/person/function in the organisation) 'owns' specific items of information. This will be reflected in the access permission to the database system derived later from the information model. That is, identifying data ownership is identifying those who will have the authority to insert new occurrences or change existing occurrences of data in the database when it is implemented and to grant access permission. Although the mechanics of this will be handled by the DBA function and application program developers, the decision authorities will lie within the user community and should be established at the earliest stage possible, that is during the data analysis (information modelling) phase of the system development life cycle.

Part 4
Relational Database Management Systems

In this part of the book, the reader is introduced in Chapter 12 to the international standard language for performing data definition and data manipulation operations with respect to relational databases, the Structured Query Language (SQL).

In the following chapter, an introduction to Relational Database Management Systems (RDBMSs) is given with the objective of giving the reader, who has not been exposed to them, an insight into the facilities they offer to various types of user; with emphasis on the facilities they provide to staff responsible for system development and maintenance.

Finally, in Chapter 14, the various phases in the life cycle of systems developed in the environment provided by RDBMSs is described, together with the activities required during each phase and the outputs from these phases.

12

Introduction to the SQL Language

12.1   Introduction

SQL, frequently pronounced 'see-kwell', but just as often, 'ess-kew-ell' (the pronunciation which has been assumed in this book) originally achieved prominence as a prototype language in support of the relational model with IBM's System R, which was that company's prototype RDBMS. IBM was not to bring out a commercially available RDBMS for some time after the system R trials in the mid seventies. DB2, its flagship RDBMS product did not become generally available until 1984/85. In the interim, a number of independent suppliers moved in, using SQL based products, to satisty a market need which IBM was responsible for stimulating in the first place. (Codd was working for IBM when he produced his seminal papers on the relational model). Principal amongst these products was ORACLE™ which was well established in the market place by the early eighties. The INGRES™ product was introduced about the same time as ORACLE, but did not initially offer SQL as its DDL/DML. It started to support SQL in 1984/5. Other major hardware manufacturers joined the SQL club rapidly, for example DEC with its RdB product (1983/4) and Data General with its DG/SQL product (1984). Another prominent independent product, SYBASE™, entered the lists in 1986. In fact, the number of products now available which support SQL is too numerous to list here. A number of DBMSs which do not support the relational model have, nevertheless, sprouted SQL 'front ends' to cash in on the language's popularity.

Thus SQL very rapidly established itself as the de facto standard DDL/DML for relational database management systems. To a certain extent this reflected IBM's dominant place in the industry, but his was by no means the only reason for the language's success. Although some of its features have been subject to valid criticism by language and relational model purists, it is a popular language with its run of the mill users, whether they be programmers or (properly trained) end users. This is because of the ease with which it can be learned and the relative speed with which complex database access procedures can be implemented using it.

In 1982, the American National Standards Institute (ANSI) applied itself to the definition of a standard relational database language and it rapidly settled on SQL as that standard. Their proposal for a standard definition of the language was finally given official publication in 1986. In the interim, many dialects of the language had appeared, just as has been the case for most other computer languages prior to their standardisation, and it would be unrealistic to expect complete conformity to the standard across all products supporting SQL for a considerable time to come.

192 *Introduction to the SQL language*

A full description of SQL requires a book to itself and a number of such books are available including[31]. All that is attempted in this chapter is to introduce the reader to the main commands and features of the language. The syntax definitions given have been kept informal. The reader will have to supplement this cursory treatment with reading of the supplier's manual in order to use SQL with any particular RDBMS product.

SQL, is available both in interactive form, for use directly at a terminal, and in embedded form, for use as embedded code in conventional procedural languages such as COBOL, Fortran and Ada. The language incorporates both data definition and data manipulation operations and also provides support for data consistency, privacy and integrity.

The interactive form of the language is dealt with first and covers the following:

- Creating and Deleting Databases
- Creating, Indexing and Deleting Tables and Views
- The SELECT Statement
- The INSERT Statement
- The DELETE Statement
- The UPDATE Statement
- Access Control
- Transaction Control

The special language features appropriate to the embedded form of SQL are dealt with next and cover:

- Connecting to a Database
- Declaring Host Program Variables
- Use of Cursors with SELECT
- Embedded UPDATE and DELETE
- Error and Exception Handling
- Dynamic Embedded SQL

The SQL statements are exemplified in their most basic form. Most dialects of SQL elaborate on these basic features of SQL commands and also include additional commands. Some examples of this are given when two typical dialects, those for the INGRES and ORACLE RDBMS products, are discussed in Chapter 13.

12.2 Example Database

The simple database used in the examples of SQL commands given in this chapter is illustrated in the ERD of Figure 12.1 and the tables (as assumed derived from the data dictionary entries corresponding to the ERD) in Figure 12.2.

Primary key attributes are shown in bold face type. The examples given in the rest of this chapter are based on these tables. The tables should be fairly self explanatory. The 'customer' table assumes that customer names are unique and can be used as primary key values. The 'customer__city' table is necessary because otherwise 'customer' would contain a repeating attribute. The 'order' table lists orders, their total value, the dates they were placed and the applicable customers. 'Line_item' lists items sold, their unit price and the quantity held in stock of each item. 'Order_item' lists the individual line items and quantities thereof against each order. 'Employee' lists employees, giving their first names and the wage each receives per hour. 'Item_maker' lists employees against the line times they have the skills to make and the average time in minutes that each employee takes to make a given line item.

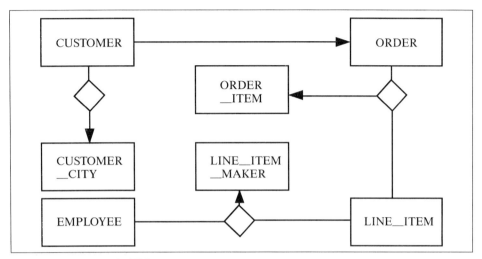

Figure 12.1   Example ERD

12.3 Creating and Deleting Databases

The SQL standard has a CREATE SCHEMA command for creating databases, but this is not as yet widely implemented. Obviously, all RDBMSs must provide a facility for creating databases. In most cases this is done by the provision of a utility program which is accessed via an operating system command. For example, in INGRES the utility is called by:

Createdb

The creator of the database using the utility program becomes the DBA for that database. The database is given a name, and access privileges to it can be defined. Note that these are to the database as a whole. Access to specific tables within a database must be defined separately using the GRANT command which will be described later in this chapter. The utility allows the database creator control over its placement in physical backing memory.

RDBMSs will also provide facilities for the deletion of databases. Using INGRES as an example once again, the relevant utility program would be called by:

Destroydb

194   *Introduction to the SQL language*

CUSTOMER

name	credit__balance	credit__limit
Jones	+10000	50000
Brown	+20000	30000
Smith	−2000	10000

CUSTOMER__CITY

customer__name	city
Jones	Leeds
Jones	Bath
Brown	Bath
Brown	Bristol
Smith	Glasgow

ORDER

order__number	order__value	order__date	customer__name
123	2000	1-3-91	Jones
124	1000	6-4-91	Jones
125	500	10-5-91	Smith

LINE__ITEM

item__name	price	stock
axe	10	1000
spade	20	1500
fork	25	2000
hoe	15	500

ORDER__ITEM

item__name	order__number	quantity
axe	123	100
spade	123	50
fork	124	34
hoe	124	10
spade	125	25

EMPLOYEE

employee__id	name	wage
AB1	Fred	3
AB2	Jim	3.5
AB3	Jim	3
AB4	John	3.4

ITEM__MAKER

employee__id	item__name	time
AB1	axe	40
AB1	spade	45
AB2	fork	35
AB3	hoe	40
AB3	axe	25

Figure 12.2 Example database

Creating, indexing and deleting tables and views 195

12.4 Creating, Indexing and Deleting Tables and Views

The data definition commands of SQL enable the basic objects of the relational model, tables, indexes and views, to be described to the RDBMS. The commands used are CREATE TABLE and CREATE INDEX for base tables, CREATE VIEW for views, and the corresponding DROP TABLE, DROP INDEX and DROP VIEW commands. The CREATE and DROP VIEW commands will be better understood when the SELECT command has been described and their description is postponed until after this has been done.

The CREATE TABLE Statement

The informal syntax for the simplest form of this statement is:

CREATETABLE tablename

      (list of column names separated by commas with their corresponding data types) optional WITH clause;

For example, the 'customer' table in the example database might be defined by the statement:

create table customer
    (name   VARCHAR(20) not null,
    credit__balance   FLOAT4,
    credit__limit   FLOAT4)
with no duplicates;

(*Note:* In this and the other SQL statement examples, the use of bold type has no syntactic significance. This has been done only to make the statements more readable by highlighting the SQL commands and operators in the statements. Nor does the fact that table names and column names are given in small letters have any significance. Again, this is only done for clarity. SQL is not case sensitive, except where character or numeric literals are used. These must be placed within apostrophes. All SQL statements in this and subsequent chapters are shown as being terminated by a semi-colon. This is not mandatory in all dialects of the language.)

The formats for each column name, which, of course correspond to attribute names for the entity type 'customer', are defined in the statement. These define the type of data allowable in the specified columns.

The syntax for this data typing can vary slightly from SQL dialect to SQL dialect, but in the above example:

- VARCHAR(20) means that the 'name' column can contain a character string of up to 20 characters in length.
- FLOAT4 means that the 'credit__balance' and 'credit__limit' columns can contain a 4 byte floating point number.

This data typing information is recorded by the RDBMS and is used by it later to support automatic checks on values to be entered into a table. Some further typical data types used by SQL include:

196   *Introduction to the SQL language*

- SMALLINT, a whole number falling in value between -32767 and +32767.
- INTEGER, a whole number capable of taking on very large values. The range of values is RDBMS dependent.
- FLOAT (or FLOAT8), An 8 byte floating point number.
- CHAR(n), a fixed length character string.
- DATE, a date in one of a number of permissible formats.

The use of 'not null' against 'name' in the above example means that all rows inserted into the table must have a value for this attribute. Any attempt to insert a row into the table without a value for an attribute defined as not null would be rejected. It is normal practice to specify not null for primary key attribute values as in the above example, but this is not mandatory.

The 'with no duplicates' clause specifies that duplicate rows will not be allowed within the table. Note that this is one of the many areas where theory and practice concerning relational databases depart company. The theory, as we saw in Chapter 5, says that all rows within a table must be unique, but, in practice, RDBMSs do not make this rule mandatory. They leave it up to the database designer to decide when and where it is practical to enforce it.

The table 'order' in the example database might be defined as follows:

create table order

(order_number	SMALLINT not null,
order_value	FLOAT4,
order_date	DATE,
customer_name	VARCHAR(20));

The 'order_date' column, giving the date that the order was placed, is defined as DATE. Most RDBMSs allow the data type DATE to be defined and support a variety of arithmetic operations on date values. A variety of formats is usually permissible for the DATE data type.

The CREATE INDEX Statement

The informal syntax for this statement is:
CREATE (optional UNIQUE qualifier) INDEX indexname
ON tablename (list of column names separated by commas);

Indexing, which was discussed earlier in Chapter 2, is a technique which can be used to speed up access to information. It is normal to index at least the primary key column(s) of a table since retrieval of data is most frequently done using them, but it is frequently useful also to index non key columns to speed up retrieval times for frequently used queries. This will be better understood after the SELECT statement has been explained.

The optional UNIQUE qualifier in the CREATE INDEX statement allows the analyst to specify that the column or columns specified must only take on unique values in each row of the table. This would normally be done for primary keys. If is was required that the primary key column of the 'customer' table in the example database be indexed and it was required that each entry in this column be unique, then the following statement would be needed:

create unique index customer__unique
on customer (name);

If we wanted to ensure that all primary key values for the table 'order__item' were unique, then the following would be required:

create unique index order__item__unique
on order__item (item__name, order__number);

The DROP TABLE Statement

The informal syntax for this statement is:

DROP TABLE (list of table names separated by commas);

If it was desired to remove the 'customer' and 'customer__city' tables from the example database then the statement would be:

drop table customer, customer__city;

This, as can well be imagined, is a very drastic command. Dropping a table deletes all information abouts its structure from the database and has the consequent effect of losing all its contents and indexes. It also deletes any views in which the table was involved.

The DROP INDEX Statement

The informal syntax for this statement is:

DROP INDEX (list of index names separated by commas);

If it was desired to drop the 'customer__unique' index created earlier, then the statement would be:

drop index customer__unique;

12.5 SQL Expressions and the SQL SELECT Statement

The major data manipulation commands in SQL are INSERT, UPDATE, DELETE and SELECT. These correspond to the basic database access operations discussed in Chapter 1. INSERT inserts rows into a base table, UPDATE modifies the contents of rows, DELETE removes entire rows and SELECT retrieves information from table rows. The SELECT command can figure in any of the others as a *sub-select* statement and it is thus dealt with first in some detail.

SQL Expressions

SQL supports expressions which allow values to be computed for use in various commands, for example to denote values to be retrieved in the SELECT statement

198 *Introduction to the SQL language*

SELECT clause, or to define values to be compared in the SELECT statement WHERE clause, both of which will be explained shortly.

Expressions can be:

A *column name,* such as 'employee__id'. A column may have to be qualified by its table name as in 'employee.employee__name' to eliminate ambiguity in certain SQL statement constructions. It can also be qualified by a table name *alias* as in 'e.name', where 'e' is an alias for 'employee'. (The use of aliases will be illustrated later.)

An *arithmetic expression.* Expressions can be formed using the arithmetic operators +, −, * (multiplication),/(division), ** (exponentiation), in descending order of precedence on column values or constants of numeric data type. Brackets can be used to force the required order or precedence in the usual manner if required. The expression:

wage*1.2

if applied to a value contained in the 'wage' column of the table 'employee' would evaluate to that value increased by 20%. The + operator can also be used to concatenate together string values. The expression:

'data' + 'base'

would evaluate to 'database'. String constants were used in this example, but columns defined as CHAR or VARCHAR data types can also have their values concatenated in this manner. Most SQL dialects also support limited arithmetic operations on 'date' data types.

* Functions: All SQL dialects support the aggregate functions count, sum, avg (average), max (maximum) and min (minimum). Examples of the use of all of these functions in expressions will be given later in this section. Most SQL dialects also support string functions allowing character strings to be manipulated in various ways. Date functions also are supported in some dialects. Functions can be included in arithmetic expressions.

The SQL SELECT Statement

The SELECT command is very comprehensive and only the most basic of the facilities provided by it will be discussed here. An informal syntax for the most common form of the SELECT statement is:

SELECT (optional DISTINCT or ALL qualifiers)
(list of column names separated by commas, or asterisk (*) meaning that all columns are to be selected)

FROM tablename(s)
optional WHERE clause
optional sub-select statement
optional ORDER BY clause
optional GROUP BY clause
optional HAVING clause;

The where clause 199

The DISTINCT or ALL qualifier indicates whether or not duplicate rows are to be returned as a result of a SELECT statement. In the absence of either, the default value is ALL and all rows resulting from the query will be returned.

The most basic form of the statement, with none of the optional clauses, simply selects all rows from a table. Thus the statement:

select *
from employee;

where the asterisk indicates that all columns are to be selected, would return all rows from the 'employee' table in the example database, thus:

employee_id	name	wage
AB1	Fred	3
AB2	Jim	3.5
AB3	Jim	3
AB4	John	3.4

If, on the other hand, the query were:

select name
from employee;

the employee names only from the 'employee' table would be returned, thus:

name
Fred
Jim
Jim
John

Note that this corresponds to the relational *project* operation which was discussed in Chapter 6. Had DISTINCT been specified as in:

select distinct name
from employee;

then only . . .

name
Fred
Jim
John

would have been returned.

The Where Clause

The WHERE clause places a restriction on the rows to be selected and thus implements the *restriction* operation of the relational model which was discussed in Chapter 6. It

200　*Introduction to the SQL language*

can include the logical operators 'and' and 'or' as well as the comparative operators '='
(equals), '!=' (not equals), '>' (greater than), '<' (less than), >=, (greater than or equal
to), <=, (less than or equal to). The statement:

select *
from cust__order
where customer__name='Jones'
order by order__number;

would return the following rows from the 'order' table in the example database:

order__number	order__value	order__date	customer__name
123	2000	1-3-91	Jones
124	1000	6-4-91	Jones

Note that the literal string value 'Jones' had to be written within apostrophes. The
ORDER BY clause simply indicated that the results were to be sorted and reported by
ascending 'order__number' values. Had it not been included, the system would have
returned the rows in the order that it found them, which would correspond to the order
in which they were originally inserted. The statement:

select customer__name, order__value, order__number
from cust__order
where order__date >='6-4-91'
and order__value <1000;

would return:

customer__name	order__value	order__number
Smith	500	125

Note that the order of the columns output to the screen corresponds to the order in which
they are listed in the query. The statement:

select item__name
from line__item
where price * stock > 10000;

would return:

name
spade
fork

that is, the names of items for which the total value of the stock in hand exceeds £10000.
Note the use of an arithmetic expression in the above statement.

The IN, BETWEEN, and LIKE Predicates

Certain additional conditions are specifiable in the where clause based on the IN, NOT

IN, BETWEEN and LIKE predicates. The query:

select distinct customer_name
from customer_city
where city **in** ('Bath', 'Leeds');

would return:

```
customer_name
_____
Jones
Brown
```

The query:

select distinct customer_name
from customer_city
where city **not in** ('Bath', 'Leeds')

would return:

```
customer_name
_____
Brown
Smith
```

The query:

select name
from customer
where credit_limit **between** 15000 **and** 40000;

would return:

```
name
___
Brown
```

The LIKE operator allows 'fuzzy' searches to be undertaken. The query:

select *
from employee
where name **like** 'J%';

would return:

```
employee-id      name      wage
_____
AB2              Jim       3.5
AB3              Jim       3
AB4              John      3.4
```

The query selected all employees whose names began with 'J'. The % symbol is a 'wild card'. Had the query used '%im', then only the rows for the two 'Jims' would have been returned. An underscore can be used to signify a single character position. Had the query

202 *Introduction to the SQL language*

used '%h__' then only the row for employee AB4 would have been returned. The significance of '%h__' is that the penultimate letter of the employee's name must be an 'h'.

Join Operations Using the Where Clause

Now suppose that a relational *join operation* were required across the 'line__item' and 'order__item' tables in order to show the unit prices of line items and the quantities of them required against order. (See Chapter 6 for a discussion of relational joins). The query:

select line__item.item__name, order__number, quantity, price
from line__item, order__item
where line__item.item__name = order__item.item__name;

would return:

item__name	order-number	quantity	price
axe	123	100	10
spade	123	50	20
spade	125	25	20
fork	124	34	2 5
hoe	124	10	1 5

In the above example some column names had to be qualified with their table names (using a period as a delimeter between them) in the SELECT and WHERE clauses to remove naming ambiguities which could otherwise have arisen in the statement. Had different column names been specified for an item name where used as a primary key in the 'line__item' table and where used as a foreign key in the 'order__item' table, this would not have been necessary. Column names must always be concatenated with their table name as above where there is any risk of ambiguity. In the column list following the SELECT clause, only one of the 'item__name' columns was specified, by concatenation with its table name (line__item.item__name). This ensured that the result was a natural join by causing a projection of only one of the 'item__name' columns.

(*Note:* The above query could have been formulated more briefly as:

select l.item__name, order__number, quantity, price
from line__item l, order__item o
where l.item__name + o.item__name;

Here, the 'line__item' and 'order__item' tables have been given the temporary aliases 'l' and 'o' respectively. These aliases hold good only for the duration of the query and are referred to as correlation names.)

The above example was of an inner join. An outer join would have given the same result since neither of the two tables contains an occurrence of an 'item__name' value which does not occur in the other.

Suppose, however, that we wish to know all employees, their names and wages, what items they make, where appropriate, and the average times they take to make these items.

Join operations using the where clause 203

This requires an *outer* join of the tables 'employee' and 'item_maker'. An inner join would return no information about employee AB4, since he does not make any line item and therefore does not appear in the 'item_maker' table. Outer joins are not universally supported in SQL dialects, but can usually be accomplished using the UNION operator where this is supported, as in the following example. (See Chapter 6 for a discussion of the UNION operator.):

select employee.employee_id, name, wage, item_name, time
from employee, item_maker
where employee.employee_id = item_maker.employee_id

union

select employee_id, name, wage, null, null
from employee
where employee.employee_id **not in**
      (**select** employee.employee_id
      from employee, item_maker
      where employee.employee_id = item_maker.employee_id);

This statement will return:

employee_id	name	wage	item_name	time
AB1	Fred	3	axe	40
AB1	Fred	3	spade	45
AB2	Jim	3.5	fork	35
AB3	Jim	3	hoe	40
AB3	Jim	3	axe	25
AB4	John	3.4	—	—

which gives all the required information. The first SELECT statement, which included a natural join of the two tables, returns the first five rows. The second returns the last row. The UNION operator adds together the two sets of rows returned by the select statements to give the result. The UNION operator normally eliminates duplicate rows from the result, but this can be overruled by the inclusion of the ALL operator, that is, UNION ALL will return all rows produced from the addition of the rows returned by the two SELECT statements. Note that this is another instance of relational database practice parting company from the theory. Note the use of nulls in the column list in the SELECT clause of the second SELECT statement. The UNION operator requires that each of the two SELECT statements have the same number of columns identified in this list. The nulls were used in the second SELECT statement to make the number of items in the two lists equal. Not all dialects of SQL will accept nulls as column names in this fashion. Note also the use of a subquery in the second SELECT statement. This is explained next.

Subqueries

SQL provides no facility for saving the results of a SELECT statement for further processing, but it is frequently useful for one query to be able to use the result from

204 *Introduction to the SQL language*

another. This is done by means of subqueries as illustrated in the following statement:

select name, credit__balance
from customer
where name **in**
     (**select distinct** customer__name
      from customer__city
      where city **in** ('Bath', Leeds'));

This will return:

name	credit__balance
Jones	+10000
Brown	+20000

The result of the subquery was to return the customer names 'Jones' and 'Brown' and these were used in the outer WHERE clause to determine the rows to be returned from the 'customer' table. Sub-queries can be nested within sub-queries.

The EXISTS predicate is used with sub-queries which evaluate to 'true' or 'false'. Suppose we need to know details of all employees who can make line items. This can be accomplished using the IN predicate with a sub-query as in:

select employee__id, name, wage
from employee
where employee__id **in**
     (**select** employee__id
      from item__maker);

It can also be accomplished by use of the EXISTS predicate as in:

select employee__id, name, wage
from employee
where exists
     (**select** *
      from item__maker
      where employee__id = employee.employee__id);

Both queries return:

employee__id	name	wage
AB1	Fred	3
AB2	Jim	3.5
AB3	Jim	3

Values for 'employee__id' are returned only where the 'exists' condition evaluates to true. Note the use of 'employee.employee__id' to *correlate* between the subquery and the from clause of the outer query. The details of employees who do *not* make line items would be obtained by:

Aggregate functions 205

```
select employee__id, name, wage
from employee
where not exists
        (select *
         from item__maker
         where employee__id = employee.employee__id);
```

would return:

employee__id	name	wage
AB4	John	3.4

Aggregate Functions

SQL supports a number of functions which operate on tables or columns within tables, such as AVG (to calculate the average of the values of a column), SUM (to sum the values in a column), MIN and MAX (to identify minimum and maximum values in a column), COUNT (to count the number of rows in a table, or values in a column). These functions can be supported by use of the GROUP BY and HAVING clauses in a SELECT statement. Some examples of queries using the aggregate functions only are given first.

```
select sum (stock)
from line__item
where item__price > 10;
```

This query will return the value 4000, this being the total number of items in stock which are priced at greater than £10 each.

```
select avg (wage)
from employee;
```

This query will return the value 3.23 (pounds), this being the average hourly wage for all employees.

```
select max (wage)
from employee;
```

This query will return the value 3.5 (pounds), this being the highest hourly wage paid.

```
select min (time)
from item__maker
where item__name = 'axe';
```

This query will return the value 25 (minutes), being the minimum time to make an axe.

```
select distinct count (item__name)
from item__maker;
```

This query returns the value 4 being the number of line__items for which at least one maker is available. Note the use of the DISTINCT qualifier. This eliminates duplicates before the count is made. This usage of DISTINCT applies for the other aggregate functions, except for the MAX and MIN functions where its use would be meaningless.

206 *Introduction to the SQL language*

The COUNT function includes a special case, COUNT(*), which is used to count rows, rather than columns, in a table. The query:

select count (*)
from order__item
where quantity > 25

would return the value 3. This form of the COUNT function cannot be qualified by DISTINCT.

The Group By and Having Clauses

It is often convenient to think of rows in a table as being divided up into groups by the values in one or more columns of the table. For example, in the 'order__item' table, it might be convenient to think of the rows as grouped by the values of 'order__number'. This means that it would be grouped into those rows associated with order number 123, those with order number 124 and those with order number 125. This kind of grouping is the function of the GROUP BY clause. Note that the grouping is purely conceptual, the table is not actually rearranged into the grouping specified by the GROUP BY clause, but it enables the aggregate functions to behave as if it were. Suppose that we need to know the number of different line items included in each current order. The query:

select order__number, **count** (*)
from order__item
group by order-number;

would return:

order__number	count (*)
123	2
124	2
125	1

indicating that there were 2 rows, therefore 2 different line items, for order number 123, 2 for 124 and 1 for 125 in the table. We could find out how frequently specific line items appeared in orders by the query:

select distinct count (item__name), item__name
from order__item
group by item__name;

which would return:

count(item__name)	item__name
1	axe
2	spade
1	fork
1	hoe

Suppose we need to find out the time it takes on average to make each line item. The query:

The SQL INSERT statement   207

select avg(time), item__name
from item__maker
group by item__name;

would return:

```
avg time        item__name
_____
32.5            axe
45              spade
35              fork
40              hoe
```

The HAVING clause is most commonly used to apply qualifying aggregate functions to groupings defined by the group by clause. Suppose that we required to know all orders where the total number of items in the order exceeded 40. The query;

select order-number
from order__item
group by order__number
having sum(quantity) >40;

would return:

```
order__number
_____
123
124
```

The way this works is that first the grouping takes place as per the group by clause. This is not visible to the SQL user, but can be thought of as resulting in:

```
order__number       quantities       item__names
_____
123                 100,50           axe, spade
124                 34,10            fork, hoe
125                 25               spade
```

The quantities are now summed for each order as per the SUM function in the HAVING clause. Finally the selection is made based on the condition in the HAVING clause.

12.6   The SQL INSERT Statement

The informal syntax for this statement is:

INSERT INTO tablename (optional column list in brackets separated by commas)
VALUES (value list in brackets separated by commas)
or (sub-select statement)

208   *Introduction to the SQL language*

For example, if it were required to add a new employee to the 'employee' table in the example database, the statement might take the simple form:

insert into employee
values ('AB5', 'Algernon', 2.75);

Note that character string values are included in quotes. The values where, as in this example, a column list it not provided, must correspond in data type and order to the columns as specified in the original CREATE TABLE statement. Values can be omitted from the value list provided that the value list is lined up in order with a column list included in the INSERT INTO clause as in the following example:

insert into employee (employee__id, wage)
values (AB5, 2.75);

A sub-select can be used instead of a value list to create one or more new rows in a table. For example, suppose that a new line item (shovel) were to be sold, two new employees (AB5 and AB6) hired to make it and new rows inserted into the 'line__item' and 'item__maker' tables. The statement:

insert into employee (employee__id)
     select employee__id
     from item__maker
     where item__name = 'shovel';

would add two new rows for the new employees, whose allocated personnel numbers were AB5 and Ab6, into the 'employee' table.

12.7   The SQL DELETE Statement

The informal syntax for the DELETE statement is:

DELETE FROM tablename
optional WHERE clause;

If the WHERE clause is omitted, all rows will be deleted from the specified table. The WHERE clause, as usual, can be used to place a restriction on the rows to be deleted. For example, if employee AB1 left the company, the following statement would delete all his details from the 'employee' table:

delete from employee
where employee__id = 'AB1';

Note that a corresponding deletion would now have to be made to the 'item__maker' table in order to maintain referential integrity. (See Chapter 7 for an explanation of referential integrity).

12.8 The SQL UPDATE Statement

The informal syntax for the UPDATE statement is:

UPDATE tablename
SET (list of 'column name=expression' statements separated by commas)
optional WHERE clause.

The UPDATE command is used to change values in table columns or insert values into them when the original INSERT statement left them as nulls. The statement:

update employee
set wage=1.1 * wage;

would increase the wages of all staff identified in the 'employee' table by 10%. The statement:

update employee
set wage=1.2 * wage
  where employee__id **in**
  (**select** employee__id
  from item__maker
  where item__name = 'axe');

would given a 20% wage increase only to employees who were capable of making axes.

12.9 The SQL CREATE and DROP VIEW Statements

(For an explanation of views, see Chapter 6)

The CREATE VIEW Statement

The informal syntax for this statement is:

CREATE VIEW viewname
(optional list of column names separated by commas)
AS select statement
WITH optional CHECK option;

Suppose that a user needs to access 'employee' data, but it is not allowed to see any employee's hourly wage per hour. Suppose also that the 'employee' table has been created. A view can be created by use of a create view statement for the user which is a 'virtual' table and which he can access by name like any real, base table, for example:

create view staff
  (employee__id, name)
as select employee__id, name
from employee;

210   *Introduction to the SQL language*

This would create the view 'staff', with columns 'employee_id' and 'name' corresponding to the columns 'employee_id' and 'name' in the base table 'employee'.

Any SELECT statement can be used to create a view, including statements which will cause the view to be created on two or more base tables. Views can also be used in the creation of further views.

The WITH CHECK option in the command applies restrictions on what can be done when using UPDATE, INSERT or DELETE commands on a view. In general, UPDATE, INSERT and DELETE operations are not allowed on a view if: it was created from more than one table; it was created from a view which itself was created from more than one table. Additionally, it is not possible to do an INSERT operation on a view which was created on a table with columns declared as not null, where these columns are not included in the view. The WITH CHECK option applies to views which are updateable. Suppose that we created a view as follows:

create view staff
        (employee_id, name)
as select employee_id, name
from employee
where wage = 3;

This view would apply only to employees earning £3 per hour. Now suppose that we perform an UPDATE statement which changes an employee's wage per hour from £3 per hour to £4 per hour, that employee's tuple would then be removed from the view. If this scenario is acceptable, then the view would be defined without specifying the WITH CHECK option. If it is not acceptable, then the view would be specified with the WITH CHECK option, thus:

create view staff
        (employee_id, name)
as select employee_id, name
from employee
where wage = 3
with check;

and it would not later be possible to perform an update on the view which changed any value in the 'wage' column.

When a table or view used in CREATE VIEW statement is dropped, that view is also dropped.

The DROP VIEW Statement

The informal syntax for this statement is:

DROP VIEW (list of view names separated by commas);

If it was desired to drop the 'staff' view created earlier, then the statement would be:

drop view staff;

Dropping a view has no effect on the base table (or tables) it was created on, but will have the effect of dropping any views which were created using it.

12.10 Access Control in SQL

All users of an RDBMS must have a *user name,* which is allocated by the DBA with overall authority for the installation. The manner in which this is done varies from RDBMS to RDBMS and does not form part of SQL. The DBA, or the creator of a table, can give and withdraw various privileges to other users by using the SQL GRANT and REVOKE statements. For example the statement:

grant select, update on employee to vocca;

would allow the user whose user name was vocca to retrieve data from the 'employee' table using the SELECT command and to update it using the UPDATE command. The other privileges which could have been granted by a DBA using the GRANT command are insert and delete, that is the use of the INSERT and DELETE commands. Later, vocca might have his privileges reduced by a REVOKE statement, for example:

revoke update on employee **to** vocca;

12.11 Transaction Control in SQL

For a general discussion of the concept of transactions, the need for lock/unlock mechanisms to maintain database consistency in a multi-user environment, and the ensuing need to protect against deadlocks, the reader is referred to Chapter 1. In the specific context of SQL, a transaction is a sequence of one or more SQL statements which must process data in the database as a single, indivisible action. The underlying lock/unlock and deadlock avoidance mechanisms supplied with an RDBMS to ensure database consistency during concurrent access are transparent to the SQL user, however he/she can indicate to the system how they are to be used. Four SQL commands are available to assist the user in maintaining database consistency, SET AUTOCOMMIT, SET LOCKMODE, COMMIT and ROLLBACK.

If the user executes the statement:

set autocommit on;

then SQL enters a mode where all statements which cause a change to the database contents have *immediate* effect.

If the user executes the statement:

set autocommit off;

then SQL enters a mode where all changes are deferred until they are *committed* by the user issuing a COMMIT command.

Whether autocommit is set to off or on, the system automatically locks data which are accessed by a user in order to change them. If autocommit is on, then the lock is removed immediately after the statement is executed. If it is off, then the locks are not removed until the changes are committed or rolled back by the user, or the system makes a decision to rollback a user's transaction in order to resolve a deadlock situation.

212 *Introduction to the SQL language*

(*Note*: The commands which can cause change to the data in the database are UPDATE, INSERT, DELETE, CREATE TABLE, DROP TABLE, CREATE VIEW, DROP VIEW, CREATE INDEX and DROP INDEX. The latter six of these commands cause changes to the data in the data dictionary (catalogue) of the RDBMS.)

The type and granularity of locking to be applied is governed by use of the SET LOCKMODE command.

If a user executes the statement:

set lockmode exclusive;

then any data accessed by that user will be locked against both read and change from all other users until either the user of the system removes the lock(s).

If a user executes the statement:

set lockmode nolock;

then other users are not locked out when that user is *reading* data. They can both read them and write to them.

If a user executes the statement:

set lockmode shared;

then other users can access the data for read purposes when that user is *reading* them, but cannot change them.

The SET LOCKMODE command is also used to specify the granularity of locking required. This varies from RDBMS to RDBMS, but will usually allow the user to specify whether he/she requires locking to be applied at the table level or at some lower level.

If a user executes the statement:

commit;

and autocommit is off, then all database changes initiated from the beginning of the transaction just completed will be applied. The beginning of a transaction is signalled by any of:

- Next statement after a COMMIT command.
- Next statement after an AUTOCOMMIT command.
- Next statement after a ROLLBACK command.
- Next statement after a system enforced rollback.
- Next statement after a SET LOCKMODE command.
- Start of an interactive session.

If a user issues the statement:

rollback;

then the current transaction is 'rolled back' to its start point. This means that the database changes called for by the transaction up to the point where it was rolled back will not be committed.

Embedded SQL 213

If the system detects a deadlock situation (see Chapter 1), then it will automatically select a transaction (or transactions) to roll back and the user(s) rolled back will be notified by an error message. The user can then restart the transaction if desired.

Some SQL dialects allow the user to specify one or more *savepoints* (or checkpoints) during the course of a transaction. A user initiated ROLLBACK statement can then be qualified by naming the savepoint to which the rollback is to take place. All changes up to that save point can subsequently be committed.

12.12 Embedded SQL

Embedded SQL uses most of the SQL commands already described for the interactive form of the language. It also includes commands which are particular to it and special forms of some of the interactive versions of SQL commands. The most important of these are described in the following paragraphs. Note that all embedded SQL statements are delimited in the source language code by 'exec SQL'.

Connecting an Application Program to a Database

The CONNECT command connects an application program to a specified database, for example:

exec SQL **connect** ford;

would connect the host program to a database named 'ford'. The DISCONNECT command is used to terminate the connection, as in:

exec SQL **disconnect** ford;

Declaring Host Program Variables for Use in Embedded SQL Statements

The DECLARE SECTION command declares host variables which are to be used in embedded SQL statements. For example:

```
exec SQL begin declare section;
      name                  character-string(20);
      credit__balance       float;
      credit__limit         float;
exec SQL end declare section;
```

would declare the host variables 'name', 'credit__balance' and 'credit__limit' to the embedded SQL pre-processor. The declarations must contain variable names and data types which are legal in the host language. The names and data types given in the above example are exemplary only.

Use of Cursors with Embedded SQL SELECT Statements

In the interactive form of SQL just described, queries could return multiple rows of data

214   *Introduction to the SQL language*

to the user's screen. Conventional languages such as COBOL and PL/1 are not in general designed to deal with multiple values, such as a set of table rows, as single operands. A mechanism is required which allows the embedded SQL to obtain rows one at a time from a table. This mechanism is provided by *cursors*. A named cursor is associated with a specific SELECT statement. When the cursor is *opened*, it causes the SELECT statement (in effect) to be executed and to retrieve rows of data. The FETCH command is then used to retrieve successive rows (those in effect retrieved by the SELECT command) *one at a time*. On each FETCH the cursor is advanced to point to the next row until, finally, the rows are exhausted or the cursor is closed. Cursors are declared by the DECLARE CURSOR command which takes the form:

exec SQL DECLARE cursorname CURSOR for SELECT statement;

The 'cursorname' can be a constant or a previously declared host language string variable. For example the statement:

exec SQL **declare** select1 **cursor for**
select *
from customer
order by name;

will create a cursor named 'select1' which is associated with the SELECT statement specified in the DECLARE CURSOR statement.

The OPEN statement takes the general form.

exec SQL OPEN cursorname;

For example, the statement . . .

exec SQL **open** select1;

when first used after the DECLARE CURSOR statement for the cursor 'select1', points the cursor to a position prior to the first row retrieved by the SELECT statement which was also defined in the DECLARE CURSOR statement. A subsequent FETCH statement of the form:

exec SQL FETCH cursorname
        INTO . . . list of host language variable names separated by commas;

will advance the cursor to point to the next row (i.e. the first row identified by the SELECT statement) and copy values from this row into the host language variables. Subsequent FETCH statements will copy from the further rows retrieved by the SELECT statement. For example, the statement:

exec SQL **fetch** select1
into name, credit__balance, credit__limit;

when used for the first time after the OPEN statement would assign the values Jones, +10000 and 50000 to the host variables name, credit__balance and credit__limit respectively. When used for the second time, it would assign the values Brown, +20000 and 30000 respectively to those variables, and so forth.

The CLOSE command takes the form:

Embedded SQL update and delete statements   215

exec SQL CLOSE cursorname;

and closes an opened cursor.

If the select1 cursor is re-opened later, it will again be pointing to a position prior to the first row identified by the SELECT statement.

Embedded SQL Update and Delete Statements

UPDATE statements may or may not use a cursor in embedded SQL. If a cursor is not used, then the command is more or less identical to the interactive version. The only difference is that it is possible to use (previously declared) host variables in the set clause. For example, supposing that the host variable 'host_credit_limit' had been declared and assigned the value 60000, then the statement:

exec SQL **update** customer
set credit_limit = :host_credit_limit
where name = 'Jones';

would change the credit limit for customer Jones from £50000 to £60000. Note the use of the colon to differentiate the host variable.

If a cursor is used then an UPDATE statement takes the general form:

exec SQL UPDATE
SET (list of 'column name = expression' statements separated by commas)
WHERE CURRENT OF cursorname;

In this case, the where clause points to the current position of the cursor. Thus, supposing that the statement:

exec SQL **fetch** select1
into name, credit_balance, credit_limit;

were the first FETCH statement executed after cursor 'select1' had been opened, as in the earlier example, then the statement:

exec SQL **update** customer
set credit_limit = credit_limit * 1.2
where current of select 1;

would increase the value of customer 'Jones' credit limit by 20%.

The DELETE command can be used with or without a cursor in a similar fashion to the UPDATE command. If no cursor is used, then an embedded DELETE statement is more or less identical to an interactive DELETE statement. The only difference, is that host variables can be used in the where clause. For example, if the host variable 'out' had been declared and assigned the value 1000, then the statement:

delete from customer
where credit_balance < :out;

216   *Introduction to the SQL language*

would remove the row for customer 'Smith' from the 'customer' table. If a cursor is used, then a DELETE statement takes the general form:

DELETE FROM tablename
WHERE CURRENT OF cursorname;

Assuming that a third FETCH statement had been executed after cursor 'select1' had been opened as in the earlier example, then the statement:

delete from customer
where current of select1;

would delete the row for 'Smith' from the 'customer' table.

Error Handling in Embedded SQL

Error handling is supported by the *sqlcode* variable which is updated each time an SQL statement is executed. (The sqlcode variable is held within a named SQL *communications area* which may contain other error and status information according to the SQL dialect and host language in use. The named SQL communications area must be included in a program using the INCLUDE command.) If it returns a value of 0, the embedded SQL statement was executed correctly. If it returns a negative value, then an error was encountered. The value of the negative number indicates the type of error which was encountered. Values greater than 0 indicate that some exceptional condition has occurred, for example, that no rows were selected as a result of a query.

(*Note*:   The meaning of the positive or negative values as returned in sqlcode varies from SQL dialect to SQL dialect and the RDBMS supplier's manuals must be consulted for this information.)

Dynamic Embedded SQL

In embedded SQL, as so far described, the SQL statements must be known to the host program at compile time, they are, in effect, hard coded into it. The Dynamic SQL extension to embedded SQL allows SQL statements to be generated dynamically during the running of a host program.

The Execute Immediate Command

For statements which do not return a value (other than values in the SQL communications area) the EXECUTE IMMEDIATE command can be used. This takes the general form:

exec SQL EXECUTE IMMEDIATE
        host string variable or literal string;

   The host string variable or literal string can contain any SQL statement other than SELECT, cursor statements or Dynamic SQL statements. If a host string variable is used, such statements can be formulated by the host program according to decisions made at run time on examination of input data. Suppose that the SQL statement:

The Prepare and Execute commands 217

create table order

(order__number	integer not null,
order__date	date,
delivery__date	date,
customer__id	smallint)

had been entered into the host string variable 'sql__statement', then the dynamic SQL statement:

exec SQL **execute immediate** sql__statement;

would result in the creation of the 'order' table. The same result would have been obtained by:

exec SQL **execute immediate**
create table order

(order__number	integer not null,
order__date	date,
delivery__date	date,
customer__id	smallint);

Note that the statement referenced by an EXECUTE IMMEDIATE statement must not contain 'exec SQL' or the delimiting semi-colon.

The Prepare and Execute Commands

It is also possible to *prepare* a dynamic SQL statement and give it a name which can be used later to execute it as many times with variations as required using the PREPARE and EXECUTE statements. These take the general forms:

exec SQL PREPARE statementname
FROM host string variable or literal string;

exec SQL EXECUTE statementname
        optional USING clause naming host variables;

The statement:

exec SQL **prepare** insert__employee **from**
        'insert into employee
        values (?, ?, ?)';

followed later in the program by the statement:

exec SQL **execute** insert__employee
using :employee__id, :name, :wage__hour;

would cause new rows to be inserted into the 'employee' table of Figure 12.2. The column values being taken from the host string variables 'employee__id', 'name' and 'wage__hour' (previously defined in a DECLARE SECTION command). Note the use of the question marks in the PREPARE statement to correlate the use of variables in the INSERT statement to the USING clause in the EXECUTE statement. The EXECUTE statement could be included in a host program loop with the contents of

218 *Introduction to the SQL language*

the host string variables being changed, probably from keyboard input, at each execution of the loop.

Dynamic SELECTS

If a dynamically defined SELECT statement is required, the problem arises that it is not possible to know in advance the data types of the columns which may be accessed by the statement. Such queries must first be prepared using the PREPARE command. The DESCRIBE command can then be used to enable the return to a progam of the data types of the result columns of the SELECT statement. Special forms of the DECLARE CURSOR and FETCH commands can then be used to retrieve rows of information from the database.

The Describe Command

The simplest form of the DESCRIBE command is:

exec SQL DESCRIBE statement name
INTO SQL__program__description__area__name;

After a DESCRIBE statement, the *SQL program descriptor area* named will contain information, inter alia, on whether or not the query named by the statement name is a SELECT statement, the number of columns which will be accessed by the query if it is, and the data type of each column. This information is used by the host program code to ensure that enough variables of the correct data type are available to hold the results of a SELECT statement before it is executed.

(*Note*:   The name and format of the SQL program descriptor area varies according to the SQL dialect and host language in use. The SQL program descriptor area's name must be included in a program using the INCLUDE command prior to issue of the DESCRIBE command.)

Suppose that 'buffer' is a host language variable into which SQL statements can be inserted by the host language code after being computed, input from a keyboard or accessed from a file. Suppose also that any legal SQL statement can be inserted into 'buffer', including SELECT statements and that the name given to the SQL program descriptor area is SQLDESCRIPTOR. The following sequence illustrates the use of the DESCRIBE command and the special forms of the DECLARE CURSOR and FETCH commands.

(i)   The host program code inserts an SQL statement into 'buffer'.

(ii)   The following embedded SQL statements are executed:

exec SQL **prepare** statement__name
from :buffer;
exec SQL **declare** statement__name
into sqldescriptor;

(iii) If the result of checking data in SQLDESCRIPTOR shows that the query addressed by 'statement__name' is not a SELECT statement then the query is simply executed by:

exec SQL **execute** statement__name;

and the program continues.

    (iv) If the check shows that it is a SELECT statement then the host program will analyse the data held in SQLDESCRIPTOR and as a result allocate variables of the appropriate data types for the requisite numbers of result columns and it will then place pointers to these variables into SQLDESCRIPTOR. The program would then continue:

exec SQL **declare** cursor1 **cursor**
for statement__name;

exec SQL **open** cursor1;

exec SQL **fetch** cursor1
using descriptor sqldescriptor;

and a row would be returned to the host program. Further rows would be fetched in the usual manner using SQLDESCRIPTOR.

Embedded SQL Preprocessors

RDBMS suppliers provide separate *preprocessors* (also referred to as *precompilers*) for each of the host languages for which they provide embedded SQL support. The source code for a program is prepared in the usual way with the SQL statements embedded into it as required using the 'exec SQL' delimiter. This code is then run through the appropriate preprocessor and the output from this is compiled in the normal manner. It is important to note that the SQL code itself is not 'compiled' in the general meaning of that term. The effect of the preprocessor is to convert the embedded SQL statements into procedure calls (in the host language) to the RDBMS software.

13
Relational Database Management Systems

13.1 Introduction

RDBMSs have been mentioned frequently in the course of this book and will be looked at more closely in this Chapter.

RDBMSs provide a total environment for the development and running of relational database systems. This is illustrated in Figure 13.1 which shows the typical RDBMS 'onion skin' architecture. The outer layer consists of the various interfaces available to system developers and users. The next layer consists of the RDBMS software which, of course, must run in the environment provided by the operating system. The databases exist under the control of this layer.

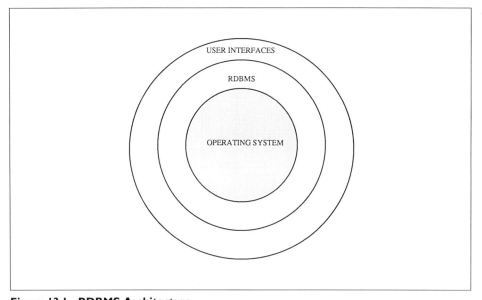

Figure 13.1 **RDBMS Architecture**

The underlying operating system facilities can be accessed by the development or end user if required, but in general are hidden by the interfaces presented to them by the RDBMS. Thus a description of an RDBMS is, for the most part, a description of the user interfaces it provides.

This Chapter begins by describing in general terms the facilities provided to various

222 *Relational database management systems*

classes of users by RDBMS products. Descriptions of two of the major RDBMS products from independent suppliers, ORACLE ^{TM} and INGRES^{TM}, are then given to illustrate how, in particular, these facilities are provided by them. Please note that these are overviews only, intended to give the reader without previous exposure to RDBMSs a practical feel for the facilities they provide, but not how to use these particular products. For this, recourse must be made to the suppliers' extensive documentation and training courses.

No attempt is made to draw technical comparisons between the RDBMS products overviewed, nor should such comparisons be inferred from this chapter. The reason for this is quite simple. RDBMS suppliers are very competitive and constantly improving their products to maintain their competitive edge. The effect of this is that the products are continually 'leap frogging' each other in terms of the facilities and performance they offer. Thus, comparisons between such products such as saying that one or other product out-performs the other, or offers a richer implementation of SQL, or has an easier to use and more comprehensive application generation facility, etc, may only hold good for a limited period of time.

RDBMS suppliers in general operate a marketing policy of 'unbundling' their products. What this means is that the RDBMS is seen as a basic product which can be extended with a number of optional extras. The point is, of course, that the extras have to be paid for in addition to the payment made for the basic product. In the descriptions of ORACLE and INGRES given in this chapter, no attempt is made to distinguish between what is 'bundled' into the basic product and what is 'unbundled'. It should also be noted that the overviews given represent a snapshot of some, but not all, of the major facilities provided by the products at the time of writing and that new facilities and/or improvements to existing facilities, whether bundled or unbundled, can be expected over time.

13.2 General Overview of RDBMSs

13.2.1 Introduction

It was remarked earlier that a description of an RDBMS amounts to a description of the interfaces it presents to users. Users with respect to RDBMSs can be classified into three principal groups, namely:

- System Developers — Analysts/Designers/Programmers

- Database Administrators

- Operational Users — Those using the RDBMS, whether directly or via its applications, in the course of their normal work for an organisation.

In this section, the typical interfaces, or tools, presented to these groups of user by RDBMSs are described. These descriptions follow some further remarks about the general architecture of RDBMS products.

13.2.2 RDBMS Architecture

In Figure 13.1 it was shown that RDBMSs fit into a typical 'onion skin' system architecture, which includes the operating system in use as its inner layer. Any RDBMS, as shown in Figure 13.2 will consist of a 'kernel' part and a set of user interfaces, or tools, which interact with that kernel. All access to a database by the user tools, or by any applications software system developed with their use, is via the kernel.

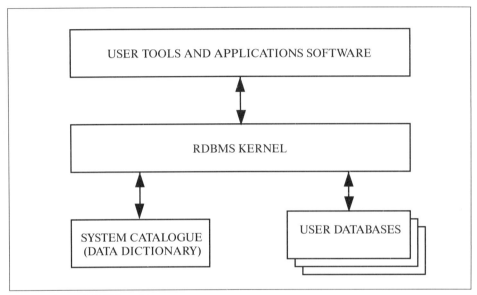

Figure 13.2 RDBMS architecture

Access to the kernel from the tools and/or applications is by means of SQL commands. There may be automatically generated, or explicitly defined by users, depending on the tool being used. A single copy of the RDBMS can support many, distinct user databases. Interaction between the kernel and the database is transparent to both users and the tools they use.

RDBMSs store databases conceptually in two parts. The storage schema which consists of table, view and index definitions, together with associated access permissions, user defined specifications affecting physical placement of data on disks and so forth, are stored in some form of system catalogue, sometimes referred to as the RDBMS's data dictionary. The actual data in a databases are stored by the kernel using the information held in the catalogue. The system catalogue is used to store other administrative information about the system and its databases. Some of their data content is directly accessible by users, in particular by the DBA. The user tools and the kernel of an RDBMS may be organised into a *client server* architecture. This arrangement assumes that users and/or application programs have access to workstations or PCs (personal computers) —the clients, which are powerful computers in their own right. These are connected via a communications network to a central processor or processor complex — the server. An RDBMS supporting the client server architecture can take advantage of this

224 *Relational database management systems*

equipment arrangement by allowing the user tools and/or applications to run in the client host processor, whilst the kernel runs in the server which also hosts the databases. The effect is to partition the processing work load across the network, thus maximising the use of the very significant computing power now available with modern, relatively inexpensive, workstations and PCs, whilst at the same time reducing the need for powerful central processors.

The general architecture of RDBMSs includes support for the homogeneous and heterogeneous communications networking and distributed database working which was described in Chapter 1. The architecture to support this varies from RDBMS to RDBMS.

13.2.3   System Development Tools

These are tools typically available to development staff using an RDBMS and can be broadly grouped under:

- SQL.
- Forms Management.
- 4GL.
- Report Generation.

13.2.3.1   SQL

The SQL language was described in Chapter 12. RDBMSs make it available to development users in a number of forms, including the following.

Interactive SQL

SQL statements can be entered at an interactive keyboard/screen for immediate interpretation and processing by the RDBMS. The results of the processing of these statements are returned immediately to the screen, or if the user chooses, can be sent to a file and/or printer. This form of the language is most commonly used where 'one off' queries of the database are required. It is also extensively used by programmers for checking their SQL statements in the interactive environment before incorporating them as embedded code into host language programs.

(*Note*:   Because interactive SQL is relatively easier to learn and use than some of the more conventional programming languages, it is sometimes marketed as an 'end user', meaning non computer literate user, language. However, it is still a complex programming language, and end users need programming aptitude and proper training in it if they are to accomplish more than the simplest of database queries using it.)

Embedded SQL

This is the form of the language is most likely to be encountered by the professional programmer. SQL statements can be embedded in traditional program code, thus allowing access to the database from programs coded in such languages as COBOL, Fortran, PL/1, Basic, Pascal, C and Ada.

System development tools 225

SQL Command Files

One or more SQL statements, as developed and tested in the interactive SQL environment, can be saved to file and later rerun.

SQL Procedures

Some RDBMs provide an enhanced version of SQL with procedural language decision making constructs, such as IF...THEN...ELSE, and WHILE...DO and the ability to declare and use variables with these procedures.

13.2.3.2 Forms Management

Most on line database applications involve the use of screen based forms for the input and retrieval of data. The forms management feature of RDBMSs enables the development of such applications with remarkable rapidity compared with traditional programming methods. They also support the subsequent running of the applications by end users. The applications developer is provided with facilities for the 'painting' of screen based forms for the insertion, update retrieval and deletion of data in the database. Facilities are provided to enable comprehensive, automatic checks to be performed on field values when the forms are used and for simple calculations to be performed on the values in form fields and/or in the database. The developed forms can be linked up with each other and with conventional or 4GL programs, enabling relatively rapid implementation of large, on line applications.

13.2.3.3 4GL

4GL stands for 'Fourth Generation Language' which is more of a marketing than a technical term. What it generally means is some facility or combination of facilities provide to the developer which enables him/her to produce sophisticated database oriented applications with minimum recourse to conventional programming techniques. In the context of RDBMSs, it generally refers to some simple block structured language which has been designed to be used in direct conjunction with embedded SQL statements and with the forms management facility.

13.2.3.4 Report Generators

A major application of databases is the production of regular or ad hoc reports from them. The output returned to a screen or printer from an interactive or embedded SQL SELECT statement is, of course, a report, albeit in a very simple format. RDBMSs extend their SQL dialects and/or their forms management facilities to enable the rapid development of more sophisticated reports than is possible by using the basic SELECT command. They also provide stand alone report generation tools which can be used for the production of even more sophisticated reports.

13.2.4 Database Administration Tools

The DBA has available for use the whole range of facilities provided to the developer as outlined above. Additionally, special facilities are available to the DBA for the regular and by exception maintenance of the databases he/she is reponsible for. These are usually provided as utility programs which the DBA can access via operating system level commands issued at the keyboard. They will include means for: setting up various system defaults; back up and restore of databases; import/export of databases from/to other systems; loading/unloading of databases from/to ASCII files; performance tuning.

13.2.5 Operational User Tools

The forms management facilities provided by RDBMSs, in addition to enabling development staff to produce screen menu/forms based applications, also provide the means by which operational staff can run and interact with these applications. Additionally, it is normal for a menu/forms based tool to be provided which can be used by the non computer literate operational user to create simple relational databases and perform insert, update, delete and retrieval operations on the data in them.

13.3 Overview of INGRES

The overview of the ASK INGRES RDBMS product which follows is structured along the same lines as the general treatment of RDBMSs just given. The following sections describe...

- INGRES Architecture
- INGRES System Development Tools
    - SQL
    - Forms Management
    - 4QL
    - Report Generation
- INGRES DBA Tools
- INGRES Operational User Tools

13.3.1 INGRES Architecture

INGRES, broadly speaking, falls into two parts, the INGRES user interfaces and the INGRES data manager. This organisation is shown conceptually in Figure 13.3. The user interfaces are provided by various INGRES tools which can be used to define and manipulate relational databases, doing so through the data manager. Applications software developed using the tools also access the database through the data manager.

Using the INGRES/NET facility as illustrated conceptually in Figure 13.4, the tools and applications at one node of a computer network can access data at remote nodes in the network as if they were available locally. Access using INGRES/NET is to one database at a time.

INGRES 227

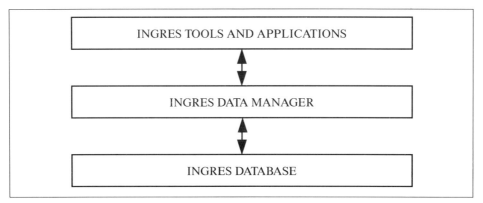

Figure 13.3 INGRES structure

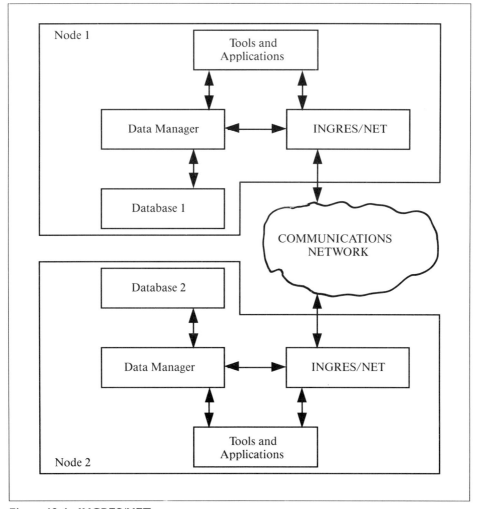

Figure 13.4 INGRES/NET

Using the INGRES/STAR facility, as illustrated conceptually in Figure 13.5, INGRES tools and applications can access different databases concurrently.

Using INGRES/NET and INGRES/STAR together, it becomes possible to access distributed databases (distinct databases residing at different nodes of a computer network) concurrently from any node in the network. The INGRES Gateways facility enables access from INGRES tools and applications to non-INGRES databases and can be used in conjunction with INGRES/NET and/or INGRES/STAR to give heterogeneous, distributed database access.

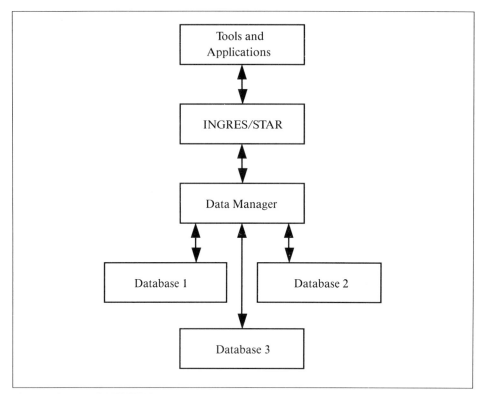

Figure 13.5 INGRES/STAR

13.3.2 Development Tools

The INGRES tools which provide the major interfaces to developers are illustrated in Figure 13.6.

(*Note*: INGRES supports two distinct query languages, the international standard SQL language and QUEL, which is particular to INGRES. Although some commentators would argue that QUEL is both the better of the two languages and closer to the theoretical considerations of the relational model. It is not discussed in this book because of its lack of general applicability to RDBMS products. INGRES includes a Knowledge Management Extension which enables rules to be defined which will trigger database procedures when some predefined event happens in the database. Although this is an extremely powerful development aid, it is not described here, again because of lack of general applicability.)

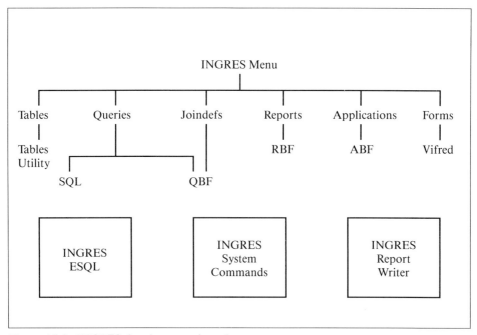

Figure 13.6 INGRES development interfaces

Entry to most of the development interfaces can be achieved using the INGRES Menu facility as indicated in the Figure. Entry is also possible directly using operating system commands. Note that INGRES introduces two further classes of users over and above those discussed earlier, namely:

The *Operating System Administrator,* who sets up the operating system environment in which the INGRES RDBMS is installed.

The *INGRES System Administrator,* who has prime responsibility for the installation and maintenance of the INGRES RDBMS.

The tools used by these users are very specialised to the product and the host operating system and these are not described.

13.3.2.1 INGRES SQL

INGRES ISQL (Interactive SQL)

(*Note*: INGRES SQL commands are not case sensitive except for string constants which must be included within apostrophes. In the examples given in this and the following sections, the use of lower and upper case and of bold faced type have no significance

230   *Relational database management systems*

other than to promote clarity in the presentation.)

The INGRES dialect of SQL supports all the SQL commands described in Chapter 12. The basic features of these commands have been extended in many cases to include extra useful options. The INGRES manuals must be consulted for these. The INGRES SQL dialect also extends the language to provide many useful commands over and above the basic commands listed in Chapter 12. Two of the most important of these are now described.

(*Note*:   Some others will be covered under 'DBA Tools' later.)

Create Procedure

INGRES SQL includes a CREATE PROCEDURE command. This allows the creation of a named database procedure definition. Database procedures can only be executed from embedded SQL, cannot contain data definition commands and cannot be nested. A procedure definition consists of the procedure name followed by a list of parameters followed by a declaration section in which local variables can be specified and, finally, a series of SQL statements bracketed by 'begin...end'. Database procedures can inlcuded local variables and decision control commands of the IF...THEN...ELSE...ENDIF and WHILE...DO...ENDWHILE variety. A number of further special commands and functions can be included with some procedures. For example, the MESSAGE command allows a message text and/or number to be returned to the calling host application program. The RETURN command returns control to the calling program and can also pass a success or failure indication via a parameter. The 'iirowcount' INGRES function can be used within a procedure to return the number of rows found by a statement. Privileges on use of database procedures can be granted and dropped to specified users thus giving the DBA another level of control over database access.

The use of database procedures improves performance, since less communication is required between application software and the INGRES data manager — the procedure is already defined to the data manager software. It reduces coding effort since the same database procedure can be called from many places in an application.

Create Integrity

This command allows integrity constraints to be placed on the columns of a base table. For example, the statement:

Create integrity on employee **is** wage $=> 3$ **and** wage $= < 5;$

would ensure that all values entered for an employee's wage per hour (as in the example table in 12.2) would have to fall between the values £3 and £5 or be rejected by the system. Integrity rules can be dropped by use of the DROP INTEGRITY command.

Terminal Monitor Command

When using INGRES ISQL, the SQL commands can be supplemented by commands supported by the INGRES Terminal Monitor. These commands are preceded by a back sloping, slash character (\).

SQL statements as they are keyed in at a terminal are stored in a query buffer. The \edit terminal monitor command can be used to put the contents of the query buffer under control of a system text editor (eg VI under Unix or EDT under Vax/VMS). If a filename is given with the command, for example:

\edit myfile;

the contents of the buffer after editing will be unaffected, but the file will contain the edited version. If no filename is specified, the contents of the buffer will be edited. The contents of a file can be loaded into the buffer using the\read command and the buffer can be written to a file using the\write command. Other terminal monitor commands include\print which prints contents of the buffer,\go which runs the SQL statement(s) in the buffer and\quit which exits from INGRES.

INGRES ESQL (Embedded SQL)

INGRES's embedded SQL covers all the commands and features described for embedded SQL in Chapter 12 including those for dynamic SQL. It also includes the EXECUTE PROCEDURE command which is used to invoke a database procedure previously named and defined by the CREATE PROCEDURE command.

Embedded SQL/FORMS

An extension to INGRES embedded SQL contains commands which allow a host program application to interact through the INGRES Forms Run Time System with predefined screen forms created using VIFRED, the Visual Forms Editor (described later).

13.2.2.2   INGRES Forms Management

The INGRES Menu

The INGRES Menu is entered from the operating system level command *ingmenu,* which will be qualified, inter alia, by the name of the database to be worked on. On entrance to the menu, the user is presented with a screen similar to that shown in Figure 13.7.

The figure is an example of an INGRES *frame.* An INGRES frame consists of two parts;

- A form which can be used for interacting with database data.
- A menu (at the bottom of the frame) which gives the user a number of choices as to what to do next.

In the Figure 13.7 case, the frame holds the main INGRES menu, which is the gateway to most of the tools that development staff will require. The purpose of each selection is self evident from the description given. A brief overview of the tools/facilities made available with each choice is given in the following paragraphs. In the great majority of cases these are made available as a succession of further frames allowing the user to input

232   *Relational database management systems*

data and make further choices. It is always possible for the user to return to a previous frame, to the frame previous to that and so on. The choices include those allowing the user to move from one INGRES tool to another where it is natural to do so without need to return to the main menu.

Database: Ford
INGRES/MENU

Tables	Create/examine tables or query/report on table data
Forms	Create/edit/use forms for customised data access
Joindefs	Ceate/edit/use join definitions on multiple tables
Reports	Create/edit/run reports
Graphs	Create/edit/plot graphs
Applications	Create/edit/run 4GL applications
Queries	Query data using QBF or a query language

Place cursor on your choice and select "Go"

Go   Tables   Forms   Joindefs   Reports   Graphs   Applications>

Figure 13.7   INGRES menu

The Tables Option

If this option is chosen from the INGRES menu, the user is guided through further frames which allow him/her to create new database tables, alter or delete existing tables or list current tables and examine their structure. The user can go on to append/update data within the tables or retrieve data from them by moving into QBF (Query by Forms) or to produce reports from them using RBF (Report by Forms).

The Joindef Option

This is an INGRES frames based facility which allows the user to create named relational

The INGRES menu   233

join operations without recourse to SQL or any other programming language. The joindefs are, in their effect, relational views on multiple tables and these views can be used in subsequent frame based operations. The user can progress in a natural way from defining joindefs to using them in QBF operations.

The Queries Option - INGRES QBF

The 'queries' option on the main menu takes the user to a further frame where a choice can be made between the use of interactive SQL supported by the INGRES terminal monitor, which was described earlier, or QBF which is now described in some detail.

QBF is an interactive, frame based interface for adding, deleting updating or simply retrieving data to/from to an INGRES relational database. Use of QBF proceeds in two steps.

- Define target database table or tables.
- Execute Queries

(*Note*: If QBF is enterered via the tables or joindef option, as discussed above, then the first step will have already taken place. 'Queries' in this usage means any kind of database access operation including updates, inserts and deletes as well as retrievals.)

On selecting QBF, the user is presented with the choice of interacting with the database via tables or joindefs or via QBFNames. On selection of the tables option the user will normally specify an existing table for access. On selection of joindef the user will normally specify an existing joindef for access. It is also possible to create or alter, etc, tables and joindefs at this point as if the table or joindef option had been chosen in the first place. Selecting the QBFNames option would enable the user to select forms for database access which had previously been created using the VIFRED utility. This utility will be described shortly.

Supposing that the 'tables' option were chosen after entering QBF, the user would be presented with a frame cataloguing all the tables and views available in the database to which he or she had access rights. Any of these tables or views could be selected as the target of some access operation. Supposing that the user wished to access the 'employee' table of Figure 12.2, first, he or she would select the table from the catalogue selected by moving the screen cursor to it and highlighting it as shown in Figure 13.8.

Next, the 'Query' choice would be made from the menu. This would result in a frame being displayed with a blank form and the following menu choices:

Append   **Retrieve**   **Update**   **Help Quit**

The first two of these correpsond in function to the SQL INSERT, and SELECT commands. The third covers the function of both the SQL UPDATE and DELETE commands.

Supposing that the 'Retrieve' option were chosen, at that point the user would be asked whether 'tablefield' or 'simplefield' were required. In INGRES a tablefield allows all the rows from a table that can be accommodated to be displayed on the screen in tabular fashion with columns of values and headers for each column. Further rows can be displayed as necessary by scrolling up and down through the table and, if there are too many columns to be accommodated on the screen, it can be scrolled sideways to view the data. A simplefield displays one row at a time and QBF automatically creates a form like display for them.

```
TABLES — Tables Catalogue

| Name          | Owner | Type  |
|---------------|-------|-------|
| customer      | vocca | Table |
| customer_city | vocca | Table |
| line_item     | vocca | Table |
| order         | vocca | Table |
| order_item    | vocca | Table |
| **employee**  | vocca | Table |
| item_maker    | vocca | Table |

Place cursor on row and select desired operation from menu
Create  Destroy  Examine  Query  Report  Find  Top  Bottom>
```

Figure 13.8 QBF table catalogue

Assuming that the simplefield option were chosen, then a frame similar to that depicted in Figure 13.9 would be displayed.

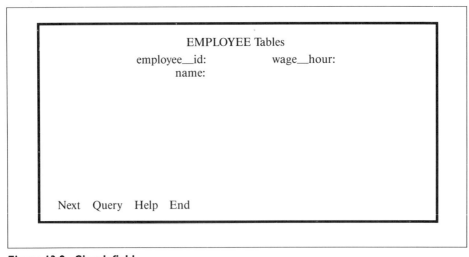

Figure 13.9 Simplefield

The INGRES menu   235

Assuming that the tablefield option was chosen, then a frame similar to that illustrated in Figure 13.10 would be displayed.

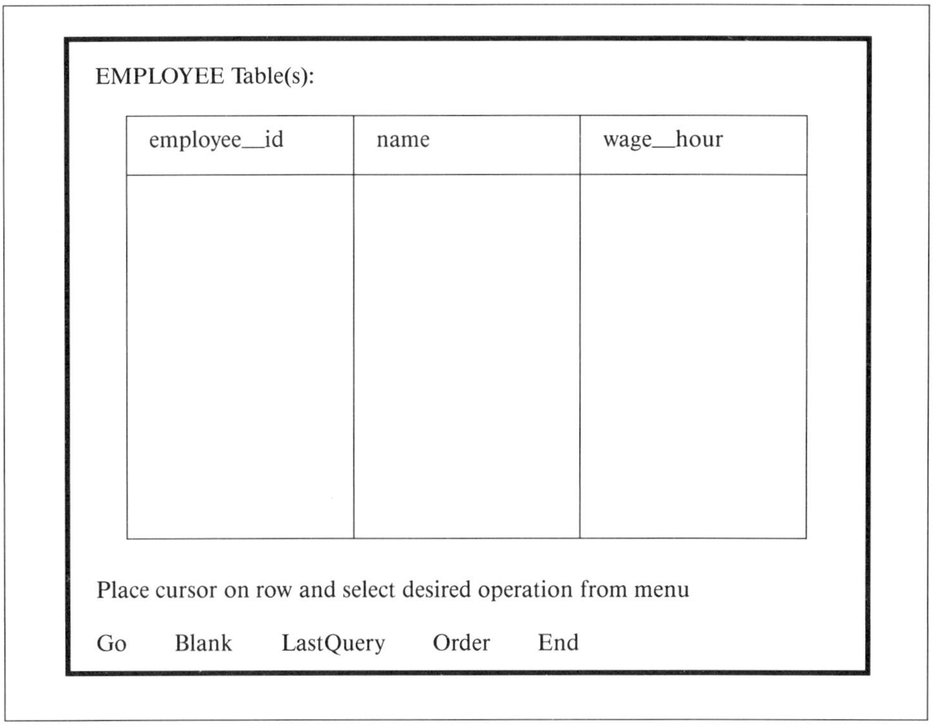

EMPLOYEE Table(s):

employee_id	name	wage_hour

Place cursor on row and select desired operation from menu

Go   Blank   LastQuery   Order   End

Figure 13.10   Tablefield

If the 'Go' option is selected, the simplest form of query is executed, this being an operation to retrieve all rows from the table, as shown in Figure 13.11.

It is possible, however, to compose more complex queries by inserting data into the columns of the tablefield prior to selecting 'Go'. For example: inserting the value 'AB1' into the 'employee_id' column and selecting 'Go' would retrieve a row giving details about the employee (Fred) with that personnel number; inserting '3' into the 'wage' column would retrieve rows for all employees earning £3 per hour, that is AB1 and AB3; inserting '3' into the 'wage' column and 'Jim' into the 'name' column would retrieve rows for employee AB3 only. The comparison operators $<$, $>$, $=$ etc. can also be used to qualify retrieval operations, for example '> 3' entered into the 'wage' column prior to selecting 'Go' would retrieve rows for all employees earning more than £3 per hour, that is employees AB2 and AB4. It is also possible to retrieve rows using pattern matching in a similar fashion to the use of the SQL 'like' operator.

All the above operations would also have been possible if the 'simplefield' option had been selected on entry to the QBF, the only difference being that rows would be returned one at a time, with scrolling being available when the query returned more than one row. Had 'joindefs' been selected rather than 'tables' at the outset, the retrieval operations would have been carried out across more than one table.

236 *Relational database management systems*

EMPLOYEE Table(s):

employee_id	name	wage_hour
AB1	Fred	3
AB2	Jim	3.5
AB3	Jim	3
AB4	John	3.4

Place cursor on row and select desired operation from menu

Go   Blank   LastQuery   Order   End

Figure 13.11   Selecting all rows from a table

Selection of the 'update' option from the menu:

Append   Retrieve   Update   Help Quit

which was displayed after entry into QBF would provide all the selection capabilities overviewed above and additionally enable the user to modify or delete data in the retrieved rows. Selection of the 'append' option would enable the user to add new rows to the tables.

From the above it can be seen that a simple database can be implemented and simple insertion, update, deletion and retrieval operations carried out on it without needing to use any other tool than QBF. However, the forms automatically created by it cannot be saved for later reuse and the user cannot tailor them to his or her particular requirements. Where reusable forms of a more sophisticated design are required by an application, the designer will choose the 'forms' option from the main menu.

The Forms Option — INGRES Vifred

INGRES Vifred (Visual Forms Editor) is a frame based utility which can be entered from the INGRES menu by selecting the 'forms' operation, or by an operating system level command. It is used to create and modify screen forms, tailored to a users needs, which can be saved for reuse. The forms created or modified using Vifred can be used by a variety of other INGRES tools including QBF (which can be entered directly from Vifred), ESQL and ABF/4GL.

The forms option 237

On entering VIFRED the user is presented with a screen frame similar to that shown in Figure 13.12. This screen lists all the forms which can be accessed by the user, giving the name of the form, its owner and a short description of the form's purpose. A list of menu choices is given at the foot of the screen as usual. The user can elect to create a new form, edit an existing form, destroy an existing form, 'run' a form (using 'Go') or ask for more information about the form selected on the screen.

VIFRED — Forms Catalogue

Name	Owner	Short Remark
staff	vocca	Default form for employee table
order	vocca	Multiple entry form for orders

Place cursor on row and select desired operation from menu

Create   Destroy   Edit   Rename   Go   Moreinfo > :

Figure 13.12   VIFRED forms catalogue

Suppose that the designer wishes to create a new form. He or she would then choose the 'create' option, and another screen would appear offering him/her the choice of starting with a default form (as shown in the earlier QBF examples) or a completely blank form. If a default form is chosen, the user will be asked to select whether it is to be from a table or a joindef and, when that selection has been made, to name the table or joindef to be used. Once again the user will be asked to choose between a simplefield (one row displayed in the form) or a tablefield (multiple rows) and the resultant default form will be displayed for editing in a 'Vifred form layout frame'. At this point, having created the default form, Vifred will allow its designer to name and save it.

238   *Relational database management systems*

(*Note*:   This name can be used to access the form from QBF under the QBFNames option which was discussed earlier.)

The menu for the Vifred forms layout frame includes the following choices:

Create   Delete   Edit   Move   Order   FormAttr   Location

The *Create* option allows the designer to create new components on the form. Vifred components are either *fields,* for entry, retrieval, etc of data, or *trim*. Trim is 'dressing' information on the form which cannot be altered when it is in use, such as field names, lines, boxes and the like.

The *Delete* option is used to delete components, for example, it could be used to delete those fields in a default form which are not required for the application the form is being implemented to serve.

The *Edit* option calls up another menu which enables the designer to modify the component pointed to by the screen cursor.

The *Move* option enables components to be re-positioned on the form.

The *Order* option enables the designer to define the order in which the fields in the form are accessed when it is used for database access.

The *FormAttr* option determines overall attributes that the form should have. For example it can be used to make the form full screen or to make it a *pop-up* form. A pop-up form, as its name suggests, is one which overlays rather than replaces an existing screen form during its operation. Pop-up forms are very useful as a means for conveying prompts and messages to the user of a forms based application and for supplementing the information contained in the main form with other information such as lists of allowable values for fields.

Each of the above options take the user into further frames with further menu options allowing him or her to specify for example: form field names which are different from but correlated with column names in the database tables; validity checks to be applied on field values when the form is used for the input of data; whether or not fields can have a null value; etc.

The Reports Option - INGRES RBF

This will be dealt with shortly under 'Report Generation'.

The Applications Option

Selection of this option from the INGRES menu takes the user into INGRES ABF/4GL which is discussed next.

13.3.2.3   INGRES 4GL

INGRES ABF/4GL (Applications By Forms/Fourth Generation Language) can be entered from the INGRES menu by selecting 'applications' or by an operating system level command. It is INGRES's prime, non-conventional programming language tool for the creation of simple to complex, on line, screen forms based applications.

The components of an ABF application are a collection of screen frames of various types. Some of these frames will have 4GL code associated with them and other frames can be called from within this code thus linking up the frames into a single application. The 4GL code can also include calls to 4GL or 3GL procedures. The application designer can specify different orders and selections of frames to suit the needs of particular users of the application.

Four types of frame can be specified:

User defined frames are the fundamental building blocks of INGRES ABF/4GL applications. They consist of a form and a menu part similar to the standard INGRES frames which have already been illustrated. The form part of a user frame is created using Vifred and incorporated into the application. The menu part of the frame is created by 4GL code written to accompany the form. This code can itself call further 4GL or conventional language procedures and can include embedded SQL statements. The selection of a menu item on a user defined frame during running of the ABF application will cause the 4GL code to be activated. It is also possible to define 4GL code which will be activated at run time when the user leaves a specified field in a form, on specific key activations by a user, or when a preset timeout period has elapsed. The first frame of any ABF application is likely to be a menu with the form part of the frame giving instructions to the user as to what he/she can do, and the menu part allowing the user to make a choice amongst the options. The designer can incorporate user help facilities into any user frame.

QBF frames can be included in an ABF application. No 4GL code is required for a QBF frame. The form part of a QBF frame is either a named form created using VIFRED or an automatically generated QBF default form which has been given a name. The QBF frame is itself given a name and can be called from 4GL code in a user frame. The menu part of a QBF frame is the standard menu provided to a user when running any QBF frame. On finishing with QBF, the user will be returned to the next frame in the ABF application. The ABF application designer can place restrictions on what the user can do using the frame during QBF operations, for example the application user may only be allowed to retrieve data from the database, not to update or append it.

Report frames reference reports created using the INGRES Report Writer (described later). The frame consists of a report and a menu for running it. No 4GL code is required for ABF report frames. When the report has been run, control is passed back to the 4GL code of the user frame which called it.

The 4GL code associated with a user defined frame can consist of one or more of the following:

- An initialisation section
- One or more menu activation sections
- One or more field activation sections
- One or more key activation sections
- One or more timeout activation sections

SQL statements can be incorporated into these sections and 4GL, conventional language and database procedures can be called from within them.

240 *Relational database management systems*

An *initialisation section*, if specified, is always placed at the start of the 4GL code. It will be activated when the 4GL code's frame is called whether from another frame or procedure or at start up of the application. The initialisation section is used to declare 'hidden' fields in the form's simplefields or 'hidden columns' in the forms tablefields. Hidden fields and columns are a convenient means for storing and manipulating data which the form user does not need to see. They correspond to conventional program variables. The initialisation section can also include a sequence of 4GL statements to be run every time the frame is activated. Suppose that a user frame contained a simplefield form, 'employee-form', equivalent to that depicted in Figure 13.9. The initialisation section:

```
initialize
        (hourly__wage = integer) =
begin
        hourly__wage = 0;
end
```

would declare a hidden field on the form for an employee's hourly wage and set it to the value zero each time the form was entered. This field could then be used by 4GL code in calculations related to an employee's wage.

A *menu activation section* is used to define the name of a menu item to appear with the frame for display on the user's screen and to specify a sequence of 4GL code statements to be activated when the user selects that menu item during running of the frame. A very simple example would be:

```
'Quit' =
begin
        message 'Quitting application...';
        sleep 5;
        exit;
end
```

This would cause the menu item 'Quit' to be displayed each time the frame was displayed and, if selected by the user during the running of the frame, would cause the message 'Quitting Application...' to be displayed on the user's screen for five seconds and the application to be terminated.

A *field activation section* is used to define what happens when a user exits from the specified field during running of the frame. Again using a simple field form, 'employee__form', based on the 'employee' table as an example, the field activation section:

```
field employee__id =
begin
        if  employee__id = NULL then
            message 'Please enter employee number';
            sleep 3;
```

Report generation   241

```
       else
            employee__form = select name, wage__hour
                             from employee
                             where employee__id = :employee__id;
                             resume;
            endif;
end
```

will check whether the user has entered a value for the employee's personnel number when he has exited from the employee__id field on the form and, if not, request him/her to do so. On entry of the number, the SQL SELECT query will transfer the appropriate column values from the 'employee' table into the form's fields.

Key and timeout activation sections can be specified in the 4GL in much the same manner as field activations.

13.3.2.4   Report Generation

INGRES provides two tools for the generation of reports, namely:

- Report by Forms (RBF) — A menu/forms driven facility for the production of the simpler ad hoc or regular reports.
- Report Writer — A programmable tool for the production of the more complex regular reports.

The Reports Option — INGRES RBF

Selecting the 'report' operation from the INGRES menu takes the user into the INGRES RBF (Report by Forms) tool, which is an interactive, frames based, interface for the production of reports from the database to screen, file or printer. On entry into RBF, the user is presented with a frame similar to that shown in Figure 13.13. Selecting an existing report from the catalogue followed by 'Go' will run the report.

Assuming that a new report were required, the quickest way to produce it would be select the 'AutoReport' option from the menu. The user would then be asked to name the table or joindef to be reported on and the file for the report to be sent to, and the report would be generated automatically and sent to the file. It could then be printed using the appropriate host operating system command. The reports produced by this means are, of course, very rudimentary. It is not possible to leave out unrequired columns from the report or to sort it into a required order or to do any aggregations on column values, etc.

Alternatively, a designer could select the 'Create' option from the menu. He or she would then be prompted through a series of frames which would allow a precise definition of the designer's requirements for the report to be specified. The resultant report definition would then be saved and could be rerun at any time. Selection of the 'Create' option would result in the following menu being displayed:

BlockMode   ColumnMode   WrapMode   DefaultMode

The first three items indicate the possible report formats which can be generated using RBF. In *BlockMode,* each row retrieved from the database is presented as a separate block

242 *Relational database management systems*

of data with the name of each column placed immediately to the left of its corresponding data value as in the following example:

employee__id:AB1   Name:Fred   Wage:3
employee__id:AB2   Name:Jim   Wage:3.5
etc.

RBF — Report Catalogue

Name	Owner	Short Remark
staff	vocca	Report showing staff details
order	vocca	Report showing order details

Place cursor on row and select desired operation from menu

Create   Destroy   Edit   Rename   Moreinfo   AutoReport   Utilities   Go

---

Figure 13.13   RBF catalogue frame

In *ColumnMode,* the data is presented in the familiar tabular form as columns across the page. *Wrap* format is similar to column format, except that if there are too many columns to fit into a page, the columns which cannot be fitted are wrapped around and fitted on the next row. If the *DefaultMode* option is taken, RBF decides on the optimum mode of presentation. RBF automatically adds date, time and page numbers to a report regardless of which format is chosen.

After the format selection has been made, RBF will present a frame showing the report layout. If the user is satisfied with this it can be saved. Alternatively, it can be modified by selecting operations from the menu in the report layout frame which includes the following choices:

Create   Delete   Edit   Move   Order   ReportOptions   Save

The first four of these perform similar functions for a report as the same choices in the

Vifred forms layout menu which was discussed earlier, allowing the designer to tailor the report's header and main body to his/her requirement. The *Order* operation takes the designer into further frames which define how the report is to be sorted and also to establish break columns, run time parameters and aggregations. Breaks mark a change in value in a report column which is designated both as a sort column and a break column. For example, if a post code (Zip Code) column is designated as both a sort and break column, then items in the report (perhaps customer's names, current order values and addresses) would be grouped together by post code and each time the post code changed there would be a break point in the report. At each break, RBF would allow for a variety of ways of visually separating the items grouped by post code and for introducing, for example, sub-totals for order values for customers in the various postal districts. The *ReportOptions* operation allows the user to specify, inter alia, the page length and form feed characteristics for the report. Reports created and saved using RBF can be further edited using the more sophisticated INGRES Report Writer tool.

INGRES Report Writer

This tool is entered at the operating system command level. Whilst RBF is adequate for the simpler type of regular or ad hoc report, major regular reports from the database such as financial statements, inventory reviews and payroll output are likely to require much more sophisticated control over the layout, format and content of the report and more sophisticated calculatuions than can be achieved using RBF.

INGRES Report Writer provides a high level language for the custom production of simple to very complex report definitions, incorporating features such as the ability to use embedded SQL statements, decision loops, the ability to declare and use variables, powerful arithmetic capabilities, handling of nulls, the inclusion of parameters to enable the user to specify specific reporting requirements at run time and complete and comprehensive control over the appearance of the report, including headers, footers and numeric and text formats.

13.3.3 DBA Tools

The DBA has available to him/her the full range of user tools already described. Additionally the role can make use of a some special SQL commands and a range of operating system level commands. Note that any user with the requisite authority can use these facilities, but, under normal circumstances, they would be used only by the DBA.

SQL Commands

The Modify Command

The INGRES MODIFY command is used, inter alia, to convert the storage structure of a table or index from its current form to some other. INGRES supports the following underlying logical storage structures for tables and indices:

- ISAM. Index sequential access method. (See Chapter 2)
- HASH. Hash-random access method. (See Chapter 2)
- HEAP. An unkeyed and unstructured storage method.

244   *Relational database management systems*

- BTREE. A dynamic, tree structured storage organisation.

All of these structures can be specified to be in compressed form, and a sorted form of HEAP storage can be specified. The selection of which to use for a given table or index has important performance implications which are fully explained in the INGRES documentation. The MODIFY command can also be used to change the physical placement of tables and indexes in or across disk volumes. A very simple example of the use of the MODIFY command is given by the statement:

modify employee
to isam **on** name;

This would ensure that the 'employee' table was stored in an underlying ISAM storage structure with 'name' as the keyed column.

Set Command

The INGRES SET command is used to set up various options for an INGRES session. It can be issued both from interactive and embedded SQL. Its options include the ability to SET ON or SET OFF:

- RESULT STRUCTURE. Used to set the default underlying storage structure for tables, that is to HEAP, ISAM, HASH or BTREE.

- JOURNALLING. Used to set journalling on or off for a specific table in the database.

Copy Table Command

The INGRES SQL COPY TABLE command allows data to be copied from a standard file onto a database table and vice versa. This is a comprehensive command with many options including the ability to specify rollback on encountering errors, to terminate or continue on errors, to specify how nulls should be handled, to specify the file type being written to, to log rows which cannot be processed to a specified file, to specify delimiters in a file being copied from, and so forth.

The following example illustrates the simplest form of the COPY command used to write data from a file into a table:

copy table employee
        (name = C20, age = c3, department = c20, xyz = d1)
from 'myfile';

The command assumes that 'myfile' consists of fixed length fields of 20, 3 and 20 characters corresponding to employee names, ages and department names respectively. Each group of three fields is delimited by a newline character. Note that the dummy column name 'xyz', which has no equivalent in the table 'employee' and which is specified as 'd1' (meaning one byte long) is simply skipped during execution of the command, thus skipping the newline delimiting character. The 'employee' table must, of course, contain the columns 'name', 'age' and 'department' formatted as specified.

The table 'employee' might be written to the file 'myfile' by the COPY TABLE

Operating system level commands 245

command as follows:

copy table employee
       (name = c0comma, age = c0comma, department = c0nl)
into 'myfile';

A table 'employee' is again assumed with columns 'name', 'age' and 'department'. The 'c0comma' format indicate that values in the 'name' and 'age' columns of the table are to be transferred to the file as variable length character strings with a following delimiting comma. The c0nl format against the 'department' column name indicates that this is to be transferred as a variable length character string followed by a new line character as a delimiter.

Operating System Level Commands

INGRES supports a number of commands which are entered at the level of the computer's operating system. These include commands specific to the DBA function. They are concerned with the overall creation of databases, their organisation, back up and so forth, and the most important of them are listed and described below.

An understanding of some of these commands must be predicated by an understanding of *journalling* in INGRES. Journals are files which record changes to tables in the database. Journalling is switched on for specified tables in the database. To enable journalling on a particular table, the journalling option in the CREATE TABLE or SET commands can be used. At reasonably frequent intervals, as determined by the DBA, a 'snapshot' of the database is taken and saved to disk or tape as back up to the online database. This is known as a checkpoint. When a database recovery is necessary, the database can be recreated from the checkpoint by applying the journals to it, that is, by applying all the changes which have taken place since the checkpoint was taken.

Auditdb

The auditdb command allows the DBA to print selected portions of journals and to create audit files of changes made to specified tables.

Createdb

This command enables the DBA to create an INGRES database. The creator of the database using createdb becomes the DBA for that database. The locations on disk(s) in which the database is to be held can be specified. Database access rights are specified in an access*db* command or, by default, a database becomes public to all users. Note that this gives access to the database as such, but not to specific tables within it. Access to tables within a database is given by the SQL GRANT command, whether by the original creator of the table or by the DBA.

Destroydb

Destroys an existing database. Obviously to be used by the DBA with extreme care. An

246   *Relational database management systems*

option exists to make the command default to a form where the DBA is always asked 'are you sure?' before it is executed.

Ckpdb

The ckpdb (checkpoint database) command is used to create a static copy of an entire database for back up purposes and marks all journal entries up to the time at which the checkpoint was taken as expired. Options exist to write the database to magnetic tape rather than disk and to enable or disable journalling of the database after the checkpoint. A checkpoint is a snapshot of the database at the time it is taken.

Rollforwarddb

This command is used to recover a database, when necessary, by applying the current journals to the last checkpoint taken. Recovery can be from disk or from magnetic tape depending on where the checkpoint was stored. Optionally a specified database or all databases in the system can be recovered. Note that the database need not be journalised to enable use of the rollforwarddb command. If it is not, the command will simply restore the database to the condition it was in when the last checkpoint was taken.

Copydb

The DBA (or any user) can make a back up copy of all base tables owned by him/her in a specified database and later, if required, restore these tables, by first making use of the copydb command. The command creates two files. The *copy.out* file contains SQL instructions to copy all the tables owned by the users to a directory specified in the copydb command. The *copy.in* file contains SQL instructions to copy files from the directory named in the copydb command into tables in the specified database, create indexes and perform modifications. Subsequent to use of the copydb command, the user must run the copy.out and copy.in files of SQL statements in order to make back up copies of the tables and restore them respectively.

Unloaddb

The operation of the unloaddb command is similar to that of the copydb command, but it operates across the entire database. In addition to base tables, views, graphs, forms, etc, are unloaded. Again, two SQL command files, *unload.ing* and *reload.ing,* are created by the command which must run by the DBA to create a back up copy of the database and to restore it respectively.

Sysmod

This command allows the DBA to instruct the system to modify the underlying logical storage structure automatically (ISAM, HASH, etc.) for database tables for optimum query processing. Sysmod can be run on a whole database or on specified tables within it.

Overview of ORACLE 247

Optimisedb

By issuing this command, the DBA causes the system to generate and store statistics for use by INGRES's internal query optimiser facility in selecting an efficient query processing strategy. The command specifies specific tables and columns within those tables within a specified database. After issuing the optimisedb command it is normal to run the sysmod command.

In addition to the above operating system level commands, and others not listed, the INGRES DBA can be expected to make extensive use of the SQL CREATE TABLE/VIEW/INDEX commands, the GRANT (privileges) command, the corresponding DROP commands and the SET command.

13.3.4 Operational User Tools

The average operational user with little or no computer experience can be trained quickly to use the QBF and RBF tools for database access purposes. Note that normal access controls to tables and views apply even where the data they contain is accessed via these tools, thus enabling the database contents to be protected from inadvertent damage by inexperienced users. Additionally, all frames which such users see in interacting with developed applications have the same 'look and feel', thus reducing the training required for operational users to use different applications.

13.4 Overview of ORACLE

The overview of the ORACLE Inc ORACLE RDBMS product which follows is structured along the same lines as the general treatment of RDBMSs given at the beginning of the chapter. The following sections describe:

- Architecture
- System Development Tools
    - SQL
    - Forms Management
    - 4GL
    - Report Generation
- DBA Tools
- Operational User Tools

13.4.1 ORACLE Architecture

ORACLE is organised into a central, *kernel* part and a variety of interfaced tools which make use of it.

The general organisation of the product is shown conceptually in Figure 13.14. The kernel part of the structure is responsible for the definition and storage of data, database access control and concurrent access handling, back up and recovery of the database and interpretation of SQL commands. Although some of the user interfaces provided by ORACLE tools do not require the use of SQL on the part of their users, the interface between all tools and the kernel is driven by SQL commands and the responses the kernel makes to them. ORACLE provides full support for communications networking and distributed databases with its SQL*Net and SQL*Star products.

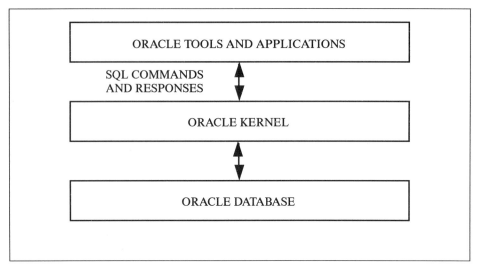

Figure 13.14 ORACLE conceptual structure

A representative set of the major user tools which interact with the kernel are shown in Figure 13.15

13.4.2 Development Tools

13.4.2.1 SQL

Interactive SQL

ORACLE supports all the SQL commands described in Chapter 12, or implements their function (such as lock control) in a different manner, and also gives explicit support for the relational model operators UNION, INTERSECT and MINUS (DIFFERENCE). The additions to these basic SQL commands provided by ORACLE's SQL are too numerous to be fully covered here, but a few characteristic examples follow.

Create Database Command (DBA use only)

This command enables the DBA to create a new database. Its options include the ability to specify a name for the database and specify the name and size of a series of files to hold it. The files which can be specified include data files which hold actual user data and redo log files which will be used to hold changes to the database since the last back up dump of it was taken.

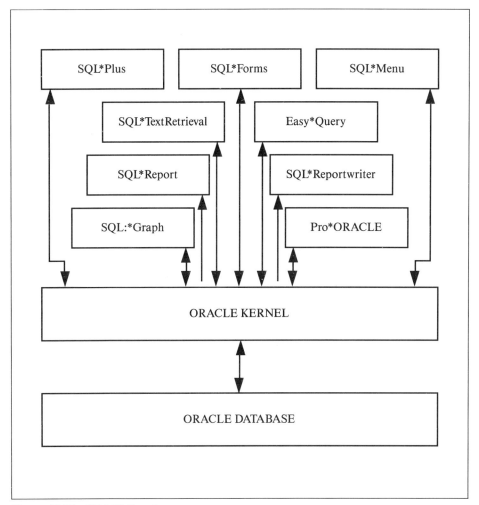

Figure 13.15 ORACLE tools

Create Sequence Command

This command is used to create a database object from which multiple users can obtain a series of unique integers. The objective of the command is to provide a means for the automatic generation of primary key values. The command includes the options to: set the interval between sequence numbers and whether they are to be generated in ascending or descending order; set the starting value for the number sequence; set maximum and minimum values; specify whether the sequence should start again when a maximum or minimum value is reached; specify that the numbers should be generated in the order of request. The dummy column 'nextval' is used in query statments to obtain the next sequence number value. The dummy column 'currval' can be used to obtain the current value of the sequence number. The name of the sequence must precede the 'currval' or 'nextval' as in 'sequence__name.currval'.

250   *Relational database management systems*

Create Database Link Command

This command allows to specify and name a link to a remote database. The user must have access to and specify a user name and password recognised by the remote database. For example, the statement:

create database link London
connect to vocca
identified by val__0
using 'D:London__Office';

would create a link named 'London' for a user with user id 'vocca' and password val__0 with a database called 'London__Office' at a remote location on the network.

Once specified, a database link enables the users to access tables within the remote database, using the link's name to qualify the remote database table names. The following statement:

select*
from employee@London;

executed by user 'vocca' would retrieve all data from the 'employee' table in the remote 'London__office' database.

Create Synonym Command

This command allows the user to create a synonym for a table, view or sequence name. The table or view or sequence can subsequently be accessed using the synonym. The synonym will normally be created as private to its creator as identified by his/her user name. The DBA, however, can create a synonym as public to all users. A synonym can also be defined for a table in a remote database link as in:

create synonym employee
for employee@LONDON

The owner of the link can now access the 'employee' table in the 'London__office' remote database by simply using the name 'employee'.

(*Note*:   There are also 'DROP' versions of all the above commands.)

SQL*Plus

SQL*Plus, which runs in the same interactive environment as the other ORACLE SQL commands, extends the language to provide a variety of useful facilities. These are too numerous for complete cover in this book, but some very frequently used examples are described in the following paragraghs.

Editing SQL Statements

When using interactive SQL at a terminal, as each SQL statement is entered it is stored in a buffer area. The statement remains there till a new statement is entered. Whilst it

Editing SQL statements 251

is in the buffer, it is possible to perform some simple edit operations on it using SQL*Plus commands, including:

APPEND (text to the end of a line)

CHANGE (delete/change text in a line)

DEL (delete current line)

INPUT (one or more lines)

The RUN command allows the command in the buffer to be executed. The SAVE command allows the buffer contents to be saved to a named file, for later repetitive running and the GET command allows the contents of the command file to be retrieved back into the buffer. The START command is used to run a command file directly. The EXIT command causes the system to leave SQL*Plus and return to the host operating system.

*SQL*Plus Report Commands*

Although ORACLE provides separate report generation facilities which will be described later, it also provides a range of SQL*Plus commands to assist with the preparation and formatting of reports of a simple tabular nature to be sent to screen or printer. These are discussed in the following paragraphs.

The Set Command

The SET command is used to control the environment in which an interactive session using SQL operates and some of its variants are used to control aspects of the format of reports, for example:

SET HEADING (Off or On)	Decides whether or not column headers are to be included in reports.
SET LINESIZE	Sets number of characters per line in a report.
SET PAGESIZE	Sets the number of lines per page of a report.
SET SPACE	Sets the number of spaces to be left between columns of a report.

The SHOW command can be used to find out the status of SET command variables.

The Column Command

The COLUMN command is used to establish various options with respect to the printing and display of a table column prior to the issue of a SELECT statement which references the table. The informal syntax for this command is:

COLUMN columnname or expression, list of options;

where columnname is the name of a column in the table to be referenced in the subsequent SELECT statement. Expressions can also be used exactly as these would appear in the subsequent SELECT statement. Many options are possible and can appear in any order in the option list. A few examples are given in this statement:

252 Relational database management systems

column comment **format** A20 **heading** 'REMARKS' **word_wrapped;**

which includes use of the options FORMAT, HEADING and WORD_WRAPPED. These options as specified in the example state that the column 'comment' in a subsequent SELECT statment is to be displayed as 20 characters wide, to have the heading 'REMARKS' and, in the event that the value obtained for it from the database exceeded 20 characters, that it was to be wrapped around at the end of the last possible complete word to fit within the 20 characters width.

The TTITLE and TTITLE Commands

The TTITLE and BTITLE SQL*Plus commands allow page headers and/or footers respectively to be displayed on each page of the report generated by the subsequent SELECT statement with automatic centring of the text. The BTITLE command also generates a date and page number on each page of the columnar report automatically.

The Break Command

The rows of a columnar report can be broken into sections by use of the SQL*Plus BREAK command. Blank lines can be left between sections or they can be started on new pages of the report. Breaks can be specified on columns, rows, pages, or the entire report. Suppose that the following BREAK statement:

break on order_number **skip** 1;

preceded the SELECT statement:

select order_number, item_name, quantity
from line_item
order by order_number;

was applied to the example 'order_item' table in Figure 12.2. The resultant report would be formatted as:

order-number	item_name	quantity
123	axe	100
	spade	50
124	fork	34
	hoe	10
125	spade	25

The Compute Command

The COMPUTE command can be used in conjuntion with the BREAK command to apply the various SQL aggregating functions (AVG, COUNT, MAX, MIN, etc.) to the specified columns at the break point. For example, the BREAK followed by COMPUTE statements:

break on order_number **skip** 1;
compute avg of quantity on order_number;

followed by the SQL statement:

select order_number, item_name, quantity
from order_item
order by order-number;

would result in the following report:

order-number	item_name	quantity
123	axe	100
	spade	50
***************		---------------------------
		150
124	fork	34
	hoe	10
***************		---------------------------
		44
125	spade	25
***************		---------------------------
		25

The Spool Command

The output obtained from SELECT statements is normally directed only to the user's screen. In order to send this output to the printer, the SQL*Plus SPOOL command is used as in:

spool myfile;

The returns from subsequent SELECT statements will now be spooled to the file 'myfile' until spooling is turned off by the statement.

spool off;

The contents of the file can then be sent to a printer using the appropriate operating system command.

If printing the contents of 'myfile' to the system default printer were required immediately, then instead of issuing the above statement, the statement;

spool out;

would be issued.

The SQL*Plus statements used to produce a report can be saved in a command file to enable repetitive running of the report.

254 *Relational database management systems*

Tracing Hierarchical Relationships Within Tables

SQL*Plus also includes the facility to trace hierarchical relationships within a database table. Suppose that a table 'employee' included a column 'manager' giving the personnel number of an employee's immediate manager and that this table were populated as follows:

personnel-number	department	job	manager
100	sales	salesman	300
400	inventory	manager	1000
200	inventory	clerk	400
500	sales	clerk	300
700	accounts	accountant	800
900	inventory	storeman	400
1000	main board	director	NULL
300	sales	manager	1000
1200	inventory	clerk	1000
800	accounts	manager	1000
1300	accounts	clerk	800

The statements:

break on department **skip** 1;

select department, personnel__number, job
from employee
connect by prior personnel__number = manager
start with manager = null
order by department;

would result in the following report being returned:

level	department	personnel-number	job
2	accounts	800	manager
3		700	accountant
3		1300	clerk
2	inventory	400	manager
3		200	clerk
3		900	storeman
1	main board	1000	director
2	sales	300	manager
3		100	salesman
3		500	clerk

The CONNECT BY clause in the SELECT statement specified the two columns to be used in establishing the hierarchical relationship amongst rows of the table. PRIOR placed before 'personnel__number' in this clause indicated the direction the tree had to be 'walked' in compiling the report. The pseudo column, 'level', in the report shows how far each row is from the starting node of the tree.

Forms management 255

Pro*ORACLE, Embedded SQL

Pro*ORACLE is the collective name given to ORACLE's embedded SQL products, each host language having its own precompiler. All the special embedded SQL commands described in Chapter 12 are supported by ORACLE including those for dynamic SQL.

PL/SQL

The optional transaction processing extension to the ORACLE RDBMS supports PL/SQL, which extends the language to include procedural language constructs such as variable declarations, assignments, conditional control, program loops and exception handling.

13.4.2.2 Forms Management — SQL*Forms

SQL*Forms is ORACLE's major, non-conventional programming tool for the creation of simple to complex, on line, screen forms based applications. It is entered by a command issued at the operating system level. The tool is used for the creation and running of custom designed forms for the insertion, update, deletion and querying of tables in a database.

The running of forms created using SQL*Forms is based on use of a standard set of function keys for the operational user. The form designer can supplement this standard function key set with further keys to accomplish specific tasks only if required. Thus, the operational user does not have to learn a new set of keystrokes each time he/she encounters a new application.

The designer of an SQL*Forms application is also presented with a standard set of function keys to accomplish specific actions and is guided through the form creation process by a series of menus on the screen.

During this form creation process the designer can incorporate various checks into a form, for example specifying validation criteria for entry of data into specific fields and/or restricting access to the database from the form to, for example, retrieval only. Automatic generation of sequence numbers for specific fields can be specified and various calculations to be carried out on data in a database can be specified for display on the form.

Forms are described in terms of:

- *Pages*. A page is the part of a form seen on a screen. A form can have many pages.
- *Blocks*. A block represents the data and text in a form which correspond to one table in the database.
- *Base Tables*. The named base table upon which a block is based.
- *Records*. A record contains the data from one row of a table.
- *Fields*. A field is a highlighted or underlined area on the screen which can display a value, normally taken from a column in the base table for a block
- *Single Record Blocks*. Single record blocks display only one record (i.e. one base table row).
- *Multi-Record Blocks*. Multi-record blocks display more than one record (ie more than one base table row).

Figures 13.16 and 13.17 illustrate how an ORACLE form might appear on the user's screen. In the first Figure two blocks, making up the first page of the form, are displayed, one based on the 'customer' table of Figure 12.2 and the other on the 'order' table. The top block holds a single record and the lower one is a multi-record block. In the example, a single customer, 'Jones' is displayed in the single record block, and all orders placed by that customer are displayed in the multi-record block.

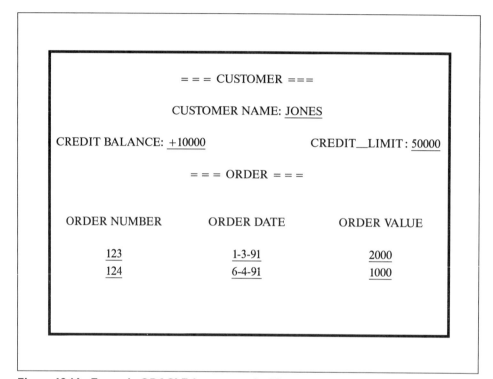

Figure 13.16 Example ORACLE form, page 1 of 2

The example shows only two rows containing orders and these fit easily on to the screen. Had there been more rows required for customer Jones' orders than could be fitted on the screen, the user would have been able to scroll up and down to see them.

The second page of the form as shown in Figure 13.17 includes a further multi-record block. This again shows the orders owned by customer 'Jones' and gives the name, unit price and quantity of each line item contained in the orders.

The user uses standard key strokes to move from page to page, block to block, record to record and field to field. Depending on what permissions have been designed into the form, its user might simply use it to browse through information about customers and their orders, might be able to insert new order or customer information, or update or delete existing information, again by the use of standard key strokes.

The facilities provided to the application designer by SQL*Forms are very comprehensive indeed and cannot be covered in full here. The next paragraphs, which introduce only a few of these facilities, are simply intended to give the reader a feel for how easy and quick it is to use the tool as compared with using traditional programming methods for creating screen form based, on line applications.

```
                    = = = ORDER ITEMS ===


ORDER NUMBER        ITEM NAME       UNIT PRICE      QUANTITY

      123              axe            £10             100
      123              spade          £20             50
      124              fork           £35             34
      124              hoe            £25             10
```

Figure 13.17   Example ORACLE form, page 2 of 2

When creating a form using SQL*Forms, the designer would first access the tool using the operating system level command *sqlforms*. This would result in a screen being displayed asking for a user name and a password. Assuming that the system was satisfied with the designer's response, a 'Choose Form' window would be displayed on the screen. The menu which this window gives to the designer includes the choice of whether to create a new form or modify or run an existing form. A field in the window allows the designer to enter a form's name. The form designer, like the user of a form is provided with a standard set of key strokes to use. These vary from system to system and from keyboard type to keyboard type within systems, but there are very few of them and their use quickly becomes intuitive. Keystrokes are specified for basic text editing within screen window fields, for cursor movement and for moving to the next and previous screen windows.

Assuming that the designer chooses to create a new form, the form's name will be typed in and the 'create' menu item will be selected. This will lead to overlaying of the 'Choose Form' window with a further, 'Choose Block' window. This window allows the designer to give a block a name, which may or may not correspond to the corresponding base table name for the block. It also provides a number of menu choices including whether to create a form from scratch or whether to create it with the assistance of an automatically produced default item form for the block. Assuming that the designer chooses the 'default' option, a further 'Default Block' window will overlay the previous two. The designer can now type in the number of table rows which are to be displayed on the form and the name of the base table to be used in its creation. The table name defaults to the name of the block. To assist in identifying the base table, the designer can call up a list of all database tables, (those which he has access rights to) in order that a selection can be made from them. At this point the screen would be similar to that depicted in Figure 13.18.

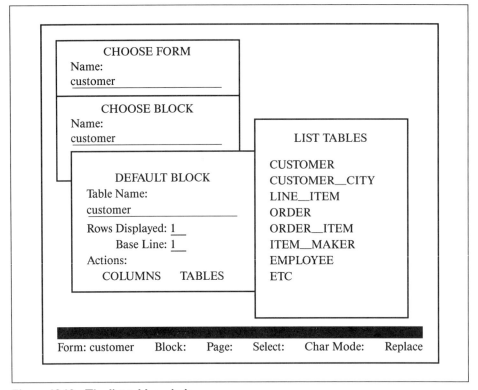

Figure 13.18 The list tables window

The designer can move through the items in the table highlighting each until the cursor is against the one required and then select it. Now, by selecting the 'columns' menu item from the 'Default Block' window, the designer will cause a further window to appear containing a list of all the columns in the selected base table. The screen now appears as in Figure 13.19. At this point the columns to be included in the form can be selected and the choice of columns can be saved to working memory using standard key strokes.

If this block is all that is required in the customer form, the designer could now return to the 'Choose Form' window and select 'Save' from that window's menu to store the form permanently. It could then be generated by selecting the 'Generate' option from the same menu and would then be ready to be run. To the user the form would look similar to that shown in Figure 13.20. The process of creating a simple form like the one just described would take much less time than it has taken to write the above paragraphs about it.

Simple form 259

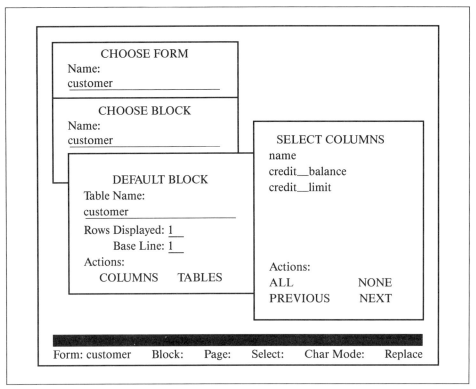

Figure 13.19 The select columns window

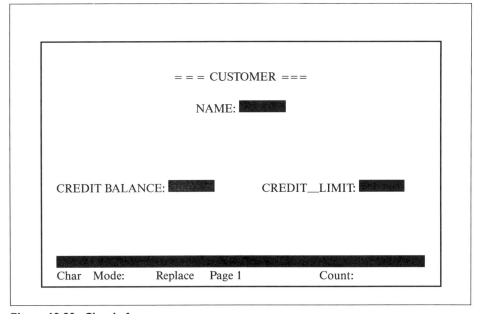

Figure 13.20 Simple form

260   *Relational database management systems*

In practice, of course, more sophisticated forms than the above are usually required. The example form could have been extended to include more pages containing more single or multiple record blocks using the simple techniques already described. It is also possible to create custom forms using SQL*Form's 'screen paint' feature, this would simply have meant making the choice of 'create' from the 'Choose Block' window's menu rather than 'default', as in the above example. Normally, a designer will initially create a form block by using the default option and later tailor it to exact requirements using the screen paint feature.

It is possible for the designer, by simple menu choices, to define very precisely the characteristics of fields on a form which will apply later when the form is being run. For example, it is possible to define: whether they are to hold characters, numbers, dates or money, etc; whether an entry in a field by a user is to be mandatory or not; whether or not a field is to be displayed to the user (it might simply be used to retrieve values from the database for calculation purposes); whether or not the user can enter and/or update data in a field or have retrieval rights only; the order in which fields will be accessed when the form is run. This list is by no means exhaustive, but gives an indication of how quite sophisticated forms based can be developed quickly without recourse to anything other than SQL*Forms windows and their menus.

*SQL*Menu*

SQL*Menu allows the designer to incorporate comprehensive user menus into ORACLE applications regardless of which tools were used in their development. It can also be used with non-ORACLE applications (though it does require the support of ORACLE kernel and SQL*Forms).

Menus developed using this tool can be a hierarchical tree structure, with selection of an item on one menu calling up a further menu and so forth down to any reasonable level of nesting. Users can progress up and down this menu structure or move directly from one menu or option to another.

Menus can be designed to be configurable dynamically according to the keyed in identity of their run time users. This feature can be used to enforce overall restrictions over the functions available to individual users of a specific application. For example one user might be allowed access to a part of an application which allows him/her to view personnel data and others might not since the appropriate menu option would not have been provided to them. The menu facility only displays those menus and options to which the user has been granted access.

Operating system commands to activate specific parts of an application can be made transparent to the user who simply has to make a selection from the menu and if the command demands the input of parameters, the user can also be prompted for these. Operating system commands can also be used directly from within the menu structure.

The designer using SQL*Menu to produce user friendly front ends for his/her applications is guided through his task by windows which include fill in fields and menus in the same simple manner as overviewed earlier for SQL*Forms.

Report generation 261

13.4.2.3 '4GL' — ORACLE Triggers in SQL*Forms

ORACLE do not use the term '4GL', but provide a similar type of capability as part of SQL*Forms, in that it is possible to design *triggers* into forms. Triggers can be defined at the form, block and field levels. Triggers cause the activation of a sequence of code after some specific event takes place during the running of a form, like entry into or exit from a specified field. The code triggered can be written in an extended form of SQL/SQL*Plus, or can be written in PL/SQL, or can cause exits to be made into procedures written in a conventional language such as COBOL or FORTRAN. It is also possible to call one form from another thus linking multiple forms into one application.

At the form level a trigger can be defined to be activated just before the form is entered or just after it is exited. It is also possible at this level to define triggers which operate gobally across the form. For example, triggers can be defined to operate: every time any block is entered in the form or every time one is exited from; prior to or after any query operation performed using a form; prior to or after any update is performed; and so on.

At the block level a trigger can be defined for activation prior to a particular block in a form being entered or after it has been exited from. Triggers can also be defined for activation pre and post any query and/or update and/or insert and/or delete operations carried out during use of a particular block in a form. Further triggers can be defined for activation before and after entry to all records and/or fields in a particular form block, including the option to activate a trigger only after a field's contents have been changed.

At the field level a trigger can be defined for activation any time a particular field within a particular block of a particular form is entered or exited, including the option of activating a trigger only when a particular field's value is changed.

The definition of triggers is supported by multiple windows with menu choices in much the same manner as has already been described for simple form design. The designer normally uses SQL statements in implementing triggers. He/she can also send messages to the user's screen giving instructions or indicating an error and can also also define inputs to be provided by the user. Triggers can also be used to exit to a procedure written in a conventional language or in PL/SQL.

13.4.2.4 Report Generation

During the description of SQL*Plus, it was shown that moderately sophisticated tabular reports could be produced using the extended commands available with the language. ORACLE also provide a further two user tools for the production of the more sophisticated reports.

*SQL*Report*

SQL*Report extends the ORACLE SQL product's capability in respect of report generation to enable the production of reports with many levels of nesting, multiple breaks on columns, a wide variety of subtotals and totals and comprehensive control over tabulation, page and margin settings, page numbering and spacing and placement of text in the reports generated.

SQL*Report actually consists of two sub-products, RPT and RPF. RPT uses SQL

262   *Relational database management systems*

statements to access the database for information to be included in reports. RPF formats this information according to a series of RPF command lines. Briefly, the process of producing a report using SQL*Report proceeds along the following lines:

Firstly, a *report control file* is produced using any standard text editor. This file contains the SQL statements required to obtain information from a database and RPF formatting command lines which determines how the information is to be presented in the report.

Next, this file is processed by RPT, which retrieves information from the database according to the SQL statements specified in the file. The result is an interim file which contains both the formatting instructions and the information to be formatted.

Finally, the interim file can be processed by RPF in order to produce the report, which can be either to a screen or to a printer. The report control file is a program which is written using the language provided by SQL*Report. This includes conventional program language constructs such as variable declaration and assignment and branch instructions as well as a special form of the SQL SELECT command, and the formatting commands.

*SQL*Report Writer*

The difference when using SQL*ReportWriter compared with using SQL*Report is that the process of creating the report is window/menu driven in a manners similar to creating forms using SQL*Forms. Use of SQL*ReportWriter is much less akin to a programming activity than use of SQL*Report and hence more accessible to the less skilled user, although a knowledge of SQL and of the general organisation of a relational database is required. It is also quicker. A report created using SQL*ReportWriter can contain the following types of objects. All individuals objects are given uniquely identfying names by the designer when he/she creates a report.

Named *Queries* define the data to be retrieved from the database. Each report must contain at least one query. A query is an SQL SELECT statement. Data from multiple queries can be combined into a single report. The queries might be unrelated, for example, the report might contain simple lists of orders and products side by side. The queries more commonly will be related. For example, to create a master/detail report the query returning the master data would be specified as the parent of the query returning detail data. In the report, the detail data would be nested within the master data as in the example given in Figure 13.21. It is also possible to define matrix reports and to parameterise the queries so that column values can be typed in by the form user for use by the SELECT statement at run time.

Named *Fields* are used to hold the results of queries or calculations. Fields correspond to the columns named in the SELECT statement and take the data type of columns by default. In creating a report, the designer is able to specify a number of settings for a field, including: the relative position of fields in relationship to each other in terms of lines and spaces; the type of calculation to be used to calculate the value of a computed field or the column name in the SELECT statement used to retrieve a value for the field; the field's display format.

Named *Groups* are collections of fields. Groups can be derived by default from a query or created by assignment of fields to the named group. Each group is normally associated with one named query, but the designer can create multiple groups within one query if extra levels of nesting are required in the report. Groups can be positioned in a report in a similar fashion to fields by relative positioning with respect to other groups. The direction of printing and spacing of records (retrieved table rows) can be specified, for example one beneath the other or as a matrix of values. Groups are the basis of page break specifications by the report designer.

```
Order Number
--------
123
                Item Name   Quantity
                _____
                axe         100

                spade       50


Order Number
--------
124
                Item Name   Quantity
                _____
                fork        34

                hoe         10
```

Figure 13.21   SQL*ReportWriter master/detail

Named *Summary* objects are simply a special kind of field defined to hold subtotal, running total and grand total calculations. Any field in a report can be summarised, including fields which hold calculations. All the usual SQL aggregate functions can be used in creating summaries.

Named *Text* objects can be used to add text to a report, including a title page, report and page headers and footers and various text objects associated with report groups. Text objects can reference fields and summaries as well as system variables such as PAGE (number) and DATE.

Named *Report* objects are complete SQL*ReportWriter report specifications. Settings which can be specified for a report as a whole include page length and width, margins and whether the report is to be output to a file, screen or printer.

For the most part, the designer of a report using SQL*Forms is prompted through the process, as stated earlier, by a series of screen windows containing menus and form like 'fill' in fields in a manner similar to that already illustrated for the creation of forms using SQL*Forms.

SQL*TextRetrieval

Unstructured text is difficult to store and retrieve in a highly structured database such as that conforming to the relational model. SQL*TextRetrieval is an ORACLE product aimed at integrating structured and textual data storage within a single database by the provision of comprehensive text retrieval options which are built round the use of SQL and fully integrated into the ORACLE product as a whole. Use of this product extends the database querying capability of ORACLE to include features normally only available in dedicated text retrieval systems, such as the ability to search for specific words and phrases and retrieve the sentences, paragraphs, pages, etc, in which they occur, the use of 'wildcards' in searches, 'fuzzy' searches, the use of boolean operators in searches, the use of alternative words (synonyms) in searches, the use of relationships between terms and so forth.

13.4.3 DBA tools

ORACLE's SQL includes a number of commands which are primarily for the use of the DBA. These include commands to CREATE and ALTER a database, to AUDIT changes to the database tables and to exert control over the logical and physical placement of underlying ORACLE database files. These and other SQL commands can be used from within the ORACLE SQL*DBA interface which also includes non-SQL commands for the general administration of databases including their back up and recovery.

13.4.4 Operational User Tools

Easy*Query

This ORACLE product is aimed directly at the novice end user. Using it, such users can build and use databases without the need for coding in SQL or any other computer language. Point and select menus are provided in conjunction with 'fill in' blank forms which guide the user in the creation, modification and deletion of database tables and views, the insertion, update, deletion and querying of data and the building of reports and graphs. Additionally, all screen forms which such users see in interacting with developed applications have the same 'look and feel', thus reducing the training required for operational users to use a variety of applications.

14

Developing Relational Database Systems

14.1 Data Driven versus Function Driven Developments

In Chapter 4 it was shown that in structured analysis the overall analysis strategy might be driven, inter alia, by the information model or by the DFD depending on the nature of the problem. This topic is now returned to in a little more detail in the following paragraphs.

Systems to be developed can be conceived of as falling within a 'spectrum' wherein at one extreme the system development needs to be *predominantly* 'data driven' and at the other it needs to be *predominantly* 'function driven'. The word predominantly was highlighted because both forms of analysis and design will alway be required to some degree. The system 'spectrum' is illustrated using some examples in Figure 14.1.

At one end of the spectrum there are systems which deal with very large volumes of different types of data for which relatively simple processing is required. Typical commercial systems such as pay-roll, inventory control and sales order entry fall into this category. They deal with very large volumes of different types of data but only relatively simple calculations are performed on those data. Even very large and complex commercial systems, such as those for banking and airline passenger booking fall into this category. They are complex because of the problems associated with the need for networking and distribution of their databases rather than from any inherent complexity of the algorithms needed to deal with the data.

Moving through the spectrum, systems are encountered which still need to hold large volumes of differing types of data, but may also require to perform complex operations on those data. Typical of such would be census systems and production control systems.

Further still across the spectrum, aircraft or ship navigation and military weapon control systems are encountered for which very difficult real time response problems must be solved in addition to the need for complex calculations on the data. Databases for such systems are currently relatively small but are increasing in significance as the technology emerges to make larger ones practical.

Finally, at the other extreme, systems, or rather stand-alone programs, may be developed to perform complex mathematical calculations on relatively small amounts of data. These are almost entirely algorithm driven.

In this book we are dealing for the most part with developments which fall within the 'data driven' area of the spectrum and for which the database concept described in Chapter 1 is appropriate. The development process for these systems should, therefore, concentrate initially on the analysis and design of the database to be provided. This is a very significant departure from the traditional approach to systems development which

266 *Developing relational database systems*

concentrates initially almost exclusively on the functionality to be delivered by the system to its users. The functions the system has to perform must be analysed and designed and, to a degree, database and function development will always have to be carried out in parallel. However, the detailed design of the system functions cannot be completed prior to the completion of the detailed design of the database and the database development must always to some extent be ahead of the development of the applications (functions) which use it. In this chapter, within the framework of this overall data driven development strategy, the phases in the development of a relational database system are examined together with the inputs, activities and outputs associated with them.

Data Driven			Algorithm Driven
Banking	Statistical Analysis	Navigation	Combinatorial Algebra
Passenger Booking	Production Control	Weapon Control	Simultaneous Equations
Inventory			

Figure 14.1   The data driven – algorithm driven 'spectrum'

14.2   The Relational Database System Project Life Cycle

Figure 14.2 illustrates, in the form of a DFD (see Chapter 4), the development processes involved in the construction of relational database systems. Note that the figure, as for any DFD, is not a flowchart and therefore does not imply a rigorous sequence of events although these can be inferred to a degree from the overall flow of the data.

It shows the three *broadly* sequential software development phases of analysis, design and coding. In real software development projects there is always a high degree of overlap across these phases.

It also shows two parallel streams of processes and outputs from processes, those starting from data analysis and those starting from functional analysis. Although relational database system development is data driven in the sense discussed in the previous section, this is intended to be a broad guideline to follow, not be treated as rigid dogma. For example, the functional analysis activity is shown in the figure to have the information model as one of its inputs. This does not mean that the information model must be fully completed prior to the start of functional analysis. What it does mean is that a specific functional area cannot realistically be analysed independently of the analysis of the database data which will be required to support that function. Once a problem area of interest with distinct boundaries has been completely analysed in the information model, work on the functional modelling for that problem area can start. These remarks about not interpreting too much rigour in the sequences shown in the figure should be borne in mind while reading the rest of this chapter.

The relational database system project life cycle 267

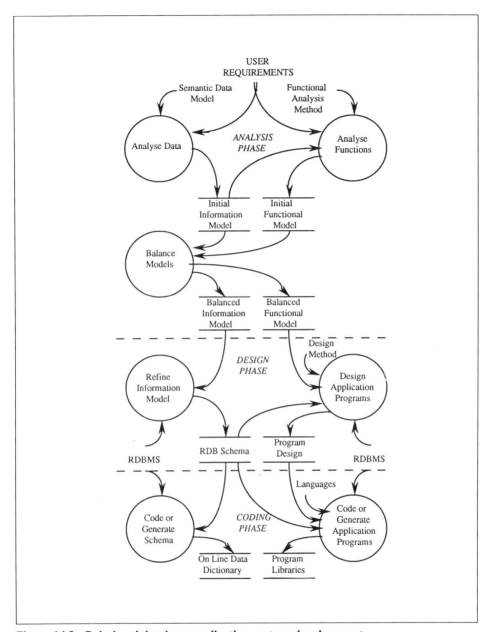

Figure 14.2 Relational database application system development

The starting points for any development are, of course, the information and functional requirements as seen in the real world of the user. From these requirements, as indicated in the figure, we proceed into the broadly sequential analysis, design and coding phases of development. These phases are overviewed briefly in the following paragraphs and will be gone into more detail in subsequent sections of the chapter.

268　*Developing relational database systems*

The Analysis Phase

Data Analysis/Information Modelling

The 'analyse data' process bubble is shown as having two inputs, a *semantic data model* and the *user requirements*. The semantic data model, with its objects, integrity rules and operators, forms the basis for the technique used by the analyst in constructing the output from this process, the *initial information model*. In this book it is assumed that the semantic data model used corresponds to the E-O model which was described in Part 3.

Functional Analysis

The 'analyse functions' process bubble is shown as having three inputs, the *functional analysis method, the initial information model* and, again, the *user requirements*. In this book, the use of DFDs, possibly supplemented by the use of STDs, as described in Chapter 4 is assumed as being the basis of the functional analysis techniques used by the analyst, but other techniques could be substituted. The reader is reminded of the earlier remark that the initial information model need not be fully complete before parts of it are provided as input to the functional analysis activity.

Balancing the Models

The 'balance models' process is shown as having two inputs, the initial information model and the initial functional model. This process was described and exemplified in Chapter 11. The outputs from it are the balanced information and functional models.

The Design Phase

Relational Database Schema Design

The inputs to the 'refine information model' process are shown as the *balanced information model* and the RDBMS to be used. The infomation model as produced during data analysis will have been designed to assist optimum communication with the users and with the 'functional' analysts. It will be an 'essential' requirements document (see Chapter 4) and will contain no implementation detail. During the design phase it will have to be refined to take into account the realities of using a particular RDBMS for the database implementation.

Applications Design

The inputs to the 'design application programs' process are shown as the *balanced functional model*, the *design method* the RDB *schema* and the RDBMS in use. It is assumed that for a project of any size the functional design activity will follow some proven design method. The RDB schema will be used by application designers in as much as the extra detail it contains is required by them to complete their designs, but it need

The analysis phase 269

not be fully complete for work on the design of the applications to start. The application designers must also take into account the facilities provided by the RDBMS in use, in deciding how the design will be implemented (by 4GL/Forms, 3GL with embedded SQL, use of simple forms facilities, etc).

The Coding Phase

Coding the Schema

The database schema must now be communicated to the RDBMS. The exact manner in which this is done will vary depending on the RDBMS in use, but in general the schema will be communicated by use of SQL (DDL) statements and stored in the RDBMS's data dictionary (system catalogue). If the information modelling analysis and design activities have been correctly carried out, there will be a one for one correspondence between the objects defined in the model and the relational database tables required, and all the information required to code the schema will be available from it.

(*Note*: CASE tools are available which can support the information modelling activity, provide automatic relational database schema generation from the information model and support subsequent maintenance of both model and schema. These are usually particular to a given RDBMS and the RDBMS supplier must be consulted as to their availability for his product. The CASE tool may be available directly from the RDBMS supplier.)

Coding/Generating the Applications

This proceeds in the conventional manner, except that certain system modules will not be coded in the conventional sense of the word, but, rather, *generated* using the RDBMSs development tools as described for typical RDBMSs in Chapter 13.

14.3 The Analysis Phase

14.3.1 Data analysis

Firstly, the real world operations of an organisation are analysed to determine the types of data of interest to that organisaton. This analysis will be based on identification of the entity types of interest to the organisation, the attributes of interest which they have and the naturally occurring relationships amongst them. The output is an *initial information model*. Since relational database developments specifically are being considered here, it is important that the information model produced be normalised in the relational model sense. The model will be based on the use of the objects, operators and integrity rules of a semantic data model. Use of the E-O semantic data model as described in Chapter 10 will ensure, to a very high degree of probability, that the model will indeed be normalised and therefore that its object types will have a one to one

270 *Developing relational database systems*

correspondence with tables in the eventual RDB schema to be derived from it. The process of constructing an information model was discusses in some detail in Chapter 11. The reader is reminded that the relevant steps needed to complete this activity are:

- Identify Enterprise Information Goals
- Identify Information Sources
- Partition the Problem
- Produce Information Models
- Integrate the Models

Ideally, CASE tools support will be available to support the information modelling activity. The information model is a key document for discussion with users as a check that their information requirements have been properly researched and understood and serves as input to the functional analysis activity.

14.3.2 Functional Analysis

For systems of any size, this activity should be based on some proven analysis method. In Chapter 4, two methods were introduced, structured analysis (SA) and object oriented analysis (OOA). Other, proprietary methods may also be used, including those from RDBMS suppliers. Ideally, as for the data analysis activity, the functional analysis will be supported by the use of a CASE tool. If OOA or a broadly similar method is in use, then the method itself dictates the production of an information model as a first step and functional analysis proceeds as outlined in Chapter 4 with the use of STDs or their equivalents. If SA or a broadly similar method is in use, then completed parts of the information model are again used as the starting point, with the production of the data transform and dynamics models, as required, following.

Because of the orientation of relational database systems to on line, terminal screen based applications, and the availability of powerful 4GL tools with RDBMSs with which such applications can be rapidly generated, the more formal analysis techniques may be supplemented by *requirements prototyping*. This involves showing the user mock ups of the screen forms he will be using and discussing and refining these with his direct involvement. This can be a very useful technique indeed because of the user interaction and involvement it promotes. What you see is what you get. However, it should be regarded as supplementary to the more formal functional analysis activity and resulting essential model documentation, not as a substitute for it. Availability of requirements prototyping facilities should not be regarded as a licence to hack.

14.3.3 Balancing the Models

This topic was covered in some detail in Chapter 11. The reader is reminded that the data flows and data stores of the DFD (or equivalent) produced as a result of the functional analysis process must be examined with the following questions in mind:

- Have any new qualifiers for existing object types in the information model been uncovered in the functional model?

Are there object types in the functional model which are not shown in the information model?
- Are these to be stored or only reported?

After the models have been balanced, the DFD will contain data stores corresponding to all the object types described in the information model and the data flows out of these stores will consist only of attributes as defined for the corresponding object types in the information model. The information model may contain further entity types and/or attributes derived from examination of the DFD.

14.3.4 Output from the Analysis Phase

On completion of the analysis phase, the project will have a well structured and unambiguous set of documents which state what the system has to do to satisfy the requirements of its users. It is very important that the users (or their agents) 'sign off' these documents. Three problems can arise with this.

Firstly, the graphical and textual notations used may be unfamiliar to the user. The only satisfactory answer to this is that key user staff be trained to understand them. Note that the key user requires only the skills to interpret the various models, not those required to construct them. If key users have been properly involved during the course of the system analysis activities, this process of education should already have taken place.

Secondly, CASE tools, if used, must also be available to the users checking the documents they contain and the users must be trained in their use for that purpose. For example, it is vastly easier and quicker to point at a particular information model object type on a screen and click a mouse to bring up a pop up window containing the relevant data dictionary entry, than to find the object type in one ERD fragment on one page of a two thousand page document, then search through the rest of the document for the relevant data dictionary entry. The point is that CASE tool providers assume that the tool itself will be used for this kind of cross referencing. If the document it contains in electronic form are output as hard copy for the user to 'sign off', the quick and convenient cross referencing capabilities they have are *not* available in that hard copy. In the more formal contract situations hard copy will almost certainly have to be provided as a deliverable, but use of the CASE tool itself should be the main means by which the customer verifies that the models are correct.

Thirdly, in the very formal contract situations normal in government and military work, the contract is likely and sensibly nowadays to specify that modern methods and supporting CASE tools be used for the analysis and design phases. But very stringent and bureaucratic requirements will also be imposed on how the results of analysis are to be presented in documents at various strictly defined milestones in the contract. It is very unlikely that the output from the CASE tool in use will conform even remotely to these specifications. This can mean that almost as much, or even more, meticulous and painstaking work will have to be done to produce the documents in the required format, than was done to produce the analysis models in the first place. There is little that can be done about this at present other than to make sure that the extra effort is planned and budgeted for at the outset of the project and to endeavour over time to persuade more of the various government procurement agencies to practice what they preach.

272 *Developing relational database systems*

14.4 The Design Phase

14.4.1 RDB Schema Design

The balanced information model is the starting point for design of the *relational database schema*. In essence this means that the information model must be refined to take into account the requirements of the RDBMS to be used.

(*Note*: This may have been anticipated by the analyst to a greater or lesser degree during the analysis phase. As stated before, there is always a degree of overlap between analysis and design activities).

For example, the names of object types and their attributes as used during analysis will have been chosen to be as meaningful as possible to assist in communication with the users. These will become table names and column names respectively in the relational database schema and may now have to be changed to conform to the syntax rules imposed by the RDBMS. This usually means abbreviating them and thus losing some of their meaning. This does not mean, however, that the original, more meaningful attribute names will now be 'thrown away'. Names agreed with the user during the analysis phase should, as fas as possible, be used in the forms through which the average user will view the database. If the supplemetary information decribed in Chapter 11 has not yet been added to the model, this must be done prior to its being encoded in the RDBMS.

14.4.2 Application Design

In designing the applications to be run against the relational database schema, the designer has a choice of four paths to follow, 'no design', structured design, object based design or a restricted form of object based design. It is likely that the designer (or design team) will have to mix and match these design methods appropriately against specific user applications and software modules within these applications.

'No Design'

Where the function to be provided is simply to insert, update and retrieve data, it may be adequately provided by the operational user interiaces provided (for example QBF in INGRES and Easy*SQL in ORACLE) and *no* design (or programming) will be required.

Structured Design

Where the function to be provided is to be implemented in a conventional, non object oriented, 3GL progamming language such as COBOL or Fortran, using embedded SQL, then structured design as overviewed in Chapter 4 is the most mature and appropriate method.

The coding/application generation phase   273

Object Based Design

Where the function to be provided is to be implemented in a more modern language such as Ada or Modula-2 which lends itself to object based implementations and for which embedded SQL preprocessors are available with RDBMS in use, then the use of an Object Based Design method is appropriate.

Restricted Object Based Design

Where the function is to be implemented in a 4 GL, then object based design in a very restricted sense (taking no account of inheritance, genericity and overloading, etc) is an appropriate design technique. Such applications are built around screen forms and a screen form can be defined as an abstract data type using the notation described in Chapter 4. This notation can be supplemented with the actual form layouts required.

14.5   The Coding/Application Generation Phase

The coding and/or generation of the application programs which will access the database will follow normal practice for the languages and/or application generation facilities provided at the installation and are not further discussed here. Some general observations follow, however, on the coding and tuning of the RDB schema.

14.5.1   Coding the RDB Schema

Assuming that the previous steps have been carried out fully and correctly, this step is the simple one of first creating a database using the SQL CREATE SCHEMA command or its equivalent and writing and executing SQL CREATE TABLE commands for each of the data dictionary entries in the final information model. Some information modelling tools will perform this relatively mechanical step automatically. The SQL commands have already been described in Chapters 12 and 13.

Assuming that the database had already been created in the RDBMS in use, then the following information model data dictionary entries:

VAN__TYPE(@manufacturer + @model + average__miles__per__gallon + service__ interval + cost__price + company__discount__price + average__depreciation__per__ annum + insurance__cost + garaging__cost + tax__cost)

VAN(@licence__plate__number + @@manufacturer + @@model + mileage + avera- ge__miles__per__gallon + serviceability__status + petrol__cost + service__cost)

taken from the transport example in Chapter 11 might, after refinement and with supplementary information addded, be encoded as:

274 *Developing relational database systems*

create table van_type
(make	varchar(30) not null
model	varchar(15) not null
mpg	float4
serv_intvl	smallint
price	float4
dscnt_price	float4
deprctn	float4
insure	float4
garage	float4
tax	float4);

create table van
(licence	char(7) not null
make	varchar(30) not null
model	varchar(15) not null
miles	float4
mpg	float4
serv_status	char(2)
petrol	float4
service	float4);

Note that the primary keys of the tables, corresponding to the identifiers of the information model object types, have been designated as 'not null'. This means that no tuple can be inserted into these tables without a primary key. The link identifier consisting of the concatenation of the 'make' and 'model' attributes of the 'van' table have also been designated 'not null'. This is because the proportion/insistency of this relationship in the direction 'van_type' to 'van' is 1:mc. An occurrence of a van_type in the 'van_type' table does not necessarily mean that any van of that type will exist in the 'van' table, but any occurrence of a van in the 'van' table must correspond to some occurrence of a van type.

In Chapter 13, it was shown that the definition of a schema involved much more than just naming of tables and columns. It was also shown that exactly what can be defined varies from RDBMS to RDBMS. Regardless of the particular RDBMS in use, the following have to be defined before the definition of a relational database schema can be regarded as complete.

- Indexes
- Access Permissions
- Duplication or Non-Duplication of Rows
- Views

These topics were discussed previously in Chapters 12 and 13 and a few more words are said about them here.

Indexes

Indexes are used to speed up update, retrieval and deletion of data in a database. Under normal circumstances it is always advisable to create an index for the primary key of a table. (The primary key of a table will, of course, correspond to the identifier of the corresponding information model object or entity type.) Decisions about the indexing of other columns are dependent on the manner in which the database wil be accessed by programmed or generated applications software, and this topic will be discussed in the next section.

Access Permissions

These are normally set up when the database schema is first defined to the RDBMS, but can be subject to review later. The granularity of access control possible varies from RDBMS to RDBMS, but, at the very least will allow the analyst/designer/DBA to specify who can access which tables and in what manner, that is, what combination, if any, of insertion, deletion, retrieval and update privileges a given user can have for a given table. Information included with the information model about data ownership (see Chapter 11) as agreed with the user community will be of great assistance in this respect.

Duplication or Non-Duplication of Rows

Defining a table as 'with no duplicates' ensures that it will be impossible to insert two occurrences of the same entity or object type into it and as such provides a powerful check on the integrity of the data being input.

Views

Views are most typically used as a means of implementing frequently used queries and in this role are much more akin to (SQL) programmed applications using the database than part of the database schema design as such. They are a necessary part of the initial schema design only where they have a permanent place in it. For example, views may be defined to restrict access to specific columns in a table for certain staff or departments in order to protect sensitive data. They then form a permanent part of the schema, that is, applications developed by or for these people or departments will use the views as they would permanently defined database schema tables.

Many other things will also have to be defined to the RDBMS for a given database, such as, journalling on tables, physical placement of tables on disks, underlying logical storage mechanisms for tables and back up and restore policies. However, these are the province of the day to day work of the DBA rather than that of the analyst/designer (always assuming that these functions are not merged) and are for the most part RDBMS dependent. Some idea of the nature of the DBAs' task in this respect can be gleaned from the special facilities made available for them in RDBMSs as described for the two representative RDBMS systems in Chapter 13, but, ultimately, the RDBMS supplier's manuals must be read and courses attended as necessary to acquire this knowledge.

14.5.2 Tuning the Relational Database Schema

A database schema, like any other piece of software, must be subject to test before it

276 *Developing relational database systems*

is brought on line. If the original information model from which it was derived accurately reflected the user's information requirements and was balanced in line with their functional requirements, then the database will support all the functionality required of it by those users. This functionality is provided by the programmed or generated application software which is developed to use the schema and, ultimately, the proof of the design of the database schema rests in proving that these applications provide the necessary user satisfaction.

However, it is possible and necessary to check as early as possible that the *performance* of the schema will meet requirements. It is not sufficient that the schema provide just the functionality required. Since this check may result in change to the schema, performance trials should take place as early as possible in the development of the system, ideally prior to significant investment of effort in the applications software which will use the schema. To run performance trials (and also to allow initial testing of the applications software) a test database population will be required.

Creating a Trial Database Population

A trial database population can be created by one of, or a selection, from the following means:

- Manual data entry.
- Initial Database Population from Current Systems.
- Automatic tuple generation.

Manual data entry is, or course, labour intensive and to be avoided if at all possible unless the data entered is to be used later in the live system. There is no necessity to write software to support this activity, since the simple form tools normally available with an RDBMS can be used.

Initial database population from current systems is the preferred method where it will be necessary later, in any case, to 'fire up' the on line database from existing filing systems (or other database systems). Most RDBMSs provide a facility to enable database tables to be loaded up from ACSII files and this can be very useful where it is possible to map such files directly to database tables, that is, where they can be arranged such that each file record corresponds to a table tuple. If this is not possible, then custom software will have to be designed and written whether to construct such matching ASCII files from the current systems or to extract data from current systems and populate the database directly from them. Note that if data is to be transferred from an existing system to the new or enhanced relational database system when it goes on trial or on line, then the existing system's documentation is almost certainly to have been part of the original source documentation for the information modelling task. Where this is the case, it is important that as a spin off from the data analysis activity, a 'file to information model' cross reference 'map' should be produced. This 'map' will relate the files, records and fields of the existing system structures which were examined during data analysis, to the information model object and entity types and attributes. The custom software for initial database population can then use the map data, which may themselves be made available as relational database tables.

The third possibility, automatic tuple generation, is the method most frequently used to generate test database populations, particularly where something equating to the eventual size of the operational database has to be simulated. Using simple programs, each table is populated automatically with dummy data corresponding as closely as possible, at least in syntax, to the real data which will eventually populate them.

14.4.2 Running Performance Trials

Performance is one of the more sensitive topics in relation to RDBMSs. The fact of the matter is, that all things being equal (including, importantly, the computing power available), a software application developed and run in an RDBMS environment is almost certain to run significantly more slowly than the equivalent application developed and run in a traditional filing system based environment. The relational model is at a level of abstraction well above the real underlying physical and logical storage mechanisms of most current hardware/operating system complexes. The RDBMS's software bridges this gap between the abstract view of data provided by the relational model and the real world lower level storage mechanisms of the system within which it runs. This software needs computer power to run and thus places an overhead on the system which has to be added to the cpu time cost of running the applications. If this fact is not faced and adequate computer power is not made available in planning for the introduction of an RDBMS, then the performance of the RDBMS based applications is likely to be disappointing. These remarks also apply, albeit to a lesser extent, where the RDBMS has to compete with systems based on a formatted DBMSs like those based on the CODASYL model, because such models are also closer to the underlying system's storage mechanisms than the relational. Nothing comes free, and the price to be paid for the benefits of relational technology must be understood as not being just that of purchasing the RDBMS, but also the purchase of sufficient computer power to support its use. The cost of this has to be traded off against the very real benefits in system development productivity to be obtained from that use. If the underlying computer power is seriously inadequate for supporting the RDBMS applications, then there is no magic solution. The real problem, the lack of computer power, must be addressed and solved.

In this section performance tuning in general is not addressed, but rather what can be achieved by detailed design of the schema in this area. The assumption is that application development is not yet complete and only a trial database population is available. The objective is to create tests, using SQL scripts, which mirror, as far as is practical, the types of access which will be made to the database tables during later live running of its applications and to identify any potential performance 'hot spots'. The test environment must be made as realistic as possible. In particular, it must emulate the sort of computer loading likely to be encountered during real operations. The focus will be on the types of access which will be made by on line systems where response time is of prime importance. The basic rules to follow are:

- Where a table will be subject to frequent insertion and/or deletion operations and relatively few retrieval or update operations, minimise the use of indexes.

- Where a table will be subject to frequent update and retrieval operations and relatively few insertion and/or deletion operations, maximise the use of indexes.

278 *Developing relational database systems*

For example, at one extreme the schema may define a table containing product information which is updated once a month but is accessed hundreds of times a day by users. If there are problems with the test response times to such retrievals, the columns in this table which are used most frequently in SQL WHERE clauses would be indexed to reduce the response time. At the other extreme, a table used to hold details about orders being taken over the telephone and thus subject to hundreds of new insertions per day, might only be used once weekly to product a management report. In this case the table would not be indexed at all until the report was required and indexes would be dropped after production of the report.

If the application of indexes alone does not remove the performance hot spots, then a check should be made first whether complex queries involving for example multiple joins and/or subqueries can be broken down into a simpler sequence of queries. At some stage, the full panoply of performance tuning facilities provided by the DBMS in use may have to be brought into play. It is impossible to be specific about that these will be, because they vary from RDBMS to RDBMS. In general it will be possible to:

- Re-arrange the physical placement of tables and indexes in backing storage for optimum performance according to the RDBMS supplier's instructions.
- Allocate more main memory to the RDBMS to reduce the amount of overlaying/paging taking place whilst it is processing database accesses.
- Allocate more space to the underlying table and index structures to reduce or eliminate overflows.

This is specially skilled work and falls very much into the province of the trained and experienced DBA. If all else fails, then the design of the schema itself may have to be re-examined. The effect of producing a fully normalised design is to produce a larger number of tables in the schema than might otherwise be the case. This may necessitate SQL queries containing multiple joins when the database is accessed and these in turn may give rise to unacceptable performance overheads with resulting poor response times. The final recourse, therefore, might be to 'de-normalise' parts of the schema to reduce the number of tables. If this has to be done, then very careful notes must be taken and detailed instructions prepared for the application analyst/designers and programmers, because they will have to cope with the update, deletion and insertion problems which will inevitably arise with the presence of un-normalised tables in the schema.

Appendix A
Object Oriented Databases

I Introduction

The topic of object orientation was introduced in Chapter 4 of the main text where the emergent methods of object oriented analysis and design and the well established discipline of object oriented programming were discussed. It was natural that those working in the object oriented (OO) field should consider the need for database management systems in support of the OO approach to system development and operation. As for OO analysis and design, the driving concepts behind the notion of object database management systems (ODBMSs) were those implicit in OO programming languages.

In Chapter 3 a number of the earlier database models were discussed and the point was made that the hierarchical and network models were arrived at by a process of abstraction from existing DBMS implementations. That is, no formally defined model for them existed before these implementations. (As opposed to the relational model which was formally defined by Codd prior to the development of any RDBMS). The position of ODBMSs is similar. No formal model exists upon which ODBMS imlpementations can be based. However, there does exist a reasonably widely-shared and tested consensus about the features which must be present in OO languages, although different languages find markedly different ways to support these features. These features have been incorporated into the various ODBMS implementations which are now emerging. In fact, the most prominent of the current ODBMS offerings are based on established OO languages. Additionally, they incorporate the features we have come to expect of any DBMS, multi-user, concurrent access control, back up and recovery, access control for security and privacy, and so forth.

In order to achieve a meaningful understanding of ODBMSs, sufficient in general to fit them within the broad context of database models which was given in Chapter 3 and, in particular, to allow meaningful comparison with the relational model, some initial insight in the way that OO languages work is necessary, at least to the point where the underlying data structures supported by them are understood. This is because, in their current implementations, ODBMSs can be regarded as (very significant) extensions to such language systems.

In this Appendix, the fundamental idea of an object as introduced in Chapter 4 is first reviewed. It then goes on to cover some of the most important features of OO language systems with emphasis on obtaining an understanding of the underlying data structures supported by them. The evolution of OO language systems into ODBMSs is then discussed. The features characteristically supported by ODBMSs are listed and discussed

280 *Object oriented databases*

and, finally, some observations are made as to the differences between the OO and relational approaches and the advantages and disadvantages of each.

2 What is an Object?

An object, in the OO concept, is a software simulation of a real world object. The software object simulates not only the existence of a real world object and the attributes of interest about it, but also those aspects of its *behaviour* in relation to other real world objects which are of interest. This simple and clarifying concept of one to one correspondence between real world objects and their software simulated equivalents is fundamental to object oriented systems in general and to object oriented databases in particular.

Objects in the real world, and hence in the corresponding software simulated world, can be concrete or conceptual, for example automobiles and business conferences. They can be very simple, like numbers or characters, or very complex, like bills of materials, engineering drawings and warships. Real world objects can be built out of other real world objects, for example an automobile consists of wheels, an engine, a radiator, door panels, and so forth. In the OO approach, the software simulation of a complex real world object can also be constructed from other software simulated real world objects and the objects from which it is constructed can themselves be constructed from further objects and so forth.

The software simulated object (we will simply say object after this) consists of an encapsulation of data describing the object, the software procedures which simulate the behaviour of that object and an interface via which that behaviour can be stimulated by other encapsulated objects. The last point is very important. The *only* way that one object can be accessed by another is via this public interface. The internal workings of an object are known only to that object itself (that is, to the designer/programmer who developed it). These internal workings, the underlying data structure representing the object (its attributes) and the programmed routines which manipulate data within that structure, when stimulated to do so at the public interface to the object, can be changed without in any way affecting any other object in the system, provided, of course, that the behaviour of the object as seen at its public interface remains as before.

3 Object Oriented Languages

3.1 Features of OO Languages

Object oriented programming languages provide an environment within which simulated real world objects can easily be specified, implemented and manipulated. OO languages support some or all of certain fundamental features, namely:

- Classes, Objects, Methods and Messages
- Object Identifiers
- Class Hierarchy and Inheritance

- Genericity
- Automatic Memory Management

(*Note:* of the above list, classes (as abstract data types) and genericity are supported by a number of languages which would not generally be classified as object oriented, for example, Ada and Modula. Genericity is not supported by all OO languages. It is only meaningful in the context of strongly typed languages, whether OO or not, and not all OO languages are strongly typed. The reader who is unfamiliar with these terms is asked to be patient, since they will be explained in the course of the Appendix.)

3.2 Classes, Objects, Methods and Messages

A *class* is a generalisation of a group of like *objects,* for example, the generalisation of individual worker objects into the class 'employee'.

The notion of a class corresponds very loosely to a semantic data model object type or a relational model table header and of an object to an occurrence of a semantic data model object type or a tuple of a table. The same distinction between type and instance of a type must be maintained. However, an OO class has a much broader meaning in as much as it encapsulates the commonly held behaviour of the generalised group of objects as well as their attributes.

A closer analogy to an OO class would be with the well established concept in conventional programming languages of a *data type* together with its permitted operators. A class can be equated with a data type and an instance of the class (an object of the class) with a program variable of that data type. For example, most programming languages support the numeric data types 'integer' and 'float' in some form or other. They also support certain permitted operators for those data types, for example, + (addition), − (subtraction), * (multiplication). If a variable is declared as being, say, integer, then it is implicit in this declaration that the relevant operators can be used with this variable. That is, in declaring the type of the variable, we are also implicitly defining the 'behaviour' which is appropriate to it. We can add, subtract, multiply, divide, etc. the values of variables of the type integer, but we cannot, for instance, use string manipulation operators (such as 'find leftmost character') with them. Integers simply do not 'behave' in that way. Any attempt to treat an integer variable as a string in this manner, or to assign the value of a string variable to an integer variable would normally be rejected by the compiler. Note also that when, as programmers, we use these system defined operators, we are unaware of the mechanism by which they are carried out. The mechanisms, whether supported by the compiler's code, by hardware, or by both can be altered, but provided that their resultant external behaviour remains the same, our programs are logically unaffected.

OO languages support system defined classes like 'integer', 'float', 'string', etc, with their corresponding operators, but also allow programmers to define classes of their own, together with the operations permissible on each class. This is analogous to allowing them to define data types of their own with their own permitted sets of operators. In OO terminology such operators are usually referred to as *methods*. Methods, of course are actually programmed routines, which in general will be either procedures or functions. In OO systems, the only actions permitted on an object of a given class are those performed when an object of another class activates one of the methods defined for the class of the object being acted upon. Such activations are accomplished by sending a *message* from one object to another. A message, of course, will actually be or embody a call to a procedure or a function.

(*Note:* The terms method and message originate from the earlier implementations of OO languages, Simula and Smalltalk ™, hence their prevalence in the literature. They are not used by more recent OO languages such as Eiffel™ and C++. They are used here to illustrate basic concepts rather than in the sense of their original language implementations.)

Thus, there are four key aspects of a class definition: the *name* of the class; its underlying data structure, that is, its *attributes;* the *methods* appropriate to the class; the public interface presented by objects of that class to objects of any other class.

Figure A.1 illustrates how, conceptually, we might define the class 'customer__account'. In the unshaded areas of the box representing the class definition, the class name and the methods available with it are named. This information is public to all objects which might wish to make use of (that is, send messages to) objects of the customer__account class. In the shaded areas of the box we have, respectively, the attributes of the class (sometimes referred to in OO terminology as *instance variables*) and the actual program routines needed to implement the methods for the class. This shaded information is *not* available to objects which might wish to make use of objects of the defined class. They can only do so via a method by sending a message which names that method. (Eiffel does, in fact, allow a class's attributes to be made public and, therefore, to be referred to from other classes.)

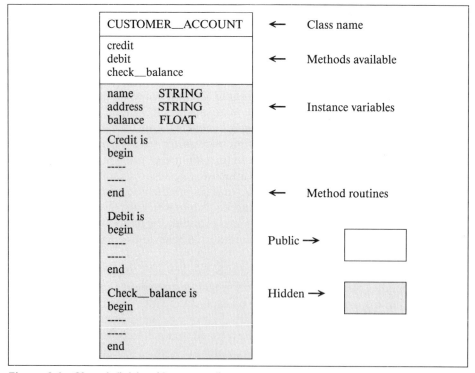

Figure A.1 Class definition (Conceptual)

Each attribue is named and its class (in effect, its data type) is given. In the above example, the classes used are STRING and FLOAT. We have assumed predefined system classes with those names. Note that by defining the class of attributes in the class definition as in the illustration, we make it possible, in principle, to determine at compile time whether operations involving these attributes are valid. Some OO languages, such as Eiffel do this and others, such as Smalltalk, do not. Where the language is not 'typed', checking for valid operations has to be carried out at run time. This is done by tagging an object to its class description when the object is created during run time. A check can then be made that any attempted operation on the object corresponds to one of the methods which is valid for its class.

3.3 Object Identifiers

3.3.1 Referencing Literal Objects

Some attributes will be of a simple predefined system class such as string, integer or float. Objects of such classes can only take on a literal value, such as 'ABCD', 7, or 7.7. Their values are equivalent to their identifications regardless of their context. They are *literal objects*, that is, they are constants, and we will refer to their classes as *literal classes*. Literal objects are always held within the system as attribute values of other objects. For example, a customer__account object as per our Figure A.1 example might have the value 'Jones', 'London' and '£10,000' for its three attributes, since these are all of literal classes. Now, other attributes could be of a more complex system defined class such as set (meaning mathematical set) or could be user defined, such as our customer__account example. These are not literal classes, since the value of an object of such classes is not equivalent to its identity (00 languages do not use the relational model concept of a primary key). They have to be identified in their context in the system, that is, by their logical position.

3.3.2 Referencing Non Literal Objects

Where a class has non literal attributes, the values held for those attributes by objects of the class will be system generated *object identifiers*. These identifiers are used by the system as references to the logical position of actual objects. This is illustrated conceptually in Figure A.2.

Object A has three attributes. One is of a literal, system defined class 'character' and its value is "c". Another is of a non literal class and is a reference to an object of that class the value of whose object identifier is C. Another still, is of a non literal class and is a reference to an object of that class the value of whose identifier is B. In the Figure, attributes of non literal classes have been asterisked. Note that object B also contains a reference to object C, that is, objects can be shared by other objects. Note also that object C has a non literal attribute whose value is 'void'. When an object is created, its attributes are initialised to some set of default values, for example, also in object C, a float attribute has been initialised to 0.0. Usually these will be system default values, but most languages will provide the means for the programmer to influence or override the system defaults to some or other extent. In Eiffel, non simple (non literal) attribute types are initialised to a 'void' since references and literal values are distinguished between and handled

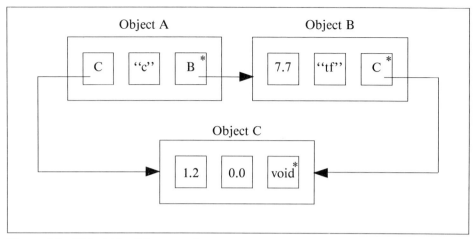

Figure A.2 Object identifiers as references

differently in that language. This attribute could remain void for the life history of the object or could eventually acquire a reference to another object of the correct class.

One should not be tempted to think that these references using object identifiers are in any way the same concept as foreign keys as used in the relational model. Object identifiers are generated automatically by the system when an object is created and are not visible to users. They can, however, be compared to the pointers used in the chain and ring structures which were discussed in Chapters 2 and 3 and which are used extensively in the hierarchical and network database models. Thus, objects, as implemented at run time in OO systems can be compared with records linked together by pointers.

3.3.4 Running OO Programs

Writing an OO program is essentially a process of defining classes as overviewed above and/or finding existing classes which can be made use of (that is, re-used) in the program. The running of an object oriented program is the initiation of a continuous process of creation, manipulation and deletion of objects of the classes defined in the program. Objects can only be created and manipulated by other objects using messages. There is no concept corresponding to the traditional programming concept of a master routine which starts everything up and controls the overall flow of the program under execution. The concept is rather one of a harmonious society of individual, well behaved objects which create other objects as they need them and ask them to carry out various tasks on their behalf. Of course, in this context, a first object must exist before anything else can happen. In Smalltalk and its derivatives, everything in the system is regarded as an object including any class itself. Therefore it is possible for a class, as an object, to have methods which can be applied to itself. Certain, built in methods are known to all classes. (They are actually inherited from a predefined system superclass called Object. Class hierarchy and inheritance will be explained in the next section.) One of these is the system defined method 'new'. When a message containing the method 'new' is sent to any class (as an object) the class will respond by creating a new object of its class, returning its

Class hierarchy and inheritance 285

identifier, which itself can now receive messages, and the program is under way. In Eiffel, the approach is somewhat different. The execution of a program begins with the creation of an initial object called the 'root' of the system, the class of the root object being specifiable, and system built in methods such as 'create' (object) and 'clone' (object) are available to the root object to start the process.

3.3 Class Hierarchy and Inheritance

A class can be defined which is a *subclass* of some previously defined class. The subclass *inherits* all the properties of the parent class. It inherits both the attributes of the parent class and its methods. Thus it can respond to all the messages to which its parent class can respond. The parent class can be a system provided literal class like 'integer' or 'string' or non literal class such as 'set', or it can be a user defined class like 'employee'.

A subclass inherits all the attributes of its parent class, but the reverse is not true. A subclass can have attributes which are not held by the parent class. For example, a subclass 'air__unit' might be defined against the previously defined parent class 'military__unit'. Air units and military units in general might have attributes in common like 'combat__effectiveness' and 'location', but an air unit would have special attributes such as 'primary__role' and 'secondary__role' (of the aircraft type the air unit is equipped with) which are not relevant to the superclass. A subclass also inherits all the behaviour (methods) of its parent class and can also have extended behaviour of its own. In the example just given, objects of the class 'military__unit' could, for example, have the methods 'attach' and 'detach' (to and from command and/or control of a superior unit) defined and implemented for them, and these methods would be applicable to all subclasses derived from 'military__unit'. However, the subclass 'air__unit' could have the additional method 'change__role' defined for it, which would not be applicable to the superclass. In some, but not all, OO languages, *multiple inheritance* is supported. Extending the above example, we might have the superclasses 'air__unit' (already a subclass of 'military__unit') and 'marine__unit' as twin superclasses of a single subclass 'marine__air__unit' which would inherit the attributes and methods of both.

Suppose that a method 'display' is defined and implemented for the 'military__unit' class which will simply display the attributes of a specific military unit such as its 'combat__effectiveness' and its 'readiness__status' on a screen. This method cannot simply be inherited without change by the subclass 'air__unit', because this class contains the additional attributes 'primary__role' and 'secondary__role' which we will assume must also be displayed. However, when we define the 'air__unit' class and we specify that it has to be a subclass of 'military__unit', we can at the same time add that the method 'display' is to be *re-defined* for the 'air__unit' class and implement that re-defined method. What we have done is to *overload* the name 'display'. It will call up different method implementations dependent on the class of the object to which it is addressed. This could be done at compile time where a typed language such as Eiffel is used, or at run time in a non typed language such as Smalltalk. Note that the term 'overloading' is used in general in the literature whenever a language permits the same operator to be used to mean different things, depending on the data type of the thing being acted upon. For example, it is common for the + (plus) operator to be legitimate both for numeric and character data types, but its action is, of course, different depending on which type it is applied to. Overloading is not particular to OO languages.

286 *Object oriented databases*

(*Note:* It is important not to confuse the OO concept of class hierarchy and inheritance, involving as it does superclasses and subclasses, with the semantic data model concept of supertype and subtype which was discussed in Chapters 3, 9 and 10, although superficially they may seem similar. An occurrence of a subtype always means that an occurrence of its corresponding supertype (or supertypes) must exist for it to be fully described, although the reverse is not necessarily true. An occurrence of an object of a given subclass has no relevance whatsoever to the occurrence of an object of its superclass (or superclasses) and vice versa.)

We have used the term 'typed' or 'strongly typed' on several occasions to describe OO languages which perform checks on programs at compile time to ensure that the method being applied via a message from one class to another class is valid for the latter. In such languages it is common for the binding of a method to a class to take place at compile time. This is referred to as *static binding*. If static binding is in force, then the executable code for a program is fixed when it is compiled. It is also possible with 'non typed' or 'weakly typed' languages, to have *dynamic binding*. With dynamic binding, decisions about whether a message (that is, the method it identifies) is valid for an object are postponed until run time. We saw earlier that such systems tag all objects with their class and can access the class descriptions to determine the validity of the message. In this case it is possible to vary the executable code to be used during the running of the program; methods do not have to be pre-bound to classes and hence to run time objects. There are advantages and disadvantages to both approaches. Static (or *early*) binding enables comprehensive and powerful checks to be carried out on a program whilst it is being compiled; dynamic (or *late*) binding makes the run time system much more flexible, but makes debugging of programs more difficult and means that powerful and comprehensive checks have to be paid for in processing overheads whilst the system is in operation.

All this may sound a bit academic until it is realised that a desirable property of objects is that they can be *polymorphous,* that is, they can 'change their shape'. For example, the same employee may, over time, progress or regress through jobs such as programmer, analyst and manager. All the methods and attributes applicable to a programmer may not be applicable to a manager and vice versa. If the programmer cannot become a manager during normal system operations, that is, during run time, then he must be recompiled as one. The system is much more flexible if an object of one class can be assigned to become an object of another class whilst the program is running, without the need for recompilation. Unrestrained *polymorphism* would be undesirable. No system could cope easily with employees who were vampires! However, polymorphism and inheritance fit neatly together as concepts. If we have a superclass 'employee' for which programmers are a subclass, analysts form a subclass of programmers and managers a subclass of analysts, then normal career progression could be simulated in the on line system. Employees could be changed into programmers, then analysts, then managers without problem. Note this concept of polymorphism constrained by inheritance works in only one direction. Managers could not become analysts without being recompiled. Note also that the term polymorphism in the OO literature is often used synonymously with overloading when used in relation to methods.

3.4 Genericity

The concept of genericity is not confined to OO languages. Genericity is also supported in modern, non OO languages such as Ada and CLU. In OO languages, a generic class can be defined which is a template from which the actual class required can be derived. A generic class is qualified by parameters, known as formal generic parameters, which themselves will normally be used to describe classes (that is, in the more conventional language case, data types). For example we could define a generic class 'Stack' and provide parameters which can be used to say whether an integer, real, character, string and so forth stack is required. A programmer writing the 'stack' class then only has to write it once to cover integer, real, character and string. At compile time, the parameter value(s) provided with a generic class will be used to construct automatically the correct code for the class(es) defined in the parameter(s). The parameter values are substituted for references to them in the code of the generic class.

3.5 Automatic Memory Management

In an OO system with objects requiring memory space being created in an unpredictable fashion during the running of a program and, just as importantly, needing to be deleted when they are no longer required in an equally unpredictable fashion, the programmer needs to be isolated from the problems of management of the computer's memory space. Thus all OO languages support automatic memory management, whereby the system looks after the problems of finding space for objects and releasing that space when an object is no longer required. Creation of an object's space by the memory manager is, of course, stimulated by the action of some object sending a message containing a system built in method such as 'new' or 'create' as discussed earlier. Deletion of an object and release of its space back into the memory pool is initiated when the memory manager detects that no references exist, in any other object, in the system to that object.

4 Evolution of ODBMSs

In OO languages as outlined above, objects can be regarded as existing for the duration of a computing session. A typical OO language application, for example, would be the implementation of a windowing system for a personal computer or a workstation. During the running of the program, the user would be able to create window objects, re-position them, re-size them, delete them and so forth. At the end of the user's session at the PC/workstation, the window objects would have no further existence. This is fine for applications where the objects created and manipulated have an ephemeral quality. However, it will not do for applications where the objects must persist from one run time session to another. We would not wish to have to create the same employee object and fill in all his/her attributes every time we started a new session, with a program whose raison d'être was the maintenance of information about employees. *Persistency* of objects between sessions is provided by OO languages in various ways, but requires specific action to be taken by the programmer to make the objects persistent. This need to address persistency, which is fundamental to most conventional commercial applications, in conjunction with the need to address the other database issues introduced in Chapter 1, has led to the introduction of the object database management systems which are discussed in the following sections.

288   *Object oriented databases*

5   Features of ODBMSs

5.1   Introductory Remarks

The various features just overviewed, which characterise OO languages, are all carried forward into ODBMSs. In fact, ODBMSs as currently available can be viewed in a simplistic way as extensions of these languages to support persistency in a comprehensive fashion and also to provide facilities characteristic of any DBMS such as multi-access, ad hoc querying, back up and restore, security and privacy, concurrent access for consistency and so on.

5.2   Difference Between ODBMS and Traditional DMBS Databases

The most obvious distinction between a database as supported by an ODBMS from one constructed using any of the more traditional database models is that it supports the storage of common *processes* as well as common data within the database. An ODBMS database will hold objects with all their attribute values, including references to other objects, but will also provide a repository for all the relevant classes of these objects. It is also a repository for the methods applicable to the objects stored. Since persistency of classes as well as objects is supported, it becomes possible for ODBMS suppliers to extend system provided classes in a more generous manner than is typical of OO languages compilers. For example, ODBMSs typically provide aggregate data structure classes such as sets, arrays, lists and dictionaries whose properties can be inherited by user defined classes, enabling one object to be a collection of things such as a list of a customer's addresses.

5.3   DDL and DML

Data definition and manipulation are provided by the OO language(s) in use by ODBMS. Data definition is the same as definition of classes (that is, it also incorporates process definition), data manipulation is equivalent to the sending of messages. In addition to access via messages, ODBMSs support both navigational access to objects and access based on the values in the objects. The first is analogous to access in hierarchical and network databases and second to access in relational databases. Versions of SQL are, in fact, supported by some products. ODBMSs, in general, support variants of one of the popular OO languages, the most common being C + + . An ODBMS may provide support for more than one OO language. (ODBMSs also provide interactive screen based interfaces to the user which allow data definition and manipulation, these will be dealt with shortly.)

5.4   Back Up and Recovery

Resilience to hardware or software failure is provided. A full replica of the database (objects and classes) can be taken whilst the system is running, followed by incremental back ups containing only those changes made to the database since the last full back up. Recovery is made, if and when necessary, by restoring the full back up and applying the incremental changes to it.

5.5 Security and Privacy

Access to the ODBMS as a whole is protected in the usual manner by user ids and corresponding passwords. This can be extended to access control to specific segments of the database, to specific privileged messages, etc.

5.6 Concurrent Access Control

Lock, unlock and deadlock avoidance mechanisms are provided in a manner similar to that provided by traditional DBMSs.

5.7 Database Networking and Distribution

Access to the database over communications networks is supported with both homogeneous and heterogeneous working within the network. Client server architectures are the norm, although some products also allow methods to be run in the server. ODBMS technology does not currently provide support for distributed databases.

5.8 ODBMS Development Tools

The major tool available is, of course, the OO language (or languages) supported by the ODBMS. Additionally, graphical interactive interfaces are commonly provided which allow the developer to define classes and create and manipulate objects of these classes directly from a terminal. Classes and objects can be saved and retrieved for use in later interactive sessions and/or used in compiled applications.

6 ODBMSs Versus RDBMSs

6.1 Basis for Comparison

Comparisons in this area are not very useful because ODBMSs and RDBMSs are based on such radically different concepts and address such radically different problem areas. However, much of the marketing literature for current ODBMS offerings and much of the hype in the technical press is based on such comparisons, with the relational model invariably being portrayed as unable to model complex objects, requiring users to be aware of complex forcign keys, needing application of 'difficult' normalisation techniques and so forth. To establish a basis for comparison we can make the following observations:

- We are comparing the merits of differing philosophies of database management, not of different programming philosophies. The key to such comparison lies in the underlying data structures supported, in particular what direct suppport is given to the respresentation of entities, their attributes and the systematic relationships which exist between them.

- Is it easier or harder to produce correct database designs using one or the other database management system or is it all much of a muchness? Does one DBMS type produce simpler data structures than the other in solving the same problem?

These issues are addressed in the following paragraphs.

290   *Object oriented databases*

6.2   ODBMS Data Structures

From a user's point of view, these are exactly the data stuctures supported by OO languages, which allow for the definition of attributes which can be literals or references as shown in Figure A.2. An object in a running system is simply such a populated data structure of the type defined by its class. When first created, its structure will be populated with default values. As time goes on these initial values, for literals and/or object identifiers, will be replaced by the sending of messages from other objects and the running of the appropriate methods.

Since a reference can point to only one object, only 1:1 relationships can be supported by the basic data structure of OO languages. It is possible, of course, for an object to have a number of attributes which are all references to the same class and therefore represent a 1:m relationship, but this number must be fixed and this degree of inflexibility would be unacceptable in most practical cases. A more flexible way to represent 1:m relationships (linkages in our E-O model terminology) is to make the object pointed to inherit the properties of an aggregate class like a set. The reference from the object on the one side of the relationship can then be to a collection of objects on the many side. Note, however, that this implementation of a 1:m relationship is *not* provided by the basic data structure of OO languages (and therefore, ODBMSs). It depends on the provision of a predefined system class 'set', or on the user defining such a class.

Consider the object types 'customer' and 'order' and the 1:m relationship 'customer places order' between them. These would be modelled by *two* tables in the relational model. Now, in order to model them in an ODBMS and provide all the information provided by the two relational tables, *five* (or possibly six) classes would have to be defined: a 'customer_set' class inheriting the properties of a 'set' class (if this is already defined, otherwise it would require definition) whose attribute would be a reference to a 'customer_class'; plus the 'customer_class' itself; then an 'order_sub_set' class inheriting the properties of a 'set' class whose attribute would be a reference to an 'order_class'; the 'order_class' itself and an 'order_set' class whose attribute would also be a reference to an order class. This works as shown conceptually in Figure A.3. Note that the customer_set and order_set objects are required in order to hold references to *all* instances of customer and order objects respectively and that all reference values would be system provided object identifiers. The approach has a considerable advantage over the relational model approach, in that it does not require the explicit use of foreign keys, but also has the distinct disadvantage that the structure is considerably more complex to design and implement than that provided by the two simple relational tables which solved the same problem.

If we now go on to consider m:n relationships, we find ourselves in greater difficulty. Even if we could accept that the system be designed to cater for fixed numbers of occurrences of these relationships (as for the possibility of fixed numbers of 1:m relationships which was discussed and dismissed above) we would have to include references in both directions. Trying to do this with aggregate objects becomes very complex because of the reference (pointer) maintenance required. (Compare this with the problems of maintaining genuine network structures which were discussed in Chapter 3.) The only practical way to represent m:n relationships is to overlay a foreign key structure on top of the basic OO language object identifier/reference based data structure. (The reader is reminded that m:n relationships are perfectly valid and frequently occurring

ODBMS representation of 1:m relationship 291

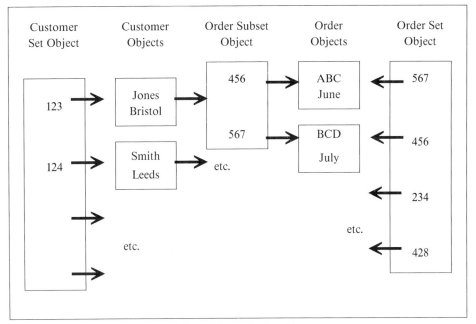

Figure A.3 ODBMS representation of 1:m relationship

entity/object types in their own right as seen from a semantic data model point of view. A system purporting to represent real world objects cannot ignore them.) That means, of course, that the related objects must have primary keys defined for them which are attributes of a literal class.

The true purpose of the use of object identifiers as references is, of course, not to establish relationships of various proportions, but to enable one object to take part in 1:1 relationships with a number of other objects each of a different class. These objects can themselves refer to other individual objects and so forth. Object identifiers are there simply to enable one object to be represented as an hierarchy of other (different) objects. This, of course, can also be done using an RDBMS by the use of foreign keys.

The fundamental difference between the OO approach and that taken by the established data models such as the hierarchical, network and relational models is that all the latter have the concept of a set *built in* to the basic data structures they support. ODBMSs cannot be made to work for the general database case unless the user defines sets of his/her own.

(*Note:* A major virtue of the OO paradigm is its comprehensive support for the concept of information hiding. As discussed earlier, this means that the internal workings of an object's class can be changed without causing a knock on effect to objects of other classes which make use of it. However, this internal change cannot necessarily be hidden from the data structure internal to the class being changed. This raises an immediate problem when persistence of objects is supported, as with ODBMSs. What happens to persistent objects if the methods and/or attributes of its class are subject to change? If one simply rules that classes with persistent objects are not allowed to change, then one of the major strengths of the OO paradigm is much diluted).

292   *Object oriented databases*

6.3   Designing ODBMS Databases

Since we are comparing ODBMSs with RDBMSs, two issues are pertinent. Firstly, is normalisation of ODBMS databases required? Secondly, are information modelling techniques still applicable?

The answer to the first question, of course, is a resounding "Yes". ODBMSs do not support repeating fields any more than RDBMSs do, therefore their database must be in 1NF. Just as enforcing 1NF in relational database designs means that two tables are required rather than one, enforcing it for ODBMSs means that at least two classes have to be defined instead of one. The ODBMS solution is simpler in that it does not require the use of foreign keys, but 1NF is still required. As we saw in Chapter 9, the further normal forms of the relational model can be viewed as sound semantic common sense. This common sense is about the semantics of real world objects and is, therefore, at least as applicable to the use of ODBMSs as to that of RDBMSs. For example, if we have an 'employee' class and a 'department' class, then it is just as wrong to include a private qualifying attribute of a department such as its location in the 'employee' class as it would be to include it in an employee table, and the same insertion, deletion and update anomalies would occur.

If the design of ODBMS databases is not to be hacked, it is difficult to see how information modelling techniques of the type discussed in Chapters 9, 10 and 11, perhaps adapted more closely to the OO paradigm, can be avoided.

6.4   Concluding Remarks

ODBMSs in their current implementations are really just extensions of OO languages. They do nothing to solve the known problems of the relational model and introduce a different set of database problems of their own. The basic data structures they support are very primitive indeed compared with RDBMSs such as ORACLE and INGRES and even with mature products following other database models such as IDMS and IMS.

OO languages as such were not designed with persistence of objects in mind. The OO paradigm has its roots in solving the problems of developing systems where the creation, manipulation and deletion of ephemeral objects such as windows and associated graphical objects is required to provide intuitively easy to use interfaces to assist users in carrying out their jobs. The use of ODBMSs in their current form is likely to be constrained to 'engineering' applications in the areas where this type of interface is very important, for example, CASE, CAD, CIM and GIS (Geographic Information Systems). These areas have become the main province of the application of OO languages. Indeed, the OO paradigm has now been adopted by RDBMS suppliers like ORACLE to enable user friendly front ends to be developed for software applications based on their main, relational product line.

To come out from this restricted market place and address the broad spectrum of commercial data processing applications, ODBMSs will have to cease to be just extensions of OO languages and directly address the problems of creating and maintaining databases of the type which have been the subject of this book. Research into OBDMSs which support the OO paradigm, but are not just OO language extensions is very active, but we are unlikely to see the practical results of this for some time to come. Even then, ODBMSs will have an enormous marketing hill to climb, given the huge investment by commercial and public organisations in relational databases. Meanwhile one is tempted to say of ODBMSs, paraphrasing the hoary old beaujolais wine joke, ''They are not great database management systems, but one admires their impertinence.''

References and Bibliography

1. James Martin, *Computer Data-Base Organisation,* (2nd Edition), Prentice Hall, 1977.

2. National Computer Centre (NCC) *Introducing Systems Analysis and Design,* Volume 2, National Computing Centre Ltd, 1979.

3. G. Wiederhold *Database Design* McGraw Hill, 1983.

4. R.E. Wagner Indexing Design Considerations, *IBM Systems Journal,* 12, No. **4**, 1973.

5. W.D. Mauren and T.G. Lewis Hash Table Methods, ACM Comp. Surv. 7, No. **1**, March 1975.

6. D.E. Knuth *The Art of Computer Programming, Volume 3, Sorting and Searching,* Addison Wesley, 1973.

7. Yourdon and Constantine *Structured Design. Fundamentals of a Discipline of Computer Program and System Design,* Prentice Hall, 1975.

8. T. DeMarco *Structured Analysis and System Specification,* YOURDON Press 1978.

9. P.T. Ward and S.J. Mellor *Structured Development for Real Time Systems,* Volumes 1, 2 and 3 YOURDON Press, 1985.

10. D.J. Hatley and J.A. Pirbhai *Strategies for Real Time System Specification* Dorset House.

11. M. Page-Jones *The Practical Guide to Structured Systems* Prentice Hall, 1980.

12. E. Yourdon *Modern Structured Analysis* YOURDON PRESS 1989.

13. C. Gane and T. Sarson *Structured Systems Analysis: Tools and Techniques,* Improved System Technologies Inc., 1977.

14. B. Meyer *Object Oriented Software Construction* Prentice Hall, 1988.

15. G. Booch Object Oriented Development *IEEE Trans. on Software Engineering,* Volume SE-12, No. **2**, Feb 1986.

16. G. Booch *Software Engineering with Ada* Benjamin/Cummings, 1983.

17. S. Shlaer and S.J. Mellor *Object Oriented Systems Analysis, Modelling the World in Data,* YOURDON Press, 1988.

References and bibliography

18. M.A. Jackson *System Development* Prentice Hall, 1983.

19. O.J. Dahl, B. Myrhaug and K. Nygaard *(Simula 67) Commom Base Language,* Publication N. S-22, Norsk Regnesentral, Feb. 1984.

20. A. Goldberg and D. Robson *Smalltalk-80: the Language and its Implementation,* Addison Wesley, 1983.

21. B. Stroustrup *The C++ Programming Language,* Addison Wesley, 1986.

22. E.F. Codd *A Relational Model of Data for Large Shared Data Banks,* CACM 13, No. 6, June 1970.

23. E.F. Codd *Further Normalization of the Data Base Relational Model,* Courant Computer Science Symposia Series, Volume 6, Prentice Hall, 1972.

24. E.F. Codd *Relational Completeness of Data Sub-Languages,* Courant Computer Science Series, Volume 6, Prentice Hall, 1972.

25. C.J. Date *An Introduction to Database Systems, Volume 1,* Addison Wesley, 1990.

26. E.F. Codd *Missing Information (Applicable and Inapplicable) in Relational Databases* ACM SIGMOD, Record 15, No. 4, Dec. 1986.

27. W. Kent *A Simple Guide to Five Normal forms in Relational Database Theory* CACM 26, No. 2, Feb. 1983.

28. R. Fagin, *Multivalued Dependencies and a New Normal Form for Relational Databases,* ACM TODS 2, No. 3, Sept. 1977.

29. P.P. Chen *The Entity-Relationship Model — Towards a Unified View of Data* ACM TODS 1, No. 1, March 1976.

30. M. Flavin *Fundamental Concepts of Information Modelling,* YOURDON Press, 1981.

31. R. van der Lans *Introduction to SQL,* Addison Wesley, 1988.

Index

Abstract Data Type	75, 80, 273, 281
Abstraction	132, 136
Ada	25, 26, 47, 75, 80, 192, 224
Aggregate function	198, 205
ALL	198
ANSI/SPARC	47
Application generation	183, 222, 273
Associative Object Type	
defined	19
equivalence to dependent entity type	143
Attribute	
as foreign key	85
as table primary key	43, 85
as identifer	17
as identifier or qualifier	135
as table column	43, 85
atomic value of	91
type and occurrence of	21
AUTOCOMMIT	212
AVG	198, 205
Back up and recovery	8, 226, 245, 246, 247, 264
Backing store	22
Base table	106, 195
BETWEEN	201
Boyce-Codd normal form (BCNF)	113, 118, 158
Candidate key	94, 118, 119
Cartesian product	95, 96
CASE Tools	51, 53, 69, 75, 129, 269, 270, 271
Catalogue	212, 223
Chain Structure	29, 33
Checkpoint	213, 245, 246
Chen P.P.	46, 129
Class (in object orientation)	75, 281
Client/server architecture	223
CLOSE (cursor)	214

298 *Index*

Closure	95, 102
Cobol	25, 35, 40, 47, 80, 192, 214, 224
CODASYL	36, 40, 47, 277
Codd E.F.	36, 81, 83, 86, 87, 95, 105, 110, 191
Cohesion	69, 75
Column	42, 83
COMMIT	211
CONNECT	213
CONNECT BY	254
Consistency	6, 192
COUNT	206
CREATE INDEX	195, 196
CREATE SCHEMA	195, 273
CREATE TABLE	171, 195
CREATE VIEW	195, 200
CURRENT OF (cursorname)	215
Cursor (in embedded SQL)	192, 213

Data definition Language (DDL)	35, 36, 90, 95
Data flow	55
Data Flow Diagram (DFD)	56
Data item	24
Data Manipulation Language (DML)	35, 36, 95, 106
Data Model	
as database model	36
as information model	16, 37
as semantic data model	37
Data redundancy	119, 123, 124, 126
Data structure	
defined by DDL	35
embedded in programs	35
introduced	20
population of	20, 33
Data type	24, 187, 195, 208, 213, 218, 219, 281
Database	
administration	13
as information pool	3
concept introduced	1
consistent view of	6
defined	3
flexibility to growth and change	11
multiple access to	4
networking and distribution of	9
reliability	8
security and privacy of	9
Database management system (DBMS)	4, 14, 35

Data dictionary 299

Data dictionary	
(in Structured Analysis and Design)	49, 55, 56, 57, 61
Date C.J.	120
DB2	83, 191
De Marco	54
Deadlock	7, 14, 213
Deadly embrace	7
DECLARE CURSOR	214, 218
DECLARE SECTION	213
DELETE	208, 215
Dependent entity type	
as binary relationship	153
defined	164
graphic notation for	143
introduced	142
Dependent object type	
defined	164
DESCRIBE	218
Difference	95, 104
Direct access file	31
DISCONNECT	213
Disk	
magnetic	23
WORM	23
DISTINCT	198
Distributed database	10, 224, 228, 248
Division	
arithmetic	198
relational	95, 99
Domain	85
DROP INDEX	195, 197
DROP TABLE	195, 197
DROP VIEW	195, 209, 210
Dynamic Embedded SQL	216
Embedded SQL	47, 213, 224, 225, 231, 255, 269
Entity	
defined	133
introduced	16
Entity Integrity	110, 123
Entity-Object (E-O) model	
and 1NF	138, 156
and 2NF, 3NF, BCNF	156
and 4NF, 5NF	159
applicability	162
defined	163
introduced	133

300 *Index*

Entity relationship diagram (ERD)	49, 56, 57, 131, 143
Entity type	
defined	133, 164
introduced	16
Entity-Relationship (E-R) Model	
as used in analysis and design methods	129
introduced	46
Enumeration	25
Environmental model	55
Equi-join	100
Essential model	54
Event	56, 62, 64
EXECUTE	217
EXECUTE IMMEDIATE	216
EXISTS	204
Extended Cartesian product	97
Fagin R.	121
FETCH	214
Fifth Normal Form (5NF)	113, 124
First Normal Form (1NF)	90, 94
Flavin M.	131
Foreign key	94, 159
Forms Management	225, 226, 231, 255
Fortran	25, 35, 47, 74, 192, 224
Fouth Generation Language(4GL)	83, 225, 231, 255, 269, 270
Fourth Normal Form (4NF)	113, 122
Functional dependency	113, 118, 120
Functional differentiation	138
Generalisation	16, 19, 133, 138
Genericity	286
GRANT	211
Granularity of locks	212
GROUP BY	206
Hashing	31
HAVING	206
Hierarchical	
database model	37
tree structure	37, 41
Host language	35, 213, 216, 219, 255
Identifier	
and degree of a relationship	137
concatenated	17
defined	135

equivalence to primary key	85
in relationships	18
introduced	17
use in accessing information	19
IN	201
Independent entity type	
defined	164
introduced	142
Independent object type	
defined	164
Indexed Files	27
Information hiding	75
Information model	
and object oriented analysis	65
distinction from semantic data model	49
in structured analysis	57
introduced	37
Ingres™	83, 191, 192, 226, 272
Inheritance	79, 285
Inner join	177, 202
INSERT	197, 207
Intersection	95, 104
Inverted File	32
Jackson M.A.	73
Join	44, 45, 95, 100, 202
Join dependency	128
Kernel (of RDBMS)	223
LIKE	201
Linkage	
defined	164
graphical notation for	144
identifier	145
introduced	142
Lock	7
Loose coupling	69, 74
Mathematical relation	86
MAX	205
Message (in object oriented language)	74, 281
Method (in object oriented language)	281
MIN	205
Multi-determinant	123
Multi-valued dependency (MVD)	113, 120, 123
Multiplicity (of relationship)	18

302 *Index*

N-tuple	86
Natural join	101, 202, 203
Network	
database model	36, 40
file structure	40
local area	9
telecommunications	9
wide area	9
Non loss decomposition	117, 118, 124, 127
Null	109, 196, 203, 210
Object (in object oriented programming)	280, 281
Object oriented analysis	65
Object oriented database management systems (ODBMS)	279, 287, 288
Object oriented design	52, 54, 73
Object oriented programming languages	52, 74, 280
Object type	
in structured analysis	58
in E-O model	134, 164
distinguished from entity type in E-O model	136
OPEN	214
ORACLE™	83, 191, 192, 247, 272
ORDER BY	200
Outer join	101, 202
Overloading	78, 80, 286
Password	9, 250
Pathological connection	69, 74
Polymorphism	286
Precompiler	219
PREPARE	217
Preprocessor	213, 219
Primary key	
as foreign key in relationship	85
in entity and referential entegrity	111
introduced	85
Process specification	55, 62
Projection	44, 45, 95, 98
Prototyping (Requirements)	270
Qualifier	
defined	165
equivalence to m:1 relationship	139
introduced	136
privacy of	149
Query language	36, 106